Documents of Medieval History 2

Adv...

G. W. S. Barrow
Professor of Scottish History, University of St Andrews
Edward Miller
Master of Fitzwilliam College, Cambridge

Published in this series:

The Birth of Popular Heresy
by R. I. Moore
The Reign of Charlemagne:
Documents on Carolingian government and administration
by H. R. Loyn and John Percival

The Reign of Charlemagne

Documents on Carolingian
Government and Administration

H. R. Loyn and John Percival

Edward Arnold

First published 1975
by Edward Arnold (Publishers) Ltd
25 Hill Street, London W1X 8LL

Cloth edition ISBN: 0 7131 5813 1
Paper edition ISBN: 0 7131 5814 X

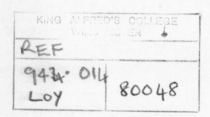
Printed in Great Britain by
The Camelot Press Ltd, Southampton

Contents

Acknowledgements

This book aims to provide an introduction to the historical sources relevant to the study of government and politics in the reign of Charles the Great. Emphasis is placed on the capitularies, newly translated by Dr John Percival, and to a lesser extent on the letters of Alcuin, a principal source of information about the politics and personalities of Carolingian Europe.

We wish to thank the following scholars for active help in the preparation of the volume: Professor Edward Miller, who first suggested that we write it, for his encouragement and editorial help, Dr Clive Knowles for his acute and positive criticism at proof stage, Professor Dorothy Whitelock (and Messrs Eyre and Spottiswoode) for granting us permission to reprint a number of Alcuin's letters from *English Historical Documents*, and Professor Lewis Thorpe (and Penguin Books, Ltd) for permission to reprint passages from Professor Thorpe's translation of Einhard and Notker.

Notes on Translations

Our aim has been to provide a text which is largely self-explanatory, and we have tried as far as possible to exclude footnotes. The following brief comments indicate our approach to some of the technical problems involved in translating material of this nature.

Place-names In most cases the modern name is known, and we have used it. Where there is no obvious identification, or where there is doubt, we print the MS name in italics.

Personal names Consistency here is almost impossible, and our practice has been to alter the MS spelling only when the name has a very obvious modern equivalent (*e.g.* Johannes becomes John), or where there is a commonly accepted modern spelling (*e.g.* Arichis for Arigisus, and names in -bert and -bald).

Weights, measures, coinage We translate *solidus* and *denarius* as 'shilling' and 'penny', except where they are used to indicate weight, in which case they are left in the original Latin. Most weights and measures are in fact left untranslated, partly because they usually have no modern equivalent, and partly because they frequently varied from place to place. The most common are the *modius*, which can perhaps be thought of as a peck, and the *sextarius* or *sextarium*, which was one-sixteenth of a *modius*. The *sicclus* occurs most frequently as a small liquid measure, and the *seiga*, which was usually a coin equivalent to the *denarius*, is at one point (p. 100) used as a unit of weight. Of the various units of land measurement the *jornalis* (*i.e. diurnalis*) was the amount of arable which could theoretically be ploughed in a day, and the *aripennis* was an area of 120 square feet (that is, half a Roman *jugerum*); the *aripennis*, like the *pictura* (*i.e. peditura* or 'footage'), was a measure commonly used for vineyards.

Terms of rank, status, etc. Our practice has been to give modern equivalents except where no obvious modern term exists or where it would be misleading to give one. The *missus* is a typical example. 'Commissioner' is often the nearest modern equivalent, but neither it nor 'envoy' conveys the full meaning. *Missus* is so common in textbooks, especially in the compounds *missus dominicus* and *missi dominici*, that we have retained it. The terms *sculdhais* and *gastaldius* have also been retained. They are both used to describe active royal executive agents, often men with special concern for royal lands or rights. *Sculdhais* was in common use in lands where the law was Germanic though not Frankish, *gastaldius* was specifically associated with Lombard Italy. During the reign of Charlemagne the subordinates of a count are regularly described as *centenarii* or *vicarii* with little if any difference of function implied. They both exercise administrative and judicial functions within territorial divisions of a county. Some indication of difference in origin is given in that *centenarius* is more common in the Germanic lands, *vicarius* in the Romanic. We have kept both terms, and also the useful *vicedominus* which describes a deputy in various kinds of secular or ecclesiastical office. Lower down in society a *casatus* or 'housed man' was a serf provided with a holding by his lord, and a *lidus* was a man of intermediate status between a freeman and a serf. In this connection one virtually insoluble difficulty must be mentioned: the word *servus*, and to a lesser extent *mancipium*, had a very wide range of meaning, and could sometimes be translated as serf and sometimes as slave. The context does not always make the meaning clear, but we have kept to the general rule that where 'serf' appears in the translation, *servus* is to be found in the Latin, and where 'slave' appears it is sometimes a translation of *servus* and sometimes of *mancipium*. For similar reasons we have translated *clericus* sometimes as 'priest' and sometimes as 'clerk', depending on the context.

Rights, fines, rents, and taxes   Two of the most difficult terms to translate have been *bannum* and *fredus*. The range of meaning of *bannum* (*-us*) is wide, including the general royal power to command his subjects, the more specific right of the king to prevent evil-doing and to punish those who disobey his orders, and the heavy fine (usually 60 shillings) imposed on such offenders. In most instances we have been able to translate *bannum* simply as 'ban' or 'our fine', and we have drawn attention to the term only when important institutional information seemed to be conveyed by it. *Fredus* signifies that part of the fines and compositions paid in the courts (normally a third in Frankish law) which belonged to the king. 'Payment for the infringement of the peace' or 'peace payments' have been used as appropriate translations. The word *census* can mean revenue in general, but more often specific rents or personal payments due to the king (sometimes in the form *census regalis* or *census noster*). We have left it untranslated on the few occasions on which it occurs.

Estates   *Villa*, like *servus*, is a major problem in this period, but it does not occur often in our selection. We have normally left it untranslated, but in the *Brevium Exempla* (pp. 98ff) we have felt justified in rendering it 'village' rather than 'manor' as the territorial element seemed more significant than the tenurial. We have used the anglicized 'manse' in spite of its modern overtones as our translation of *mansus*, the term for a regular holding. *Fiscus* as an administrative unit of the royal estates we have translated 'crown lands' or 'crown estate', though where it means the royal purse we have used the convenient word 'fisc'.

There are many passages in the documents which are ambiguous or imprecise, or where the text we have is hopelessly corrupt: we have quoted the original Latin where we feel it may be helpful, but where no obvious historical issue is involved we have normally trusted our own judgement. The aim of the translations generally is to convey the precise meaning of the Latin and, where possible, to preserve something of its character and even, on occasion, of its somewhat awkward structure.

Introduction

THE reign of Charles the Great is by any standard one of the most important in the history of Europe. It marks a culminating point in the sub-Roman period. It also provided in fact as well as in theory an inspiration and example to later medieval monarchies; so much of what we take to be typically medieval in institutional life as well as in cultural life in the West can be traced back directly to the empire of Charles the Great. In this brief introduction to our selection of documents we aim to establish the context in which the achievement of Charles may be fairly set, to say something of the political and governmental aspects of the reign, and to note some of the features of the coronation of 800 and of the subsequent undoubted decline of the empire.

The easiest of the basic problems to treat is the military and political setting of the reign. Charles was a formidable and highly successful soldier and leader of soldiers. Without his military skill the political success which culminated in the creation of an empire would not have been possible. His was a dynamic reign and his empire depended in large part on the force at the centre of his own physical energy. When this slackened in his own last years and more so under his weaker successors, the cracks in the apparently unified edifice quickly appeared. Even so the achievements were great. He consolidated the Frankish hold over the other Christian Germanic kingdoms and communities of western Europe; and he further extended his political hold until all the continental Germanic peoples on the mainland of western Europe were subject to his rule. The ultimate boundaries of Charles's empire were racial and linguistic, Roman and German; and the whole vast area was rounded off by the strong military local presence at the borders with the Danes, the Slavs, the Avars, the south Slavs, the Greeks, the Moslems, and to some degree the Bretons.

The most important single step in the consolidation of the Germanic Christian communities came early in his reign. Charles succeeded to the Frankish kingdom in 768 jointly with his brother Carloman who inherited the lands to the southeast, Burgundy and Alamania. The arrangement worked badly, but Carloman died in 771 before civil war broke out. North Italian interests had been partly responsible for the fraternal strains. The Lombard kingdom in northern Italy enjoyed a somewhat tangled relationship with the papacy which had, since the early 750s, exercised political mastery over the former imperial territories of the exarchate of Ravenna. Charles invaded Lombardy in 773–4 to defend papal interests, defeated the Lombard king, Desiderius, at Pavia, forced him to retire to a monastery, and assumed the iron crown of Lombardy in person. This was a highly successful move. Charles was now king of the Franks, king of the Lombards and unmistakably protector of the papacy. Nothing illustrates better than Charles's assumption of the Lombard crown the strength of the new-found Christian kingship. Christian sanction could overcome ancient tribal loyalties. Elsewhere in Europe Charles also made a reality of his position as royal protector of Christian peoples. Bavaria had been Christianized and to some degree Romanized earlier in the eighth century. Charles was able to bind Duke Tassilo to him by feudal bonds and Christian oaths. Bavaria was an outpost against non-Germanic peoples and its subordination marked a step towards the unification of the Christian Germanic peoples. In similar fashion, though with limited success, Charles intervened in Spain where the northern fringe remained Christian and Teutonic in spite of the overthrow of the Visigothic kingdom by the Moslems. In 778 Charles advanced as far south as Saragossa. The disaster to the rearguard at Roncesvalles was countered by the successful creation late in the eighth century of a Spanish March as a buffer against possible Moslem attack.

It is arguable, however, that for Charles himself, his main political achievement (at least before AD 800) came in his forcible extension of Frankish rule and Christianity over other continental Germanic peoples. His own territories, his homelands, lay in the Austrasian Frankish lands, especially around Aix-la-Chapelle. His near neighbours to the east were the continental Saxons, still pagan and relatively untouched by Roman traditions. For more than thirty years Charles faced a series of political and military crises on this frontier. From the first campaigns of 772 up to 780 his object was to keep the Saxons quiet by means of punitive raids. After 780 conquest was the objective. The campaigns were ugly and violent, involving a wholesale massacre of prisoners in 782, a series of terrorist marches, compulsory transfer of population on a large scale, and Christian propaganda. The Church was used in the interests of the Frankish monarchy. Priests were supported by a system of tithes and laws, based on ecclesiastical administration. The confessional was used in the most repressive days as a political weapon. Strong reaction by the pagan Saxon prince, Widukind, led to fierce fighting, but the settlement of 797 when Saxon laws were brought into conformity with Frankish laws marks an attempt at true pacification. In the last Saxon campaigns, made after Charles had become emperor, loyalist Saxons took part on Charles's side. Christianity spread rapidly. Bishoprics were established at Bremen, Munster and Paderborn, 804–6, and later at Hamburg, Hildesheim, Minden, Osnabrück, Verden and ultimately at Magdeburg. Success in Saxony came about partly by military vigour and persistence, partly by the open involvement of the Church and the cause of Christianity in the campaigns.

By the turn of the century, Charles's empire extended along the River Elbe to the Danube and on to the Adriatic. Some of his most vigorous and profitable campaigns were conducted against the Avars who occupied the fertile lands of the middle Danube, modern Hungary. They were decisively defeated in 791, and Charles established special military march-lands along the eastern frontier, notably the Wendish March in the northeast and the March of Carinthia to the southeast. No systematic attempt was made to Christianize the non-Germanic peoples, though in fact the remnant of the Avars was converted.

This brief political sketch is enough to illustrate the extent and range, and also in some measure the nature, of Charles's military and political successes. We have now to consider the question of his relationship with Rome and the papacy, and the problems surrounding his coronation as emperor in AD 800. No German barbarian leader had achieved such success, and none had shown himself so zealous a defender of Christendom. It is tempting to interpret the imperial coronation of 800 as a natural outcome of his triumphs, particularly when these are associated with his attempts to maintain law and order in a Roman style, with the weakness of the empire at Constantinople (ruled by a woman, Irene, since 797) and with the immediate situation at Rome.

From 772–96 the papal chair had been occupied by Pope Hadrian, who had worked very closely with the Frankish king. Hadrian was succeeded by Pope Leo III who had to face political unrest at Rome which resulted in 798 in an outbreak of sedition and violence against the pope, who turned to the Franks for protection. Charles, encouraged by his ecclesiastical advisers, marched to Rome, presided over a tribunal at which the pope of his own free will protested his innocence of the charges brought against him, and was crowned emperor in the basilica of St Peter on Christmas Day, AD 800. The act of coronation was performed by the pope, and later generations were to take this as a sign of special powers possessed by the papacy in relation to the making of the emperor. Einhard tells us that Charles would not have entered the basilica if he had known that the coronation was to take place, but it is highly unlikely that Charles's apparent hesitations were due to an awareness of future constitutional implications. His sentiments are best explained as conventional expressions of diffidence and seemly humility.

The implications and consequences of these events of AD 800 remain a matter for active discussion. It appeared that the Germanic and Romanic peoples in western Europe achieved political consolidation in the face of the other two political powers that had emerged as inheritors of the ancient Græco-Roman civilized world—the eastern empire, centred at Constantinople, and the Moslem world. Christian unity had indeed been achieved in the West so that the heathen might not mock the Christian. Ideas concerning a Christian empire, an *imperium christianum*, were current at Charles's court at Aix-la-Chapelle before AD 800, and the influence of St Augustine's conception of a city of God—in no matter what garbled a form—was far from negligible. Yet there is evidence to suggest that the empire was in a sense personal rather than an attempt to create a single united institution; in 806 a firm decision was taken to divide the empire at

Charles's death among his sons, and it was only the dynastic accident of the survival of one son alone that ensured the integrity of the empire into a second generation. In 843 a political partition of the Carolingian domains was made along lines that were to be familiar throughout the succeeding centuries of the Middle Ages, and Charles's grandsons succeeded to power in France, in Germany and in the Middle Kingdom.

Valid interpretation depends to a great extent on our view of the inner nature of Charles's empire and of his personal position. Was it the empire of the West, vacant since 476, or a co-emperorship with Constantinople of a universal Roman empire, or even the sole emperorship of the Roman empire? Was the title of no significance except to a handful of antiquarians at Aix or at Rome or did it bring political advantage in the West? Did the idea of an empire mean anything to the Franks or the Lombards—or to the Church? Is there any validity in the argument that the coronation cemented the alliance between the pope and the emperor and symbolized the creation of the theocratic Carolingian state? These questions—and many others like them—are propounded in order to assess the importance of the coronation to Europe generally. There is a sense in which the events of AD 800 mark the culmination of the previous four centuries of western history and also the beginning of a new era.

It is true that many strands in the history of western Europe seem to be brought together in the new empire of Charles the Great—developments of long standing in the Mediterranean world, the eastern empire, and Germany, and intimately within the Frankish orbit itself alliances between Church and State and between the Frankish monarchy and the papacy. Mediterranean developments are basic to the whole story. Movements in world trade, associated with the sweeping Moslem successes of AD 632–732, left Frankia and the western world substantially landlocked in the eighth century; only a trickle of trade through Venice and the imperial Italian territories maintained a trace of the old Mediterranean commercial vigour. The result was a steady increase in the importance of land and the revenues and services dependent upon land. The cash nexus was weak. Charles's own family owed their own authority to their landed strength in the most Germanic part of the Frankish realm. His grandfather, Charles Martel, victor over the Moslems at Poitiers in 732, had himself taken over much Church land in order to provide payment for his cavalry officers. It was normal to reward a royal servant with a benefice, to grant him payment in land and local revenue. Similar developments in non-Byzantine Italy led to a social uniformity in the western world, cut off from the life-line of Mediterranean commerce and fluid wealth. At the same time the true imperial heirs of Rome, the emperors at Constantinople, were growing further estranged from the West and particularly from the papacy. This was a gradual and somewhat reluctant process on both sides. To the popes in eighth-century Italy the choice in the search for physical protection must often have been seen to lie between a civilized empire and a barbaric Frankish kingdom. Military and religious reasons led to estrangement from Constantinople. The eastern imperial forces, the Greeks or Byzantines as we may now term them, were unable to give the papacy effective aid against the Lombards. The popes were forced to look north for protection. They appealed to Charles Martel who was hesitant about acting against the fellow Germanic power of the Lombards. Appeals to Martel's son, Pippin, were more successful, resulting in the early 750s in Frankish armed intervention and the virtual creation of the papal states from imperial territory. The Greeks were worried on their own eastern frontiers and in the north by the Bulgars, and could not give their full attention to their Italian interests. Religious sentiments, too, contributed to Byzantine estrangement. The strong Isaurian ruling house of the eighth century was iconoclastic, that is to say it disapproved of what it considered excessive veneration of images in churches. Opinion in the West was much opposed to the policy of the puritan emperors, so much so that at one stage jurisdiction over the churches of south Italy was withdrawn from the papacy. Italy became something of a centre of refuge for opponents of iconoclasm, and ecclesiastical opinion became better prepared for a change in masters. When in the last years of the century the eastern empire passed into the hands of Irene, who took the imperial title to herself, Italian and especially Roman sentiment was even further alienated from the court at Constantinople.

Meanwhile, as religious differences emerged between the eastern empire and the papacy, so the position of the Frankish kings as defenders of western orthodoxy became more pronounced. The English had been converted to Christianity in the seventh century. Inspired by their new faith they formed the active spearhead of the missions that brought the Christian faith to the continental German to the east of the Rhine in the course of the eighth century. The Anglo-Saxon missionaries remained in touch with their insular homeland and also maintained close ecclesiastical contact with Rome. They depended for military and political support on the rulers of the Frankish people. In the 740s the greatest of them, St Boniface, was instrumental in effecting reform in the Frankish Church itself. St Boniface was martyred by the Frisians in 755, but the work of conversion continued, and was indeed intensified. The forcible conquest and conversion of the continental Saxons was the last step in a process of Christianization of the Frankish Germanic border and the east. The papacy was actively involved in the whole process, giving advice, material help, and sanction in the way of ecclesiastical title. St Boniface himself was created the first archbishop of Mainz in 733. We miss one vital element in the creation of the Carolingian empire if we fail to appreciate the full importance of the cooperation achieved by the papacy, the Frankish soldiers, and the Anglo-Saxon missionaries in their German enterprises.

Within the Frankish kingdom itself the missionary enterprise on the border had great impact on the relationship between the Church and the State. The attitude of the Church towards the State throughout the sub-Roman period tended to be somewhat passive. Following the teaching of St Augustine men recognized the State as necessary because of the sinful nature of humanity and yet at the same time as a means of providing a remedy for sin. Among the western communities the Church was forced, nevertheless, to play an increasingly large part in government, its role increasing as Roman territorial authority dwindled. In eighth-century Frankia political circumstances came to exaggerate this process. Bishops possessed great local prestige and for the most part worked closely with the king. Missionary efforts and internal reform brought Church and State close together. Under Charles the Great contact was even more intimate. His military campaigns against the Saxons and the Moslems took on some of the attributes we later associate with crusades. Bishops were employed extensively as government officers. Some of the best and most vigorous intellectual elements of the age were gathered together at his court at Aix. Alcuin, the greatest scholar of the day, was recruited specially from York to give intellectual strength to the teaching and writing at the Frankish court. There was a powerful theological element right at the centre of Charles's kingdom and empire. Bishops and clerics were actively involved in society; awareness of the implications of this involvement tempered their traditional passive attitudes to society and helped to popularize the conception of a new Christian commonwealth, a true *civitas dei* on earth. Charles's government in consequence took on a distinct theocratic tinge: the idea of a crime against a state blurred into the notion of a sin against God.

The ugly side of this close cooperation may be seen in the course of the Saxon campaigns where, as we have already mentioned, the confessional itself was used as a political weapon. The best ecclesiastical thinkers were alarmed at the excesses. Alcuin protested that tithes were destroying the faith among the Saxons. Charles himself tempered the abuses of royal control, particularly after his imperial coronation. He had a deep personal interest in theology, and did not hesitate to support his Frankish theologians even against the pope if occasion appeared to demand such action.

In general, however, the interests of the Franks and the papacy came to coincide. From the time of Gregory the Great, AD 590–604, the papacy had been a considerable force in European political life. By nature and tradition it belonged to the world of Mediterranean civilization but that world itself was altering its shape and nature. The astounding success of the Moslem invasions left the greater part of the Near East and the provinces of North Africa and the greater part of Spain in non-Christian hands. Some counter to these sensational losses was provided by the conversion of the Anglo-Saxons and continental Germans. On the world scale the axis of Christianity was veering north away from the Mediterranean. Papal interests were less at one with those of the emperor at Constantinople. By the conversion of territories to the north and the east, Frankia assumed a central position in western Christendom: and the papacy had been active and creative in the principal missionary efforts.

Even so, as we have seen, direct contact was hesitant in the first half of the eighth century. Political events in the early 750s precipitated matters. Frankia was ruled by Pippin the Short, father of Charles the Great. He was not king but mayor of the palace ruling in the name of a symbolic king, a *roi fainéant*, a descendant of the Merovingian dynasty. The only other powerful Christian kingdom on the Continent was Lombardy, the heavily Romanic kingdom of north Italy, ruled by a German dynasty and people, which had relatively recently adopted the orthodox Catholic faith of the Romans. There was a delicate balance of political power in Italy between the Lombard kingdom, imperial lands answerable to the emperor at Constantinople, Lombard duchies and imperial cities in the south, and the papacy. The heart of imperial power lay in the so-called exarchate of Ravenna, a substantial corridor of land running from northeast to southwest across north-central Italy, from Ravenna to Rome. In 751 the balance of power was destroyed when the Lombards in a sudden campaign defeated the imperial troops and occupied Ravenna. The threat to the papacy was immense. If the rest of the Greek possessions in Italy were to fall to the Lombards, Rome itself faced the future as a mere Lombard bishopric. The only possible counterpoise lay in the north. Pope Zacharias appealed to the Franks. A series of letters was exchanged and a bargain was struck. The Franks promised military intervention and in return the papacy issued a decree which ended the Merovingian farce and established the legitimacy of Pippin and his descendants as a Christian dynasty. In a famous judgement Zacharias announced to Pippin:

ut melius esset illum regem vocari, qui potestatem haberet, quam illum, qui sine regali potestate manebat. *[that it was better that he who had the power should bear the royal name, than he who remained without the royal power.]*

The last of the Merovingians was shorn of his locks (the long hair was the special distinguishing feature of the dynasty), and sent packing to a monastery. Pippin was acclaimed king and anointed with holy oil as Christian king by St Boniface. Two years later renewed Lombard threats (a mere show of force had been enough to remove the danger in 751) prompted the new pope, Stephen II, to cross the Alps to renew the compact. Pippin on this occasion was consecrated by the pope himself, and his sons (including the young Charles) were also anointed and a papal anathema launched against those who would disturb their rule. Pippin received the title of *patricius* which gave him special standing in the city of Rome. He invaded Lombardy, imposed peace, and handed over the exarchate to papal rule, the pope acting apparently as representative of the Roman republic. A second invasion in 756 made sure that the Lombard king, Aistulf, obeyed the terms. At some stage during these long negotiations the Donation of Constantine, the document that was later to have great impact on medieval political thought, received its historic form. By the terms of this document the papacy was to exercise the rights in the legitimate transmission of the empire. Thus, in the short space of four or five years the foundations were laid both for the 'Carolingian' dynasty as Christian kings of Frankia and for the temporal power of the papacy. The Christian Church had emerged as a civilizing agency strong enough to overcome the Germanic tribal traditions implicit in the strange Merovingian situation. Charles's career and achievements, culminating in the creation of a Christian empire, appear almost as the natural logical outcome of the political settlement, 751–6.

For all the emphasis on its unity, there was in practice great diversity in the empire of Charles the Great. Each district had its own laws, a product of the individual development and racial peculiarities of the vast territories under Frankish control. As early as 781 Charles had taken pains to create his two sons Louis and Pippin kings respectively of Aquitaine and Italy (the old Lombard kingdom). They remained subordinate to their father but provided a means of controlling government and military affairs in more manageable units. The Church provided one important unifying element. In the purely secular field Charles relied on royal officers known as *comites* or counts as his chief instrument in achieving unity. The counts ruled over administrative areas that could vary from the size of a parish to that of a province. They were powerful men, comparatively few in number considering the extent of territory concerned; there were probably never more than 250–300 of them at any stage in Charles's reign. Within his territory the count was responsible to the king for the collection of taxes, the supervision of justice and the carrying out of royal administrative orders, particularly in relation to the running of the royal estates. He had to be present every year at a great assembly, the 'Field of May', when the chief men in the realm met, usually at a royal manor or township, to decide on the year's campaign or to hear important judgements. To supervise the counts Charles made extensive use of special commissioners, known as *missi dominici*. Charles was not the first to use such men but he was the first to regularize their employment. A commission, generally consisting of one layman and one cleric, bishop or abbot, would be sent to a particular district where its members had little personal material interest to make sure that local government was being carried out in satisfactory manner, that the counts were not abusing their powers, that the king's estates were well run and that the church was in good condition. The *missi* were to order the counts to read their capitularies carefully (that is to say the government orders issued centrally by Charles the Great) and to reflect on the oral instructions given to them. The capitularies were indeed published in the local courts and may be read as a powerful attempt to keep the centre in touch with the localities. Occasional courts of inquiry were held to codify laws: definition was the first step towards centralization and unification. The *missi* themselves did not develop into a permanent institution. They needed constant supervision, the driving force coming from Charles's court. They also provided a powerful link between the centre and the localities, a gallant attempt to achieve an effective articulation of government.

It would be wrong to imagine a universal and uniform county system in the Carolingian empire. There were also important exceptions to the working of ordinary government. Some landlords were granted exemptions from normal government. They were granted immunities, particularly immunities from the royal courts. In practice this meant that they took on the function of the court in relation to their own districts. They maintained law and order, collected proper dues and taxes, and saw that the necessary number of fighting men were sent to the royal host. In return they acquired the not negligible proceeds of justice. The dangers are obvious. Once control from the centre slackens it is hard to bring powerful immunities under the control of a king or a great prince; but in Charles's reign such privileges were almost exclusively ecclesiastical and confined to great ecclesiastical landlords, bishops and abbots. Indeed Carolingian immunists, *missi*, bishops and missionaries became intimately involved in the workings of the State. Charles, by extensive use of his clerics, at their best learned and able men with no families to provide for, brought the Church a step nearer recognition of a divine purpose behind secular government.

No discussion of Carolingian government would be complete without some reference to the military basis upon which the political structure rested. The Franks from their early days of settlement had been able to summon troops either by insisting on the obligation of every free man to serve or by forcible recruitment. They maintained in fact the principle of general summons, grouping households into units of four or five in order to ensure greater efficiency. The eighth century brought new complications. A cavalry force became essential. In both Roman and German traditions the military was considered the highest of service. The Carolingians themselves built up their power by skilful use of military retainers. Under Charles constant warfare and preparation for warfare exaggerated the problem. The economy would not support paid military leaders. Charles therefore consciously fostered the nascent institutions of vassalage. Tassilo, the duke of Bavaria, became Pippin's vassal, and later was brought into strict vassalic subjection to Charles himself. But these institutions flourished not only at the top level of society but throughout the free Frankish society as well. Charles deliberately encouraged the formalization of the relationship between lord and man as a means of creating his new order. Christian oaths were used solemnly to bind the man and his lord in a reciprocal relationship, and the institutions extended deep into the Church as well as into the secular world. A vassal would normally be rewarded for his service with land, a *beneficium*. At this stage benefices and vassalage were not normally hereditary, though the trends and indeed the dangers were evident and obvious. Within the framework of the empire in Charles's days, the bond of vassalage was used consciously as a means of increasing royal military strength and general prestige.

9

The opening years of the ninth century were years of confidence for the new empire. Charles deliberately emphasized his new title and exacted special oaths of loyalty from his vassals. In 806, however, native Frankish custom proved too strong to overcome any possible new unitary principles. The emperor arranged to partition his territories among his three sons with no known provision for imperial succession. Complicated negotiations with Byzantium brought some recognition of Charles's personal position though no formal ratification was achieved. The death of two of his sons left the survivor, Louis the Pious, as the natural heir, and Louis was crowned by Charles himself as co-emperor in 813. Under the rule of the ecclesiastically-minded Louis (814–40) imperial ideas were in many ways strengthened though the substance of power and authority dwindled. Efforts were made to preserve the unitary succession to the empire in 817 and again in 823 but in practice the empire was falling apart. Succession problems and revolts made partition inevitable. This was effected among Charles's grandsons in 843 when the new emperor, Lothar, took control of the Middle Kingdom, old Austrasia, Burgundy and Italy, while Louis the German succeeded to Saxony, Suabia and Bavaria, and Charles to Neustria, Aquitaine and the Spanish March. An uneasy balance was followed by sporadic civil war but the main preoccupations lay with local problems and defence against barbarian invasions. By hereditary accident there was a temporary reunion of the Carolingian inheritance under the feeble Charles the Fat (885–8), but by the end of the century Carolingian unity had perished. Only the papacy retained some conception of the unity of Christendom. In the middle of the century Pope Nicholas I made far-reaching claims to papal overlordship. During the first half of the tenth century the imperial title itself passed to Italian princelings dominated by the pope. The poverty of the West was too great to support unity over the extensive territories brought into the empire of the dynamic Charles. Outside pressure of barbarian attack forced power into the hands of local lords. Internal dissensions and civil wars ruined what slim hope there was of dynastic unity. Particularist feelings grew strong and western Europe split along regional lines while authority fragmented within the regions. Until the rise of the Saxon house in the tenth century, the Church and the aristocracy seemed to be the true beneficiaries of the Carolingian peace.

I Biographies and Annals

WE have chosen short selections from six biographical works, from the two ninth-century lifes of Charles the Great, from a life of Pope Leo III (795–816), and from the less well-known biographies of Charles's son, Louis the Pious, and of his grandsons.

Lives of Charles the Great

Both the lives of Charles the Great, the *Vita Caroli* of Einhard and the *De Carolo Magno* of Notker the Stammerer, monk of St Gall, have been edited and translated many times. They are now available in a reliable and attractive modern English version by Lewis Thorpe, *Two Lives of Charlemagne*, (Harmondsworth 1969). The best modern edition of Einhard (with translation into French) is by L. Halphen, *Vita Caroli* (Paris 1938, 3rd edn. 1947). Good texts are also available in the series *Monumenta Germaniae Historica (MGH)* where Einhard has been edited successively by G. H. Pertz (Berlin 1829), by G. Waitz (Hanover 1880), and by O. Holder-Egger (Hanover 1905—a revision of Waitz's work—and 1911). Halphen's edition and Lewis Thorpe's translation are both based on the critical edition of the most important single early manuscript made by Ph. Jaffé, *Bibliotheca rerum Germanicarum*, vol. IV; *Monumenta Carolina* (Berlin 1867, and again with minor emendations by W. Wattenbach, 1876). Notker's text is edited by Pertz (*MGH* 1829, above) and by Jaffé (*Bibliotheca rerum Germanicarum*, 1867, above). It is also edited in vol. VI of the *St Gallische Geschichtsquellen*, by G. Meyer von Knonau (St Gallen 1918).

1 Einhard

Einhard was born about AD 775, was brought up at the monastery of Fulda, and from 791 or 792 to 828 was at the royal, and later the imperial court—first of Charlemagne and then of Charlemagne's son, Louis the Pious. Einhard retired from the political scene about 828, and died at Seligenstadt on 14 March 840. He wrote his *Life of Charles* some time in the early 830s, giving an educated layman's view of Charles, drawing when necessary from classical models to make his point. His work was divided into five books and, as well as his own short, modest introduction, a further introductory note by Walafrid Strabo, written between 840 and 849, has survived, in which that scholar takes credit for the headings and for dividing the *Vita* into chapters for easy reference.

The first book deals with the early Carolingians, describing the background of Charles's own succession at first jointly with his brother Carloman and then as sole king of the Franks. Book II discusses the wars and political campaigns of Charles; Book III the emperor's private life, including a description of his coronation; Book IV the emperor's last years and death, and finally, Book V Charlemagne's last will and testament. We have chosen extracts from Lewis Thorpe's translation of Book II—the Saxon wars, Spain (including the Roncesvalles episode, the focal point of so much medieval romantic legend), Bavaria, the Huns, and the Northmen—and from Book III (personal details and the outcome of Charles's visit to Rome) to illustrate Einhard's style and method. The personal description of the emperor in Book III is based on Suetonius' description of a number of Roman emperors, and was used later by an anonymous monk of Caen as the basis for his own description of William the Conqueror of England. The passage concerning the visit to Rome, with its account of the coronation, should be read alongside the descriptions in the *Liber Pontificalis* and the *Annals*.

Source: Thorpe, pp. 61–72, 76–82 (Book II, chs 6–7, 9, 11, 13–15, 17; Book III, chs 22–5, 27–9).

Book II

The opening chapters of Book II deal with Charles's campaigns in Aquitaine and Lombardy. Chapter 6 concludes with Einhard's summary of the results of the successful campaigns in the early 70s.

The outcome of this conflict was that Italy was subdued, King Desiderius was carried off into exile for the remainder of his life, his son Adalgis was expelled from Italy and everything stolen by the Longobard kings was restored to Hadrian, the ruler of the Church of Rome.

Now that the war in Italy was over, the one against the Saxons, which had been interrupted for the time being, was taken up once more.[1] No war ever undertaken by the Frankish people was more prolonged, more full of atrocities or more demanding of effort. The Saxons, like almost all the peoples living in Germany, are ferocious by nature. They are much given to devil worship and they are hostile to our religion. They think it no dishonour to violate and transgress the laws of God and man. Hardly a day passed without some incident or other which was well calculated to break the peace. Our borders and theirs were contiguous and nearly everywhere in flat, open country, except, indeed, for a few places where great forest or mountain ranges interposed to separate the territories of the two peoples by a clear demarcation line. Murder, robbery and arson were of constant occurrence on both sides. In the end, the Franks were so irritated by these incidents that they decided that the time had come to abandon retaliatory measures and to undertake a full-scale war against these Saxons.

War was duly declared against them. It was waged for thirty-three long years and with immense hatred on both sides, but the losses of the Saxons were greater

[1] The Saxon wars lasted from AD 772–804.

than those of the Franks. This war could have been brought to a more rapid conclusion, had it not been for the faithlessness of the Saxons. It is hard to say just how many times they were beaten and surrendered as suppliants to Charlemagne, promising to do all that was exacted from them, giving the hostages who were demanded, and this without delay, and receiving the ambassadors who were sent to them. Sometimes they were so cowed and reduced that they even promised to abandon their devil worship and submit willingly to the Christian faith; but, however ready they might seem from time to time to do all this, they were always prepared to break the promises they had made. I cannot really judge which of these two courses can be said to have come the more easily to the Saxons, for, since the very beginning of the war against them, hardly a year passed in which they did not vacillate between surrender and defiance.

However, the king's mettlesome spirit and his imperturbability, which remained as constant in adversity as in prosperity, were not to be quelled by their ever-changing tactics, nor, indeed, to be wearied by a task which he had once undertaken. Not once did he allow anyone who had offended in this way to go unpunished. He took vengeance on them for their perfidy and meted out suitable punishment, either by means of an army which he led himself or by dispatching a force against them under the command of his counts. In the end, when all those who had been offering resistance had been utterly defeated and subjected to his power, he transported some ten thousand men, taken from among those who lived both on this side of the Elbe and across the river, and dispersed them in small groups, with their wives and children, in various parts of Gaul and Germany. At long last this war, which had dragged on for so many years, came to an end on conditions imposed by the king and accepted by the Saxons. These last were to give up their devil worship and the malpractices inherited from their forefathers; and then, once they had adopted the sacraments of the Christian faith and religion, they were to be united with the Franks and become one people with them. . . .

At a time when this war against the Saxons was being waged constantly and with hardly an intermission at all, Charlemagne left garrisons at strategic points along the frontier and went off himself with the largest force he could muster to invade Spain. He marched over a pass across the Pyrenees, received the surrender of every single town and castle which he attacked and then came back with his army safe and sound, except for the fact that for a brief moment on the return journey, while he was in the Pyrenean mountain range itself, he was given a taste of Basque treachery. Dense forests, which stretch in all directions, make this a spot most suitable for setting ambushes. At a moment when Charlemagne's army was stretched out in a long column of march, as the nature of the local defiles forced it to be, these Basques, who had set their ambush on the very top of one of the mountains, came rushing down on the last part of the baggage train and on the troops who were marching in support of the rearguard and thus were protecting the army which had gone on ahead. The Basques forced them down into the valley beneath, joined battle with them and killed them to the last man. They then snatched up the baggage, and, protected as they were by the cover of darkness, which was just beginning to fall, scattered in all directions without losing a moment. In this feat the Basques were helped by the lightness of their arms and by the nature of the terrain in which the battle was fought. On the other hand, the heavy nature of their own equipment and the unevenness of the ground completely hampered the Franks in their resistance to the Basques. In this battle died Eggihard, who was in charge of the king's table, Anshelm, the count of the Palace, and Roland, lord of the Breton Marches, along with a great number of others. What is more, this assault could not be avenged there and then, for, once it was over, the enemy dispersed in such a way that no one knew where or among which people they could be found. . . .

Next there suddenly broke out a war in Bavaria,[2] but this was very soon over. It was occasioned by the pride and folly of Duke Tassilo. He was encouraged by his wife, who was the daughter of King Desiderius and thought that through her husband she could revenge her father's exile, to make an alliance with the Huns, the neighbours of the Bavarians to the east. Not only did Tassilo refuse to carry out Charlemagne's orders, but he did his utmost to provoke the king to war. Tassilo's arrogance was too much for the spirited king of the Franks to stomach. Charlemagne summoned his levies from all sides and himself marched against Bavaria with a huge army, coming to the river Lech, which divides the Bavarians from the Germans. He pitched his camp on the bank of this river. Before he invaded the province he determined to discover the intentions of the duke by sending messengers to him. Tassilo realized that nothing could be gained for himself or his people by his remaining stubborn. He went in person to beg Charlemagne's forgiveness, handed over the hostages who had been demanded, his own son Theodo among them, and, what is more, swore an oath that he would never again listen to anyone who might try to persuade him to revolt against the king's authority. In this way a war which had all the appearance of becoming very serious was in the event brought to a swift conclusion. Tassilo was summoned to the king's presence and was not allowed to go back home afterwards. The government of the province over which he had ruled was entrusted from that moment onwards not to a single duke but to a group of counts. . . .

The war which came next was the most important which Charlemagne ever fought, except the one against the Saxons: I mean the struggle with the Avars or Huns. He waged it with more vigour than any of the others and with much greater preparation. He himself led only one expedition into Pannonia, the province which the Huns occupied at that period. Everything else he entrusted to his son Pippin, to the governors of his provinces and to his counts and legates.

[2] AD 787–8.

The war was prosecuted with great vigour by these men and it came to an end in its eighth year.

Just how many battles were fought and how much blood was shed is shown by the fact that Pannonia is now completely uninhabited and the site of the Khan's palace is now so deserted that no evidence remains that anyone ever lived there. All the Hun nobility died in this war, all their glory departed. All their wealth and their treasures assembled over so many years were dispersed. The memory of man cannot recall any war against the Franks by which they were so enriched and their material possessions so increased. These Franks, who until then had seemed almost paupers, now discovered so much gold and silver in the palace and captured so much precious booty in their battles, that it could rightly be maintained that they had in all justice taken from the Huns what these last had unjustly stolen from other nations. . . .

The last war which Charlemagne undertook was against those Northmen who are called Danes. They first came as pirates and then they ravaged the coasts of Gaul and Germany with a large fleet. Their king, Godefrid, was so puffed up with empty ambition that he planned to make himself master of the whole of Germany. He had come to look upon Frisia and Saxony as provinces belonging to him; and he had already reduced the Abodrites, who were his neighbours, to a state of subservience and made them pay him tribute. Now he boasted that he would soon come with a huge army to Aix itself, where the king had his court. There was no lack of people to believe his boasting, however empty it really was. He was actually considered to be on the point of trying some such manoeuvre, and was only prevented from doing so by the fact that he died suddenly. He was killed by one of his own followers, so that his own life and the war which he had started both came to a sudden end.

These, then, are the wars which this powerful king, Charlemagne, waged with such prudence and success in various parts of the world throughout a period of forty-seven years, that is, during the whole of his reign. The Frankish kingdom which he inherited from his father Pippin was already far-flung and powerful. By these wars of his he increased his kingdom to such an extent that he added to it almost as much again. Originally no more land was occupied by the eastern Franks, as they were called, than the region of Gaul which lies between the Rhine, the Loire, the Atlantic Ocean and the sea round the Balearic Islands, together with the part of Germany which is situated between Saxony, the Danube, the Rhine and the Saal, which last river divides the Thuringians and the Sorabians. To this must be added, too, the fact that the Alamanni and the Bavarians formed part of the Frankish kingdom. By the campaigns which I have described, Charlemagne annexed Aquitaine, Gascony, the whole mountain range of the Pyrenees and land stretching as far south as the River Ebro, which rises in Navarre, flows through the most fertile plains of Spain and then enters the Balearic Sea beneath the walls of the city of Tortosa. He added the whole of Italy, which stretches for a thousand miles and more in length from Aosta to southern Calabria, at the point where the frontiers between the Greeks and the men of Benevento are to be found. To this he joined Saxony, which forms a very considerable part of Germany and is considered to be twice as wide as the territory occupied by the Franks, while it is just about as long; then both provinces of Pannonia, the part of Dacia which is beyond the Danube, Istria, Liburnia and Dalmatia, with the exception of its maritime cities, which Charlemagne allowed the emperor of Constantinople to keep, in view of his friendship with him and the treaty which he had made. Finally he tamed and forced to pay tribute all the wild and barbarous nations which inhabit Germany between the rivers Rhine and Vistula, the Atlantic Ocean and the Danube, peoples who are almost identical in their language, although they differ greatly in habit and customs. Among these last the most notable are the Welatabi, the Sorabians, the Abodrites and the Bohemians, against all of whom he waged war; the others, by far the greater number, surrendered without a struggle. . . .

Charlemagne took upon himself the task of building a fleet to ward off the attacks of the Northmen. For this purpose ships were constructed near to the rivers which flow out of Gaul and Germany into the North Sea. In view of the fact that these Northmen kept on attacking and pillaging the coast of Gaul and Germany, Charlemagne placed strong-points and coastguard stations at all the ports and at the mouths of all rivers considered large enough for the entry of ships, so that the enemy could be bottled up by this military task force. He did the same in the south, along the shore of southern Gaul and Septimania, and along the whole coast of Italy as far north as Rome, against the Moors who had recently begun piratical attacks. The result of this measure was that during his lifetime no serious damage was done to Italy by the Moors, or to Gaul and Germany by the Northmen. The only exceptions were Civitavecchia, a city in Etruria, which was captured and sacked by the Moors as the result of treachery; and certain islands in Frisia, near to the German coast, which were looted by the Northmen.

Book III

This personal description of Charles follows an account of his family life, his marriages, his respect for his mother, with whom, we are told, 'he never had a cross word, except over the divorce of King Desiderius' daughter, whom he had married on her advice.' He educated his daughters as well as his sons, and was exceptionally possessive about them, keeping them in his household until the day of his death. Einhard tells us that he had a number of unfortunate experiences as a result, but that he shut his eyes to all that happened. He was not naturally cruel, and Einhard blames the occasional severities (rather unfairly) on the influence of Queen Fastrada.

The emperor was strong and well built. He was tall in stature, but not excessively so, for his height was just seven times the length of his own feet. The top of his head was round, and his eyes were piercing and unusually large. His nose was slightly longer than normal, he had a fine head of white hair and his expression was gay and good-humoured. As a result, whether he was seated or standing, he always appeared masterful and dignified. His neck was short and rather thick, and his stomach a trifle too heavy, but the proportions of the rest of his body prevented one from noticing these blemishes. His step was firm and he was manly in all his movements. He spoke distinctly, but his voice was thin for a man of his physique. His health was good, except that he suffered from frequent attacks of fever during the last four years of his life, and towards the end he was lame in one foot. Even then he continued to do exactly as he wished, instead of following the advice of his doctors, whom he came positively to dislike after they advised him to stop eating the roast meat to which he was accustomed and to live on stewed dishes.

He spent much of his time on horseback and out hunting, which came naturally to him, for it would be difficult to find another race on earth who could equal the Franks in this activity. He took delight in steam baths at the thermal springs, and loved to exercise himself in the water whenever he could. He was an extremely strong swimmer and in this sport no one could surpass him. It was for this reason that he built his palace at Aix and remained continuously in residence there during the last years of his life and indeed until the moment of his death. He would invite not only his sons to bathe with him, but his nobles and friends as well, and occasionally even a crowd of his attendants and bodyguards, so that sometimes a hundred men or more would be in the water together.

He wore the national dress of the Franks. Next to his skin he had a linen shirt and linen drawers; and then long hose and a tunic edged with silk. He wore shoes on his feet and bands of cloth wound round his legs. In winter he protected his chest and shoulders with a jerkin made of otter skins or ermine. He wrapped himself in a blue cloak and always had a sword strapped to his side, with a hilt and belt of gold or silver. Sometimes he would use a jewelled sword, but this was only on great feast days or when ambassadors came from foreign peoples. He hated the clothes of other countries, no matter how becoming they might be, and he would never consent to wear them. The only exception to this was one day in Rome when Pope Hadrian entreated him to put on a long tunic and a Greek mantle, and to wear shoes made in the Roman fashion; and then a second time, when Leo, Hadrian's successor, persuaded him to do the same thing. On feast days he walked in procession in a suit of cloth of gold, with jewelled shoes, his cloak fastened with a golden brooch and with a crown of gold and precious stones on his head. On ordinary days his dress differed hardly at all from that of the common people.

He was moderate in his eating and drinking, and especially so in drinking; for he hated to see drunkenness in any man, and even more so in himself and his friends. All the same, he could not go long without food, and he often used to complain that fasting made him feel ill. He rarely gave banquets and these only

17

on high feast days, but then he would invite a great number of guests. His main meal of the day was served in four courses, in addition to the roast meat which his hunters used to bring in on spits and which he enjoyed more than any other food. During his meal he would listen to a public reading or some other entertainment. Stories would be recited for him, or the doings of the ancients told again. He took great pleasure in the books of Saint Augustine and especially in those which are called *The City of God*.

He was so sparing in his use of wine and every other beverage that he rarely drank more than three times in the course of his dinner. In summer, after his midday meal, he would eat some fruit and take another drink; then he would remove his shoes and undress completely, just as he did at night, and rest for two or three hours. During the night he slept so lightly that he would wake four or five times and rise from his bed. When he was dressing and putting on his shoes he would invite his friends to come in. Moreover, if the count of the Palace told him that there was some dispute which could not be settled without the emperor's personal decision, he would order the disputants to be brought in there and then, hear the case as if he were sitting in tribunal and pronounce a judgement. If there was any official business to be transacted on that day, or any order to be given to one of his ministers, he would settle it at the same time.

He spoke easily and fluently, and could express with great clarity whatever he had to say. He was not content with his own mother tongue, but took the trouble to learn foreign languages. He learnt Latin so well that he spoke it as fluently as his own tongue; but he understood Greek better than he could speak it. He was eloquent to the point of sometimes seeming almost garrulous.

He paid the greatest attention to the liberal arts, and he had great respect for men who taught them, bestowing high honours upon them. When he was learning the rules of grammar he received tuition from Peter, the deacon of Pisa, who by then was an old man, but for all other subjects he was taught by Alcuin, surnamed Albinus, another deacon, a man of the Saxon race who came from Britain and was the most learned man anywhere to be found. Under him the emperor spent much time and effort in studying rhetoric, dialectic and especially astrology. He applied himself to mathematics and traced the course of the stars with great attention and care. He also tried to learn to write. With this object in view he used to keep writing-tablets and notebooks under the pillows on his bed, so that he could try his hand at forming letters during his leisure moments; but, although he tried very hard, he had begun too late in life and he made little progress.

[After a brief account of Charles's attitude towards the practice of the Christian Church, Einhard gives us the following very important account of Charles's visit to Rome and his coronation.]

Charlemagne cared more for the church of the holy apostle Peter in Rome than for any other sacred and venerable place. He poured into its treasury a vast fortune in gold and silver coinage and in precious stones. He sent so many gifts to the pope that it was impossible to keep count of them. Throughout the whole period of his reign nothing was ever nearer to his heart than that, by his own efforts and exertion, the city of Rome should regain its former proud position. His ambition was not merely that the church of St Peter should remain safe and protected thanks to him, but that by means of his wealth it should be more richly adorned and endowed than any other church. However much he thought of Rome, it still remains true that throughout his whole reign of 47 years he went there only four times to fulfil his vows and to offer up his prayers.

These were not the sole reasons for Charlemagne's last visit to Rome. The truth is that the inhabitants of Rome had violently attacked Pope Leo, putting out his eyes and cutting off his tongue, and had forced him to flee to the king for help. Charlemagne really came to Rome to restore the Church, which was in a very bad state indeed, but in the end he spent the whole winter there. It was on this occasion that he received the title of emperor and Augustus. At first he was far from wanting this. He made it clear that he would not have entered the cathedral that day at all, although it was the greatest of all the festivals of the Church, if he had known in advance what the pope was planning to do. Once he had accepted the title, he endured with great patience the jealousy of the so-called Roman emperors, who were most indignant at what had happened. He overcame their hostility only by the sheer strength of his personality, which was much more powerful than theirs. He was forever sending messengers to them, and in his dispatches he called them his brothers.

Now that he was emperor, he discovered that there were many defects in the legal system of his own people, for the Franks have two separate codes of law which differ from each other in many points. He gave much thought to how he could best fill the gaps, reconcile the discrepancies, correct the errors and rewrite the laws which were ill-expressed. None of this was ever finished; he added a few sections, but even these remained incomplete. What he did do was to have collected together and committed to writing the laws of all the nations under his jurisdiction which still remained unrecorded.

At the same time he directed that the age-old narrative poems, barbarous enough, it is true, in which were celebrated the warlike deeds of the kings of ancient times, should be written out and so preserved. He also began a grammar of his native tongue.

2 Notker the Stammerer

Notker was a monk of St Gall who wrote a life of Charlemagne in 883 or 884 at the command of Charlemagne's undistinguished descendant, Charles the Fat. Much of this so-called biography is taken up in a series of anecdotes, some of which may be well-founded, although others were no more than the accepted good stories of the day. He divided his work into two books, the first of which consisted of 34 chapters on Charles's piety and character, the second of which, in 21 chapters, dealt with his military exploits.

We have chosen extracts from Lewis Thorpe's translation of Book I which cast light on the personality of Alcuin, and on the energy and personality of Charles himself. The extracts selected from Book II indicate how longingly the late ninth-century writer looked back to the good peace and security which he considered typical of the empire of Charles. Professor Bullough rightly points out that Notker tells us in general 'more about how Charles was remembered than about the man he had been.' *The Age of Charlemagne* (London 1965), p. 15.

Source: Thorpe, pp. 101–2, 127–8, 132–4, 157–8 (Book I, chs 9, 30, 34; Book II, ch. 13).

Book I

I must not seem to forget or to neglect Alcuin. I have therefore recorded this true statement about his industry and his accomplishments: of all his pupils there was not one who did not distinguish himself by becoming a devout abbot or a famous bishop. Grimald, my own master, studied the liberal arts under him, first in Gaul and then in Italy. Lest I should be accused by those who know the facts of telling a lie when I say there was no exception to this, there were, it is true, among his pupils two sons of millers in the house of St Columban who did not seem proper persons to be promoted to the command of bishoprics or of monasteries; but through the influence, as it is thought, of their master, these two acted one after the other with great assiduity as stewards of the monastery of Bobbio.

In this way the most glorious Charlemagne saw that the study of letters was flourishing throughout the length and breadth of his kingdom. All the same, despite his superhuman efforts, he grieved because this scholarship was not reaching the high standards of the early fathers, and in his dissatisfaction he exclaimed: 'If only I could have a dozen churchmen as wise and as well taught in all human knowledge as were Jerome and Augustine!' The learned Alcuin, who considered even himself ignorant in comparison with these two, became very indignant at this, although he was careful not to show it, and he dared to do what no one else would have done in the presence of Charlemagne, for the emperor struck terror into everyone. 'The maker of heaven and earth himself,' he said, 'has very few scholars worth comparing with these men, and yet you expect to find a dozen!' . . .

It was a rule in those days that whenever the emperor had ordered some building project to be carried out—the construction of bridges, ships or causeways, or the cleansing, paving or levelling of muddy roads—the counts of the empire could operate through deputies and lesser officials, always provided that only minor works were concerned. From major works, and especially new constructions, no duke, count, bishop or abbot could be excused, whatever the pretext. The arches of the great bridge at Mainz can be quoted as an example of this rule. All Europe, so to speak, laboured side by side at this bridge in orderly cooperation; and then the fraudulent behaviour of a few malevolent people, who were determined to amass some ill-gotten gain from the ships passing underneath, brought about its destruction.

If there were any churches belonging to the royal domain which needed to be decorated with carved ceilings or wall-paintings, this was attended to by the bishops and abbots of the neighbourhood. If, on the other hand, new churches had to be built, all bishops, dukes, counts, abbots, those in charge of churches in the king's gift and anyone who held a public office worked at them ceaselessly from the foundations to the roof. This is proved not only by the cathedral at Aix, which was built by human hands, yet with the inspiration of God. It is also proved by the mansions belonging to men of various rank which were erected round the palace of Charlemagne in such a way that, shrewd as he was, through the windows of his private apartment, he could see everything they were doing, and all their comings and goings, without their realizing it. In the same way all the houses of his nobles were built high off the ground, so that the retainers of his nobles, the personal servants of those retainers and every other passer-by could be protected from rain and snow, cold or heat, and yet the nobles themselves could not hide from the eyes of the ever-vigilant Charlemagne. The description of this cathedral I leave to your own court officials, for I myself am tied here in my monastery. . . .

My mention of the long cloak which the emperor Charlemagne wore when he went out at night brings me now to his clothing in time of war. The dress and the equipment of the Old Franks were as follows. Their boots were gilded on the outside and decorated with leather laces more than four feet long. The wrappings round their legs were scarlet. Underneath these they wore linen garments on their legs and thighs, of the same colour, but with elaborate embroidery. Long leather thongs were cross-gartered over these wrappings and linen garments, in and out, in front and behind. Next came a white linen shirt, round which was buckled a sword-belt. The sword itself was encased first in a sheath, then in a leather holder and finally in a bright white linen cover which was hardened with shining wax, so that protection was given to the middle of the leg when men drew their swords to kill people.

The last item of their clothing was a cloak, either white or blue, in the shape of a double square. This was so arranged that, when it was placed over the shoulders, it reached to the feet in front and behind, but hardly came down to the knees at the sides. In the right hand they carried a stick of applewood, a strong and formidable weapon, remarkable for its even knots, with a handle of gold or silver, worked with decorative engravings. I am a lazy man myself, more sluggish than a tortoise, and I have never travelled to the land of the Franks, but I saw Charles III, the king of the Franks, in full regalia, in the monastery of St Gall. Two gold-petalled flowers stuck out from his thighs. The first of these rose up so high that it was as tall as the king himself; the second, growing gradually upwards, adorned the top of his trunk with great glory and protected him as he walked.

When the Franks, in their wars with the Gauls, saw these latter resplendent in their short striped cloaks, as happens so often in human fashion they were delighted with this novelty. They abandoned their ancient customs and began to imitate their enemies. For a time the emperor did not forbid this dress, although he was a strict man, for it seemed more suited for fighting in battle. Later on he noticed that the Frisians were abusing the freedom he had permitted, for he caught them selling these little short cloaks at the same price as the large ones. He then gave orders that at this price no one should purchase from them any but the bigger cloaks, which were at once very broad and very long. 'What is the use of these little napkins?' he asked. 'I can't cover myself with them in bed. When I am on horseback I can't protect myself from the winds and the rain. When I go off to empty my bowels, I catch cold because my backside is frozen.'

In the preface to this little book, I promised that I would follow only three authorities. Werinbert, the most important of these, died seven days ago, and this very day, the thirtieth of May, we, his bereaved sons and disciples, must pay tribute to his memory. Here then I bring to an end my short treatise on the piety of our lord Charlemagne and his care of the Church, which is based on the reminiscences of that priest.

The next book, which tells of the wars fought by the emperor Charlemagne with such ferocity, is taken from the tales told by Adalbert, who was the father of the same Werinbert. Adalbert was present with his master Kerold in the fighting against the Huns, the Saxons and the Slavs. When I was a child, he was already a very old man. He brought me up and used to tell me about these events. I was a poor pupil, and I often ran away, but in the end he forced me to listen.

Book II

At about this time, when the emperor was just completing his campaign against the Huns and had received the surrender of the peoples whom I have just mentioned, the Northmen started their invasion and began to cause great anxiety to the Gauls and the Franks. The unconquerable Charlemagne turned back and strove to invade them in their own homes, marching overland through a hostile and trackless countryside. Either the will of God held him back, so that, as the scripture says, 'He might make trial of Israel' [Judges 2.22] or else our own sins stood in the way, for all his efforts ended in frustration. In a single night, for example, to the great discomfort of the whole army, 50 pairs of oxen belonging to a single abbot died of a sudden attack of pest. Charlemagne, who was the wisest of men, decided to abandon his plan, preferring not to disobey scripture by 'trying to move against the current of the stream'. At a moment when Charlemagne was travelling on a protracted journey across his own wide empire, Godefrid, the king of the Northmen, encouraged by the emperor's absence, invaded the territory of the Frankish kingdom and settled down in the neighbourhood of the Moselle. Godefrid's own son, whose mother the king had only recently repudiated, so that he might marry another woman in her place, caught up with him just as he was calling his falcon off a heron, and cut him through the middle with his sword. Then, just as happened long ago when Holofernes was slain, none of the Northmen dared to rely any longer upon his courage or his weapons, but all sought safety in flight. In this way the land of the Franks was liberated without any great effort being made, and no one could boast to God as the ungrateful Israel had done. The unconquered and unconquerable Charlemagne gave thanks to God for his decision, but he complained bitterly because some of the Northmen had escaped through his absence. 'I am greatly saddened,' said he, 'that I have not been thought worthy to let my Christian hand sport with these dog-heads.'

Once when he was on a journey Charlemagne came unheralded to a certain town which lies on the seashore in southern Gaul. While he sat eating his supper incognito, a raiding party of Northmen made a piratical attack on the harbour of this town. As their ships came in sight, some said that they were Jewish merchants, others that they were Africans or traders from Britain. Charlemagne in his wisdom knew better. From the build of the ships and their speed through the water he recognized them as enemies rather than merchants. 'Those ships are not loaded with goods,' he said to his men. 'They are filled with savage enemies.' When they heard this, they rushed off to the ships at full speed, each striving to be the first to reach them. They were not successful. As soon as the Northmen learned that the man whom they were accustomed to call Charles the Hammer [an apparent confusion with Charles Martel] was in the neighbourhood, they sailed away at incredible speed. They were not content with avoiding the swords of the pursuers; they were determined to hurry out of sight, too, for fear that their whole fleet might be driven back, or even destroyed and broken up into small pieces. Charlemagne, who was a God-fearing, just and devout ruler, rose from the table and stood at a window facing east. For a long time the precious tears poured down his face. No one dared to ask him why. In the end he explained his lachrymose behaviour to his warlike leaders. 'My faithful servants,' said he, 'do you know why I wept so bitterly? I am not afraid that these ruffians will be able to do me any harm; but I am sick at heart to think that even in my lifetime they have dared to attack this coast, and I am horror-stricken when I foresee what evil they will do to my descendants and their subjects.'

May the protection of Christ Our Lord prevent this from ever coming to pass!

3 Charles the Great and Pope Leo III

The *Liber Pontificalis* consists of a series of lives of the popes, starting with St Peter. For the Carolingian period the individual biographies may be treated as contemporary or near-contemporary sources. The standard and authoritative edition by L. Duchesne (Paris, two vols. 1886–92) has been reissued with a supplementary volume of emendations and critical comments (Paris 1955–7).

The following extract is taken from the life of Pope Leo III (795–816), and relates to the dramatic events at Rome in AD 800 which included the exculpation of the pope from charges brought against him and culminated in the imperial coronation of Charles the Great at St Peter's on Christmas Day.

Source: Duchesne, vol. II, pp. 5–8.

[Leo has been miraculously restored to health after suffering mutilation at the hands of his enemies.]

When this was noised abroad the faithful flocked to him from all the Roman cities; and taking with him a company of people from those cities, bishops and priests, clerics of Rome and leading men of the cities, Leo set out to visit the most excellent lord Charles, king of the Franks and Lombards and patrician of the Romans. And the most Christian and orthodox, most eminent and merciful king, as soon as he heard of it, sent Archbishop Hildebald, his chaplain and Count Aschericus to meet him, and after that his son, the most excellent king Pippin, along with others of his counts; and finally the mighty king himself came to meet him, and received him in respect and honour, with hymns and holy chants, as the vicar of the blessed apostle Peter. Tearfully they embraced and kissed one another; the pontiff began the *Gloria in excelsis Deo*, and it was taken up by all the clergy; a prayer was said over the whole assembly, and then the most blessed lord and mighty king, Charles, gave thanks concerning the pontiff to God, who had, through the intercession of St Peter and St Paul, the chiefs of the apostles, wrought such a miracle upon his servant and brought the evil men to nought.

And when the most serene king had entertained him for some time in great honour, these same evil men and sons of the devil, after having caused such terrible and wicked damage by fire to the possessions and property of St Peter the apostle, contrived in the face of God's disfavour towards them to lodge false charges against the most holy pontiff and to send them in pursuit of him to the king—charges which they could in no wise prove, since in their desire to see the Holy Church humiliated they had made unspeakable accusations which arose from their own treachery and wickedness. However, when the pontiff had stayed with the most merciful and mighty king in great and appropriate honour, there came together there from all parts the archbishops, bishops, and other clergy, together with the council of the same most pious and mighty king and all the chief men of the Franks, and with the great honour that was fitting they sent him forth with God as his guide to return in state to his apostolic see. And city by city, as though they were bringing the apostle himself, they escorted him as far as Rome. And the people of Rome, in great joy at receiving back their shepherd, all came together on the eve of St Andrew the apostle—the leading clerics and the rest of the clergy, the chief men and the senate and all the soldiers, and the whole people of Rome, together with the nuns and deaconesses, the most noble matrons and all the women, and with them also all the colonies of foreigners, the Franks, Frisians, Saxons and Lombards—and joining together at the Milvian bridge they received him with standards and crosses and holy chants, and took him to the church of St Peter the apostle, where he celebrated the rites of the mass and all together partook in faith of the body and blood of Our Lord Jesus Christ.

On the next day, when they were celebrating the birth of St Andrew the apostle, in accordance with the ancient custom, he came into Rome itself amid great rejoicing and entered the Lateran palace. And after some days the most faithful emissaries who had accompanied him in pontifical service—Hildebald and Arno, most reverend archbishops, Cunipertus, Bernard, Atto and Jesse, most reverend and holy bishops, Erflaicus, bishop elect, and Helmgoth, Rottecarius and Germario, most glorious counts—took their seat in the great hall of the same lord, Pope Leo, and for a week and more made inquiry of those most wicked criminals, Paschales and Campulus along with their followers, and the malice which they bore towards their own pontiff; and there was nothing that they could say against him. Then, arresting them, the emissaries of the great king sent them away to the Franks.

After some time the mighty king himself, when he had joined him in the church of St Peter the apostle, and had been received with great honour, caused all the archbishops and bishops, the abbots and all the nobility of the Franks, and the Roman senate to meet together in the same church. And seated side by side, the mighty king and the most blessed pontiff requested the most holy archbishops and bishops and abbots to be seated, and the rest of the clergy and the leaders of the Franks and Romans to stand, so that they might hear the charges which had been made against the gentle pontiff. And all the archbishops and bishops and abbots, when they heard them, declared with one voice: 'We do not dare to judge the apostolic see, which is the head of all the churches of God. For it is by it and by its vicar that all of us are judged. It is not itself judged by anyone, and this has been the custom from of old. Rather, we shall give canonical obedience to whatever the supreme pontiff himself may decide.' Then the venerable pontiff said: 'I follow in the steps of my predecessors as pontiffs and am ready to purge myself of such false charges as have lately maliciously sprung up against me.'

25

On the next day, in the same church of St Peter the apostle, there assembled together all the archbishops and bishops and abbots, and all the Franks who were in the service of the same mighty king, and all the Romans as well in the same church of St Peter the apostle, and in their presence the venerable pontiff, clasping the four holy gospels of Christ, went up into the pulpit in the sight of all and said in a clear voice under oath: 'Of all these false charges which have been laid against me by the Romans who maliciously persecuted me I have no knowledge, nor am I conscious of having done such things.' And when this was done a prayer was offered, and all the archbishops, bishops, abbots and all the clergy gave praise to God and to Our Lady Mary, eternally virgin mother of God, and to St Peter the chief of the apostles and all the saints of God.

After this, when the birthday of Our Lord Jesus Christ arrived, they all assembled again in the church of St Peter the apostle. And on this occasion the venerable and gentle pontiff crowned him, with his own hands, with a most precious crown. Then all the loyal Romans, seeing the great love and care which he showed for the Holy Church of Rome and for its vicar, inspired by God and by St Peter who holds the keys of the kingdom of heaven, cried out aloud with one voice: 'To Charles, most pious Augustus crowned by God, mighty and peaceable emperor, long life and victory!' Before the holy tomb of St Peter the apostle it was said thrice over with the invocation of many saints, and by all the company he was established as emperor of the Romans. Whereupon the most holy priest and pontiff anointed Charles his most excellent son as king with holy oil, on the very day of the nativity of Our Lord Jesus Christ.

[After the ceremony the new emperor presented various gifts to St Peter's and to other churches in Rome.]

After this, when those most evil criminals Paschales and Campulus and their followers were brought into the presence of the most pious lord emperor, and the most noble Franks and Romans and all the rest were in attendance and acquainting themselves with their evil plans and deeds, then Campulus rounded on Paschales, saying: 'It was a bad day when I saw your face, seeing that you brought me to this peril.' And the others did the same, and by condemning one another each of them made his own guilt plain. And when the most pious emperor had seen that they were so cruel and evil he sent them in exile to a part of Frankia.

Lives of Louis the Pious and his sons

Important information about Charlemagne is given in both of the surviving biographies of his son, Louis the Pious (by Thegan and by Astronomus). Our selections are based on the standard modern collection, edited by R. Rau, *Quellen zur karolingischen Reichsgeschichte*

(Berlin 1955), vol. V in *Ausgewahlte Quellen zur Deutschen Geschichte des Mittelalters*; also *MGH, Scriptores* II, ed. G. H. Pertz, pp. 590–604 (Thegan) and pp. 607–48 (Astronomus). The work of Nithard appears in Rau's collection (pp. 383 ff), and in Pertz's edition, pp. 649–72 (revised by E. Muller, Hanover and Leipzig 1907). A convenient and useful edition of Nithard is given in Ph. Lauer, *Nithard: Histoire des fils de Louis le Pieux* (Paris 1926).

4 Thegan's life of Louis the Pious

Thegan (or Theganbert) was a Frank of noble kindred, archdean *(chorepiscopus)* of Trier and prior of the church of St Cassius in Bonn. He wrote the life of Louis the Pious towards the end of Louis' reign in the late 830s.

We include chapters 5–12 of the *Thegani Vita Hludowici Imperatoris*, which deal with arrangements for the succession to the empire; the death of Charles the Great; and the succession itself.

Source: Pertz, pp. 591–3; Rau, pp. 218–23.

5 Now the emperor, Charles the Great, ruled beneficently and well, and loved his kingdom. In the forty-second year of his reign (AD 810) his son Pippin died at the age of 33 and in the following year Charles, his eldest son by the aforementioned Queen Hildegard, died. Only Louis was left to succeed to the government of the kingdom.

6 When the emperor saw that his last day was drawing near (for he was now very old), he called his son Louis to him together with all his army, his bishops, abbots, dukes, counts and their subordinates; and in a general gathering at the palace of Aix he spoke with them peaceably and honourably, urging them to show loyalty to his son and asking all of them, from the greatest down to the least, whether it was pleasing to them that he should bestow his own title of emperor upon his son Louis. They all exultantly replied that this was God's will. This done, he arrayed himself on the following Sunday in his royal attire and placed a crown upon his head, and went forth brightly decked and adorned as befitted his rank. He made his way to the church which he himself had founded and built, and came to the altar dedicated to Our Lord Jesus Christ, which had been set up in a position higher than that of the other altars; on this he ordered a gold crown to be placed—not the one which he wore on his own head, but another. And when he and his son had prayed for a long time, he spoke to him in the presence of the whole multitude of his pontiffs and nobles, exhorting him above all else to love and fear Almighty God, to keep his commandments in all things, and to govern the churches of God and defend them against evil men. To his sisters and brothers younger than himself, to his nephews and nieces and all his kinsmen he ordered him at all times to show unfailing mercy. He should, moreover, honour the priests as his fathers and love the people as his sons, should curb the proud, lead evil men into the way of salvation, and should be a

supporter of the monasteries and a father of the poor. He should appoint loyal and God-fearing ministers, to whom unlawful rewards would be hateful, should withdraw his favour from no man without due cause, and should at all times show himself blameless in the sight of God and all his people. And when he had spoken these words, and many besides to his son before the whole assembly, he asked him if he were willing to obey his commands; and his son replied that he would gladly obey them, and with God's help would abide by all the instructions which his father had given him. Then his father ordered him to take up the crown which was on the altar with his own hands, and to place it upon his head as a reminder of all the instructions which his father had given him. And he did as his father bade him. This done, they heard the rites of the mass and then went to the palace, and so long as he remained with him the son supported his father wherever he went. Some days afterwards his father honoured him with many splendid gifts and sent him off to Aquitaine. Before they separated they embraced and kissed each other, and for joy at their love were moved to tears. The son went on his way to Aquitaine, and the lord emperor kept his kingdom and his title with honour, as was fitting.

7 After they had separated, the lord emperor began to devote all his time to prayer and alms-giving and the correction of books; and on the last day before his death he had accurately corrected the four gospels of Christ, which are inscribed with the names of Matthew, Mark, Luke and John, alongside the Greek and Syriac versions.

In January of the following year, the forty-sixth of his reign [AD 814], the lord emperor succumbed to a fever, which came upon him after his bath. The sickness increased from day to day, so that he took no food or drink except for a little water to refresh his body; and when on the seventh day his suffering became acute he ordered his close friend Bishop Hildebald to come to him and administer the sacrament of the body and blood of Our Lord to comfort his passing. This done, the sickness continued to trouble him for that day and the following night; and at dawn of the next day, knowing what was about to happen to him, he stretched out his right hand and with what strength he could muster pressed the sign of the holy cross upon his forehead, and marked it on his breast and all his body. Finally, he drew his feet together, stretched his arms and hands across his body and closed his eyes, singing softly the following verse: 'Into thy hands, O Lord, I commend my spirit [Psalm 31.5].' And immediately after this, being now at a ripe old age and full of days, he passed peacefully away; and on that same day his body was buried in the church which he himself had built at the palace of Aix, this being his seventy-second year, of the seventh indiction.

8 After the death of the most glorious emperor, Charles, his son Louis came from the region of Aquitaine and made his way to the palace of Aix, and succeeded without any opposition to all the kingdoms which God had bestowed

upon his father. This was the eight hundred and fourteenth year of Our Lord's incarnation, and the first year of his reign. So he took his seat in the palace in succession to his father, and as his first and most urgent task he ordered all his father's treasures, of gold, of silver, of precious stones and of furnishings of every kind, to be shown to him. To his sisters he gave their lawful portion, and what remained he gave for his father's soul. He sent the greater part of the treasure to Rome during the papacy of the blessed Leo, and all that remained after this he distributed among the clergy and the poor, and among strangers, widows and orphans, keeping nothing for himself except one silver table made in the form of three shields joined together: this he kept out of love for his father, though he paid for it with a further sum which he gave in his father's memory.

9 After this, ambassadors came to him from all his kingdoms and provinces, from foreign peoples and all who had been under his father's authority, declaring their intention to show peace and loyalty towards him and freely and spontaneously offering him their obedience. Among them came ambassadors of the Greeks, accompanied by Amalharius, bishop of Trier, who had been ambassador of Charles of pious memory to the prince of Constantinople (whose name for the moment escapes me).[3] As they came in they found the lord Louis seated on his father's throne as God had ordained. He received them kindly, gratefully accepted their gifts, and held friendly talk with them as long as they were with him. Some days later he conferred high honours upon them and sent them home again, dispatching his envoys before them to make ready whatever they might need in whatever part of his kingdom they might be.

10 In the same year the prince ordered all the enactments concerning the churches of God which had been made in the time of his predecessors to be renewed, and he himself confirmed them with his own hand and signature.

11 Meanwhile ambassadors came from Benevento to place the whole Beneventan territory under his control, and promised to pay many thousands of gold pieces every year by way of tribute: this they have continued to do until the present day.

12 At this time also came Bernard, the son of his brother Pippin, who offered himself as his vassal and swore allegiance to him. The lord Louis gladly received him, bestowed great gifts and honours upon him, and allowed him to return again in safety to Italy.

5 Astronomus' life of the Emperor Louis

The anonymous writer was by his own testimony a member of Louis's court at the time of his royal master's imperial coronation. He is generally called 'Astronomus' because

[3] It was Michael: see below the corresponding passage in 'Astronomus' (**5:23**).

of his self-confessed skill in astronomy. His account of the early part of Louis' career during Charles's lifetime is especially important because he used a work, now lost, which was written by the monk Adhemar, and which may have contained a history of Aquitaine.

We include two short sections of the life, chapters 9–12, which illustrate the relationship between Louis, king of Aquitaine since 781, and his father, and chapters 20–3, which deal with the succession problems.

Source: Pertz, pp. 611–12, 617–19; Rau, pp. 270–73, 286–93.

9 When the winter [AD 799] was over the king his father sent for him to come with as many of his men as he could, and join him in his campaign against the Saxons. Louis set out without delay, and came to him at Aix; and the king went with him to Friemersheim, on the banks of the Rhine, where he held a general gathering. Louis stayed with his father in Saxony until the feast of St Martin; then he left Saxony with his father, and when the greater part of winter was over returned to Aquitaine.

10 In the following summer King Charles again sent to him with instructions to go with him to Italy, but the plan was changed and he was ordered to stay at home. But when the king had gone to Rome and was there receiving the imperial insignia, King Louis went off again to Toulouse and from there marched into Spain. As he was approaching Barcelona he was met by Zaddo, the duke of that city who had recently been deposed, but King Louis did not hand the city back to him. Going on beyond it he came to Lerida, which he subdued and sacked; and after this, and the sacking and burning of other towns, he advanced as far as Huesca. Here the fields were full of crops, and a force of soldiers was sent in to cut down, lay waste and burn them, and everything found outside the city was used to feed the flames. With this accomplished he returned home as winter was approaching.

11 When summer returned the most glorious emperor, Charles, set out for Saxony, instructing his son to follow him there with a view to spending the winter in that region. Louis hastened to do so, and came to Neuss, where he crossed the Rhine and then hurried on to join his father. But before he could reach him he was met at a place called *Ostfaloa* by his father's messenger, with instructions not to tire himself out with further travelling but rather to set up camp in a place convenient to himself and wait there for his return. The whole Saxon people, he said, had been subdued, and the victorious emperor, Charles, was already on his way back. When his son met him, Charles embraced and kissed him again and again, thanked him and praised him repeatedly, and kept emphasizing the value of his loyalty, declaring how fortunate he was to have such a son. Finally, at the end of this long and bloody Saxon war, which they say lasted for all of 33 years, King Louis was released by his father and returned with his men to his own kingdom to spend the winter.

12 When winter had passed the emperor Charles took advantage of the fact that he was now free of foreign wars and began a tour of the parts of his kingdom bordering on the sea. When King Louis learned of this he sent Hademarus as envoy to Rouen, asking his father to make a detour into Aquitaine to visit the kingdom he had given him, and suggesting that he should come to the place called Chasseneuil. His father received the suggestion with courtesy and thanked his son for it, but declined to agree to it, requesting instead that Louis should come to meet him at Tours. When Louis arrived there he was received by his father with great rejoicing, and accompanied him on his return to Frankia as far as Ver, where he parted from him and returned to Aquitaine. . . .

20 About this time, since Pippin, king of Italy had died earlier and since more recently his brother Charles had also departed this life, he conceived the hope of ruling the whole empire. His falconer Gerricus had been sent to consult his father on some necessary matters, and while Gerricus was staying at the palace awaiting the answers to his questions he was advised by Franks and Germans alike that the king should come to his father and be at hand to support him: it seemed to them, they said, that his father was now entering old age, that he had taken the unhappy death of his children very badly, and that in view of this his health was likely to decline very rapidly. Gerricus passed this on to the king, and the king to his counsellors, and some of them, indeed nearly all of them, felt that it was the best course. But the king took a more lofty view, and rather than run the risk of putting his father under suspicion as a result of such an action, decided for the moment to do nothing. But God, for fear and love of whom he had been unwilling to act, in keeping with his custom of ennobling those who love him more highly than they could conceive, arranged the matters more wisely. Those people whom it had been his custom to harass with war now asked for peace, and the king willingly granted it, with the provision that it be for a two-year period. Meanwhile the emperor Charles, seeing that he was now declining into old age, and fearing that he might be taken from the world and leave in confusion a kingdom which by God's grace was so nobly ordered (it might, he feared, be buffeted by storms from outside or vexed by internal divisions), sent word to summon his son from Aquitaine. When Louis arrived he received him kindly and kept him by him all the summer, instructing him in those matters which he thought needful: he advised him on how he should live, how rule, how order his kingdom and how keep it in order; and finally he crowned him with the imperial crown and made it known that with Christ's favour the supreme authority would lie with him; and with this business done he allowed him to return home, and in November Louis left his father and made his way back to Aquitaine. His father was now near to death, and began to suffer from frequent and unfamiliar ailments: it was as though by such indications death was announcing that its approach was now imminent. At last, with the disorders struggling so with each other and sapping his strength, his weakened constitution gave way and he took to his bed; and daily, even hourly, drawing nearer to death, he formally divided up his property as he wished and breathed his last, leaving for the Frankish kingdom an almost unbearable sorrow. Yet in his successor was proved the truth of that saying with which those who suffer from such troubles are wont to console their spirits: 'A righteous man is dead, and it is as though he had not died: for he has left a son to succeed him like himself.' The most pious emperor Charles died on the twenty-eighth of January in the year of Our Lord Jesus Christ's incarnation eight hundred and fourteen. As though by some presentiment the emperor, Louis, had at this time summoned a general gathering of his people, to meet on the feast of the purification of Mary, Holy Mother of God, at the place called Doué.

21 On the death of his father of pious memory, Rampo was sent to Louis by those who were concerned with the burial, that is, his children and the chief men of the palace, to inform him quickly of the death and to avoid any delay in his coming. When Rampo arrived at Orleans, Theodulf, the bishop of the city and a most learned man in all respects, divined the reason for his arrival and took pains to inform the emperor by sending off a messenger with all speed, with instructions simply to ask him whether he should wait until he came to the city or come and meet him somewhere on his way there. The emperor perceived the reason for the question immediately, and instructed the bishop to come to him. Then, as he received news of the sad event from one messenger after another he decided on the fifth day to make a move, and set out with as large a retinue as short space of time would allow. The greatest fear was that Wala, who had been in very high standing with the emperor Charles, might devise some mischief against the new emperor; but he came to Louis with all speed, and in humble submission committed himself fully to his service in accordance with the Frankish custom. And after he had joined the emperor all the chief men of the Franks followed his example, and vied with each other in crowds to go and meet him. At last he arrived safely at Herstal, and on the thirtieth day after he had left Aquitaine he successfully set foot in the palace of Aix. Now, although he was by nature a most gentle man, he had for a long time been concerned at the behaviour of his sisters in his father's household, which was the one blemish that marred the royal house. Wishing to remedy the trouble, but at the same time taking care not to revive the scandal which had occurred over Hodilo and Hiltrudis, he dispatched Wala and Warnarius, and also Lantbert and Ingobert; they were to come to Aix, take precautions to see that things of this kind should not occur, and keep to await his own arrival any who through conspicuous immorality or outstanding arrogance were guilty of treason. Some of these, in fact, had approached him as suppliants on his journey, and had asked for and obtained pardon. His further order was that the people should stay where they were and await his arrival there without fear. But Count Warnarius unbeknown to Wala and Ingobert called his nephew Lantbert to him, and

instructed Hoduinus, who was guilty of the crime in question, to come to him, ostensibly to arrest him and submit him to the royal punishment. But Hoduinus, whose conscience was already troubling him, was quick to see the trap, and because he was unwilling to turn aside from his course, not only earned ruin for himself but brought it upon Warnarius as well. For, coming to him as he had been ordered, he killed Warnarius himself, gave Lantbert an injury in the leg which left him incapacitated for a long time, and finally died by his own sword. And when this was reported to the emperor his heart was so moved with pity at the death of his friend that Tullius, one of the men concerned, who until now in the emperor's mood of clemency had seemed worthy of pardon, was punished by the loss of his eyes.

22 So the emperor came to the palace of Aix, and was received with much welcome by his kinsmen and by many thousands of Franks, and was for the second time declared emperor. This done, he expressed his thanks to those responsible for his father's burial, and to console his kinsmen who were overcome with the bitterness of their grief, he offered the appropriate words of comfort. But he was not slow either to perform what was due to his father's memory. When his father's will was read there was nothing of his property but was shared out according to his apportionment: for he left nothing that was not formally bequeathed. What he wished to be distributed among the churches he had divided up into 21 separate shares listed under the names of the appropriate metropolitans. Such things as belonged to the royal regalia he left to those who came after him. He also prescribed what should be given in accordance with Christian custom to his sons, grandsons and daughters, and not only to the royal manservants and maidservants but also to the poor in general. All these things the lord emperor, Louis, carried out exactly as they were written.

23 After this the emperor decided that the whole company of women, which was very large, should be removed from the palace, save only for a very small number which he thought appropriate for the royal service. Each of his sisters also withdrew to the property which she had received from her father; those who had not yet obtained property in this way were provided for by the emperor, and they too turned their attention to what they had been given. After this the emperor received the embassies which had been sent to his father but now came to him; he listened to them attentively, entertained them sumptuously and sent them on their way with lavish gifts. The chief among them was that of the emperor Michael of Constantinople, to whom the lord Charles had sent Amalharius, bishop of Trier and Abbot Peter of Nonantola to confirm a treaty of peace. Now they had returned, bringing the envoys of the said Michael, namely the *protospatharius*[4] Christopher and Gregory the deacon, who had been sent to the emperor Charles with replies to all matters on which he had written.

[4] A high court official: literally 'captain of the sword-bearers'.

When the emperor sent them on their way he sent with them his own envoys, Northbert, bishop of Reggio and Richoinus, count of Poitou, to ask the new emperor, Leo, for a renewal of the old friendships and for a confirmation of the treaty. In the same year he held a general gathering at Aix, and sent out loyal and trusty men to all parts of his kingdom, who were instructed, on his behalf, to hold fast to justice, to right wrongs and to render to all men their just and proper due. And he summoned Bernard, his nephew, who had for some time been king of Italy, to come to him; and when he did so he loaded him with gifts and sent him back to his kingdom.

6 Nithard's history of the sons of Louis the Pious

Nithard was a wealthy layman, the son of Angilbert (the Homer of Charles the Great's court), and the grandson, though illegitimate, of Charles himself. Nithard was the lay abbot of St Riquier, and died in battle near Angoulême on 14 June 844. He began to write this work about 841.

We include the opening chapters of the *Nithardi historiarium libri IIII* which deal with the succession problems after the death of Charles the Great and also the text of the oath of Strasbourg, 14 February 842. Both selections illustrate the political and personal problems facing the Carolingian dynasty within a generation of the death of the founder of the empire. References are given to the edition by Lauer mentioned above.

Source: Book I: Lauer, pp. 4–8; *Book III*: Lauer, pp. 102–8.

Book I

1 Charles of happy memory, rightly called the great emperor by all nations, died at a ripe old age about the third hour of the day [28 January 814], leaving the whole of Europe flourishing in all prosperity. So much did he surpass the men of his day in every branch of wisdom and virtue that to all the inhabitants of the world he was at once an object of fear, of love and of wonder, and so his rule over all his empire, as all could plainly see, was honourable and beneficial in every respect. Most remakable of all his achievements, to my mind, was that he alone was able by the judicious use of fear so to keep in check the fierce hearts and iron wills of the Franks and barbarians that they dared not act openly in all the empire save in the public interest. He ruled successfully as king for 32 years, and held the reins of empire with great success for 14 years more.

2 The heir to this lofty authority was Louis, the last surviving of his legitimate sons. As soon as Louis heard for certain that his father was dead he came immediately from Aquitaine to Aix; here the people came to him from all parts and he received their allegiance without any opposition, resolving to deal later with those whose loyalty seemed more doubtful. As a first act of his reign he

ordered the vast properties left by his father to be divided into three, and spent one part on the funeral and shared the other two between himself and his legitimate sisters, whom he then ordered to leave the palace immediately and go to their monasteries. To his brothers Drogo, Hugo and Theodoric, who were still of tender years, he gave a place at his table and instructed that they should be brought up with him in the palace. To his nephew Bernard, the son of Pippin, he granted the kingdom of Italy: shortly afterwards Bernard rose in rebellion, was captured by Bertmund, prefect of the province of Lyon, and deprived of his sight and his life. Fearing that his brothers might rouse the people and do the same, Louis instructed them to appear at the public gathering, where he had them given the tonsure and sent them to monasteries for safe keeping. This done, he arranged lawful marriages for his sons, and divided the whole empire between them, so that Pippin received Aquitaine, Louis Bavaria, and Lothar the promise of the whole empire after his death: to Lothar also he granted the title of emperor along with himself. During this time Queen Irmengard their mother died, and shortly afterwards the emperor Louis married Judith, who bore him Charles.

3 When Charles was born his father was at a loss what to do for him, now that he had divided the whole empire between his other sons, and when, in his anxiety, he petitioned his sons on behalf of the child, Lothar agreed under oath that his father should give to him whatever part of the empire he wished, and swore to be his guardian and protector in the future against all his enemies. Later, however, at the instigation of Hugo [count of Tours], whose daughter he had married, and of Mathfrid [count of Orleans] and others, he regretted this undertaking and sought ways of retracting it.

Book III (*The Oaths of Strasbourg, 14 February, AD 842*)

Before taking the oath, they addressed the assembled people, the one in the German tongue and the other in the 'Roman'.[5] Louis, being the elder, spoke first:

'How often Lothar tried to destroy myself and this my brother after the death of our father, by harassing us to the point of extermination, you know well. And since neither brotherhood nor the Christian faith, nor any other consideration, was enough to bring peace between us and at the same time leave justice unimpaired, we were compelled finally to submit the matter to the judgement of Almighty God, being ready to accept His decision concerning our several rights. In this, as you know, we were by God's mercy victorious, and he, being defeated, withdrew with his men where he could. Whereupon we for our part were filled with brotherly love, and with compassion for our Christian people,

[5] *Romana (lingua)*, which we have translated as 'Roman' or 'the Roman tongue' to suggest an intermediate stage between Vulgar Latin and the Romance languages.

and were unwilling to pursue and destroy them; instead, we gave orders that for the future, as in the past, each man should receive the justice to which he was entitled. But our brother was not content with the divine judgement, and did not cease after this to pursue us with armed bands, and to ravage our people with fire and pillage and slaughter. For this reason, therefore, we have been compelled to meet, and because we believe that you have come to doubt the strength of our loyalty and brotherly affection we have decided to swear an oath to one another in your presence. We do so, not from any dishonourable motive, but in order that, if God with your help grant us peace, we may be assured of a common benefit. If, however (which God forbid), I should presume to break the oath which I shall swear to my brother, I release each one of you from my service and from the oath which you swore to me.'

And when Charles had made the same statement in the 'Roman' tongue, Louis, being the elder, began and swore to observe the following:

'Pro Deo amur et pro christian poblo et nostro commun salvament, d'ist di in avant, in quant Deus savir et podir me dunat, si salvarai eo cist meon fradre Karlo et in aiudha et in cadhuna cosa, si cum om per dreit son fradra salvar dift, in o quid il mi altresi fazet et ab Ludher nul plaid nunquam prindrai, qui meon vol, cist meon fradre Karle in damno sit.'[6]

When Louis had completed the oath, Charles swore to the same effect in the German tongue:

'In Godes minna ind in thes christianes folches ind unser bedhero gehaltnissi, fon thesemo dage frammordes, so fram so mir Got geuuizci indi mahd furgibit, so haldih thesan minan bruodher, soso man mit rehtu sinan bruher scal, in thiu thaz er mig so sama duo, indi mit Ludheren in nohheiniu thing ne gegango the, minan uuillon, imo ce scadhen uuerdhen.'

And the oath which the people swore, each in their own tongue, was in the 'Roman' tongue as follows:

'Si Lodhuuigs sagrament que son fradre Karlo jurat conservat et Karlus, meos sendra, de suo part non l'ostanit, si io returnar non l'int pois, ne io ne neuls cui eo returnar int pois, in nulla aiudha contra Lodhuuuig nun li iu er.'[7]

And in the German tongue:

'Oba Karl then eid then er sinemo bruodher Ludhuuuige gesuor geleistit, indi

[6] 'For the love of God and for our Christian people and for our common safety I shall from this day forth assist this my brother Charles/Louis with all the wisdom and strength that God may give me, in the bringing of aid and in all other matters in which a man should rightly assist his brother, provided he does the same for me, and I will not willingly enter into any agreement with Lothar which may be harmful to this my brother Charles/Louis.'

[7] 'If Louis/Charles observes the oath which he has sworn to his brother Charles/Louis, and if Charles/Louis my lord for his part does not keep it and I am unable to prevail upon him to do so, then neither I myself nor anyone upon whom I can prevail shall give him any assistance against Louis/Charles.'

Ludhuuuig, min herro, then er imo gesuor forbrihchit, ob ih inan es iruuenden ne mag, noh ih noh thero nohhein, then ih es iruuenden mag, uuidhar Karle imo ce follusti ne uuirdhit.'

This done, Louis made his way to Worms along the Rhine by way of Speyer, and Charles by Wissembourg around the Vosges.

Annals

The source of outstanding importance for the chronology of events in the reign of Charles the Great is a composite record known as the Royal Annals, the *Annales Regni Francorum*. For the later part of Charles's reign (after 793 with a change of authorship in 808) the annals were constructed soon after the years in which the events recorded took place. The earlier annals, dealing with the years 741–93, present greater complications. They appear to have been assembled from a variety of entries in monastic Easter tables and put together at some stage under the direction of the royal court between 787 and 793. Existing manuscripts of the Royal Annals consist of later (often revised and altered) copies which make detailed comparison with other contemporary records at times difficult. The annalistic tradition continued among some religious communities but in fact the so-called 'minor annals' only rarely add anything of significance to the full account in the Royal Annals. One great exception which we have included in this collection is the comment on the imperial coronation from a manuscript now preserved in the Vienna National Library (codex 515). The set of annals from 794–803 which is preserved in this manuscript used always to be referred to as 'The Annals of Lorsch' because of its supposed connection with Ricbod, abbot of Lorsch and bishop of Trier. Modern investigation (ably summarized by Professor Bullough in *EHR* LXXXV, 1970, p. 65) has shown that these annals are contemporary, that they were written year by year by two scribes, probably in the Alemannic area and not at Lorsch.

Our selections from the Royal Annals are based on the standard modern collection, ed. R. Rau, *Quellen zur karolingischen Reichsgeschichte* (Berlin 1955), vol. V in the *Ausgewahlte Quellen zur Deutschen Geschichte des Mittelalters*: also *MGH, SS*, vol. I, rev. edn. G. H. Pertz and F. Kurze (Hanover 1895). A useful introduction to the annals is given in Rau, pp. 1–7 and in D. Bullough, *The Age of Charlemagne*, p. 13. A clear modern translation into English is provided by B. W. Scholz (with Barbara Rogers) in *Carolingian Chronicles* (Ann Arbor, Michigan 1970). We have chosen extracts relating to the Tassilo incidents, to the Avar expedition, and to the imperial coronation to illustrate the nature and tone of the record. Our final extract is taken from the Vienna manuscript edited (as the 'Annales Laureshamenses') by G. H. Pertz, *MGH, SS*, vol. I (1826), pp. 37–9.

7 The Royal Annals

Source: AD 757: Pertz-Kurze, pp. 14–17; Rau, pp. 16–19. AD 788: Pertz-Kurze, pp. 98–101; Rau, pp. 64–7. AD 800 and 801: Pertz-Kurze, pp. 110–16; Rau, pp. 72–7.

AD 757 The Emperor Constantine[8] sent to King Pippin, among other gifts, an organ, which was brought into Frankia.

And King Pippin held his assembly at Compiègne along with his Franks. And there came there Tassilo,[9] duke of Bavaria, to place himself in vassalage by the clasping of hands; he swore innumerable oaths, placing his hand upon the relics of saints, and promised fealty to King Pippin and his aforementioned sons, the lords Charles and Carloman, to be their vassal with right mind and with steadfast devotion according to the law, as a vassal should be towards his lords. So the said Tassilo confirmed his pledge upon the bodies of St Denis, St Rusticus and St Eleutherius, as well as those of St Germain and St Martin, that all the days of his life he would keep the promise that he had sworn; and his chief men who were with him confirmed the oath, it is said, both in the places mentioned and in many others.

AD 788 Then the lord king Charles assembled a synod at the aforesaid palace of Ingelheim. And there came there Tassilo, on the orders of our lord the king, along with his other vassals; and the loyal Bavarians began to assert that Tassilo had not kept his faith, but that, after handing over his son and other hostages and swearing the oaths, he had later shown himself deceitful, being persuaded by his wife Liutberga. This Tassilo was unable to deny, but confessed that he had later sent envoys to the Avars, and had won over to his side some vassals of the aforesaid lord the king and had conspired against his life; he ordered his men when they swore the oaths to do so in pretence only and to retain a different intention in their hearts; and, what was more, he confessed to saying that even if he had ten sons he would prefer to lose all of them rather than abide by his agreements and hold fast to the oath that he had sworn; he even said that it would be better to die than to live on such terms. And when all these things were proved against him the Franks and Bavarians, Lombards and Saxons, and those from all the provinces who had assembled at the synod, being mindful of his former evil deeds, and how he had abandoned the lord king, Pippin, on active service and so committed the crime known in the German tongue as *herisliz*, decided to condemn the said Tassilo to death. But when all of them with one voice cried out that he should receive the capital sentence, the aforesaid lord and most pious king Charles was moved with pity, for the love of God and because

[8] Constantine V Copronymus (741–75).
[9] cf. **13** (Boretius 28), and also the annal of AD 788 below.

he was his kinsman, and obtained consent from his and God's faithful subjects that the man should not die. And when asked by the same most merciful lord and king what he wished to do, the said Tassilo requested permission to take the tonsure and enter a monastery, so that he might do penance for his great sins and seek the salvation of his soul. His son Theodo was judged in the same way, and was given the tonsure and sent to a monastery; and a few Bavarians who wished to persist in their enmity to the lord king Charles were sent into exile.

In the same year hostilities broke out between Greeks and Lombards, that is, between Hildebrand, duke of Spoleto and Grimald, whom the lord king Charles had made duke of Benevento. Wineghisus was sent with a small band of Franks to take cognizance of all that they had done; and with God's help victory was won by the Franks and the aforementioned Lombards. Another battle occurred in a similar fashion between the Avars at ——[10] and the Franks who were then living in Italy; with God's assistance the Franks were victorious and the Avars routed in disgrace, having fled without achieving any success. A third battle occurred between Bavarians and Avars in the plain of Ips; there were present Grahamannus and Audaccrus, envoys of the lord king Charles, along with other Franks, and with God's help the Franks and Bavarians gained the victory. All these things were treacherously plotted by the aforementioned Duke Tassilo and his evil wife, the godless Liutberga. The Avars engaged in a fourth battle, wishing to exact vengeance of the Bavarians; there too were envoys of the lord king Charles, and with God's protection victory went to the Christians. The Avars took to flight and a great slaughter ensued, while others lost their lives by drowning in the Danube.

After all this the lord king Charles came in person to Regensburg, and there set in order the frontiers, or marches, of the Bavarians, that with God's protection they might be safe against the aforementioned Avars. On his return from there he celebrated Christmas in the palace at Aix, and Easter also.

AD 796 Pope Hadrian[11] died, and Leo, as soon as he had succeeded him, sent envoys to the king with gifts; with them he sent the keys of St Peter's tomb and the standard of the city of Rome. But Heiricus, duke of Friuli, sent his men into Pannonia under Wonomyrus the Slav and laid waste the Ring of the Avars, who, with their chieftains exhausted by internal quarrels, had been at peace for a long time. The Khan and the Jugur[12] were set against one another in a private feud and killed by their own men; the treasure of the old kings, which had been collected over many generations, was sent to the lord king Charles at the palace of Aix. On receiving it, this wisest of men and God's most generous steward gave thanks to God the giver of all good gifts, and sent the greater part of it to

[10] The name of the place is missing in the manuscript.

[11] Hadrian died on 25 December 795; Leo III continued in office until 816.

[12] Titles of rank. The Khan (or Khagan) was the head of state; Jugur and Tudun (below) are names for subordinate princes.

the churches of the apostles at Rome, through Angilbert his beloved abbot; the remainder he bestowed upon his chief men, both clergy and laymen, and upon his other faithful subjects.

In the same year, in accordance with his promise, the Tudun came to the king along with a great number of Avars and surrendered himself, his people, and his country to the king; both he and his people were baptized, and having received gifts returned home with honour.

The king collected his forces and marched into Saxony, having sent his son Pippin, king of Italy, with an army into Pannonia. While he was in Saxony two embassies arrived from Pippin: the first announced that the Khan had come to him, along with other chieftains whom the Avars had appointed after the death of the previous ones; the second, that Pippin and his army were occupying the Ring. Having marched through Saxony the lord king withdrew with all his forces into Gaul, and at the palace of Aix joyfully received his son Pippin when he returned from Pannonia bringing with him the remaining part of the treasure.

There he celebrated Christmas and Easter.

AD 800   The king released the monk of Jerusalem[13] and set him on his journey home, sending with him Zacharias, a priest of his palace, to take his gifts to the holy places. He himself left his palace of Aix in the middle of March and travelled along the shore of the Gallic ocean; he put a fleet on the sea itself, which was at that time infested with pirates, and set up guard posts, and then celebrated Easter at St Riquier. Then, setting out from there, he travelled along the coast again to Rouen, and crossing the River Seine at this point came on to Tours, to pray in the church of St Martin. Here he remained for some days because of the illness of his wife, the lady Luitgardis, who died and was buried here: this was on 4 June.

Then he returned to Aix by way of Orleans and Paris. On 6 July there was an unusually severe frost, and another on the 9th; neither of them, however, did any harm to crops.

At the beginning of August he came to Mainz and announced a journey to Italy; and setting out from there he came with his army to Ravenna. There he organized an expedition against Benevento and after a week's delay set off for Rome, ordering his son Pippin to take an army and ravage the Beneventan territory. On the day before he arrived at Rome, Pope Leo and the Romans came to meet him twelve miles from the city at Mentana, and received him with great humility and honour; and having eaten with him there the pope preceded him into the city. On the next day he stood on the steps of the church of St Peter the Apostle, sent the standards of the city of Rome to meet the king, and set crowds of citizens and foreign visitors at appropriate points to sing his praises when he came; and he himself, with his clergy and bishops, received the king as

[13] Sent to Charles by the patriarch of Jerusalem in the previous year.

he dismounted from his horse and ascended the steps, and after offering a prayer escorted him into the church of St Peter the apostle amid singing from all the people. All this was done on 24 November.

A week later the king summoned an assembly and explained to all of them why he had come to Rome, and after this he daily devoted his energies to carrying out the things for which he had come. The greatest and most difficult of these was the matter with which he began, namely, to examine charges which had been brought against the pontiff. He, however, since there was no one willing to testify to these charges, went up into the pulpit of the church of St Peter in the sight of all the people, with a gospel in his hand, and calling upon the name of the Holy Trinity cleared himself on oath of all the charges laid against him.

On the same day Zacharias came to Rome on his way back from the East, along with two monks, one from the Mount of Olives and one from the monastery of St Sabas, whom the patriarch of Jerusalem had sent to the king with Zacharias, to bring to him for blessing the keys of the Holy Sepulchre and of Calvary, and also those of the city itself and of Mount Sion, along with a standard. These men the king graciously received, and having kept them with him for a few days sent them away with gifts. This was in April; Christmas he had spent in Rome. And the number of the years changed to 801.

AD 801   On the holy day of Christmas itself [i.e. AD 800], at a mass before the tomb of St Peter the apostle, Pope Leo placed a crown upon the king's head as he rose from prayer, and all the people of Rome cried out: 'To Charles Augustus, mighty and peaceable emperor of the Romans crowned by God, long life and victory.' And after the acclamation he was adored by the pope in the manner of the old emperors, and setting aside the title of patrician was named emperor and Augustus.

A few days later he gave orders for those who had deposed the pontiff in the previous year to be brought before him; and when they had been examined according to the law of Rome they were found guilty of treason and condemned to death. But the pope was moved with holy compassion and pleaded with the emperor on their behalf; and so their life and members were spared to them, but because of the magnitude of their crime they were sent into exile. The leaders of this conspiracy were the *nomenclator*[14] Paschales and the treasurer Campulus, together with many other nobles living in the city of Rome, all of whom received the same sentence.

Then, having ordered the public, ecclesiastical and private affairs of the city of Rome, of the pope himself, and of the whole of Italy (for throughout the winter the emperor did nothing else), and having sent an expedition for the second time against the Beneventans, he himself with Pippin his son set out from Rome after Easter, on 25 April, and came to Spoleto.

[14] A dignitary of the papal court whose duty it was to receive petitions and envoys.

41

While he was there, on 30 April at the second hour of the night, a great earthquake occurred which badly shook the whole of Italy. The movement caused the greater part of the roof of the church of St Paul the apostle to fall down, beams and all, and in some places the mountains fell upon cities. In the same year tremors were felt in some places along the Rhine, both in Gaul and in Germany, and because of the mildness of the winter there was a pestilence.

From Spoleto the emperor came to Ravenna, and after staying there for some days went on to Pavia. There it was announced to him that envoys of Harun Amir al Mumminin, the king of the Persians,[15] had entered the gates of Pisa. Sending men to meet them he had them presented to him between Vercelli and Ivrea. There were two of them: one was a Persian from the East, an envoy from the Persian king, and the other a Saracen from Africa, an envoy from the Emir Abraham, who ruled on the borders of Africa at Fostat. They informed him that the Jew Isaac, whom the emperor had sent to the Persian king four years before along with Lantfrid and Sigimund, had returned with rich gifts: Lantfrid and Sigimund had both died. Then he sent Ercambald the notary into Liguria to prepare a fleet to transport the elephant and the other things which he had brought with him. He himself, after celebrating the feast of St John the Baptist at Ivrea, crossed the Alps and returned to Gaul.

In the same summer the city of Barcelona in Spain was taken after a two year siege; Zatun, its commander, and many other Saracens were captured. In Italy the city of Chieti was similarly taken and burned, and its commander Roselmus captured; the forts which belonged to the city were received in surrender. Zatun and Roselmus were brought on the same day to the emperor's presence and condemned to exile.

In October of the same year the Jew Isaac returned from Africa with the elephant and entered Porto Venere; and because he could not cross the Alps on account of the snow he wintered in Vercelli.

The emperor celebrated Christmas in the palace at Aix.

8 The Vienna Manuscript

The important entry relating to the coronation was written after the end of 801.
Source: Vienna National Library Codex 515; *MGH*, vol. I (1826), pp. 37–9 (the 'Annales Laureshamenses').

AD 798 This year King Charles was in Saxony; he spent the winter, and also celebrated Easter, at New Herstal. It was the king himself who gave the place this name, so we have heard, because the houses in which they stayed had been

[15] Harun al Raschid (786–809); the title Amir al Mumminin means 'Prince of the Faithful'.

built by the host. In the summer of the same year he came with his army to Bardowiek, and all the people there submitted themselves to him; and he took such prisoners as he wished and as many hostages as he desired. Meanwhile those of our Slavs who are called Abotridi assembled together with the *missi* of our lord the king against the Saxons who lived in the northern part of Albingia, and laid waste and burned their territory. The Saxons came together in one force, and a mighty battle was joined; and although the Abotridi were pagans, yet they were strengthened by the sure help of Christ and of our lord the king, and were victorious over the Saxons; and there fell to them in that battle two thousand nine hundred and one. Then these Slavs came to Thuringia to our lord the king, and he honoured them magnificently as they deserved. After this our lord the king returned to Frankia, taking with him such of the Saxons as he wished and allowing such as he wished to depart. He himself arrived at the palace of Aix, where he spent the winter.

AD 799   Once more the lord king Charles celebrated Easter at his palace of Aix. And the Romans, inspired by the devil, laid hands on the lord pope Leo during the great procession, that is to say on 25 April, and cut out his tongue; and they wished also to gouge out his eyes and put him to death, but by God's good grace they did not carry out the evil plan which they had begun. In the same year our lord the king entered Saxony and stayed at Paderborn, and was visited there by the lord pope, Leo, whom earlier the Romans had wanted to kill; and our lord the king received him with respect, bestowed many gifts and honours upon him, and afterwards sent him back in peace and with great array to his own see. The *missi* of our lord the king provided an honourable escort, and sent those who had plotted against his life to our lord the king: they are now in exile, as they deserve. And our lord the king took a great multitude of Saxons, along with their women and children, and settled them in various parts of his territories; and he divided their lands among his loyal subjects, that is to say his bishops, priests, counts and others of his vassals. And there at Paderborn he built a church of wondrous size, and caused it to be dedicated; and after this he returned in peace to the palace of Aix, and there remained.

AD 800   That winter he stayed at the palace of Aix, and about the time of Lent he went to visit his estates and also those places where the bodies of saints are buried. At length, just after Easter, he came to Tours, where rests the body of the blessed St Martin; he had with him his sons Charles and Pippin, and his son Louis also came to join him there. It was there too that Luitgardis, the wife of our lord the king, had died. Having made his solemn devotions there he returned in peace to his own home. And when summer came he gathered together his nobles and all his loyal subjects in the town of Mainz, and when it was made known to him that there was peace throughout all his territories he recalled the injury which the Romans had inflicted on Pope Leo; and he set his face to go to Rome, and this he did. And he held there a mighty gathering of his bishops and abbots, along with his priests, deacons and counts and the rest of his Christian people, and there appeared before them those who wished to condemn the pope; and when the king discovered that it was not for any just cause that they wished to condemn him, but through malice, then it seemed right, both to the most pious prince Charles himself and to all the bishops and holy fathers who were there assembled, that if it was his wish and he requested it he should purge himself, not according to their judgement, but of his own free will. And so it was done; and when the oath had been completed, the holy bishops, with all the clergy and Prince Charles himself and all his devoted Christian people, began the hymn: 'We praise thee, O God; we acknowledge thee to be the Lord.' And when this was done the king himself and all his loyal people with him gave praise to God, because it had been granted to them to have Pope Leo preserved in body and spirit. And he spent the winter at Rome.

AD 801 Because the name of emperor had now fallen into disuse among the Greeks, who now had a woman to rule over them, it seemed good, both to Pope Leo himself and to all the holy fathers who were at the council, as well as to the rest of the Christian people, that they should bestow the title of emperor upon Charles, king of the Franks. He it was who held Rome itself, where the Caesars had always resided, along with all the other residences which he had in Italy and Gaul and Germany; and seeing that Almighty God had given him possession of all these it seemed right to them that with God's blessing and at the request of all his Christian people he should have the title. This request King Charles was unwilling to deny, but in all humility, and in deference to God and to the wishes of his clergy and all his Christian people, he accepted the title of emperor, with the blessing of the lord pope, Leo, on the day of the Nativity of Our Lord Jesus Christ [i.e. AD 800]. Then as the first of his acts he restored the Holy Church of Rome, which had been divided upon itself, to peace and concord, and there celebrated Easter. And when summer approached he made his way to Ravenna, where he administered justice and peace, and then came home to Frankia.

AD 802 In this year the lord Charles Caesar remained quietly at the palace of Aix among his Franks, with no summons of the host; but mindful of his duty to the poor who lived in his kingdom and who were not able to enjoy his justice to the full he did not wish to send his poorer vassals from within the palace to do justice in return for rewards, but instead he chose from his kingdom archbishops and bishops and abbots, with dukes and counts, who now had no need to receive gifts from the innocent, and sent them throughout his kingdom, so that they might administer justice to the churches, to widows, orphans and the poor, and to all the people. And in the month of October he called together a full synod in the aforementioned place, and there caused to be read to the bishops and priests and deacons, all the canons, which the holy synod received, together with the decrees of the pontiffs; and he ordered them to be fully expounded in the presence of the bishops, priests and deacons. Likewise at the same synod he brought together all the abbots and monks who were there; and they met together and read the rule of the holy father Benedict, and learned men expounded it in the presence of the abbots and monks. And from thenceforth a general order was issued to all the bishops and abbots, priests and deacons and all the clergy, that each one in his place should live according to the precepts of the holy fathers, whether in bishoprics or in monasteries or in all the holy churches, that those subject to canon law should live in accordance with it, and that whatever fault or shortcoming was found among clergy or people should be corrected in accordance with the authority of the canons, and that whatever in monasteries or among monks was done contrary to the rule of St Benedict should be corrected in accordance with the same rule. And while this synod was being held, the emperor also gathered together his dukes, counts and the rest of his Christian people, together with the lawmakers [*legislatoribus*], and caused all the laws of his kingdom to be read to them; and each man was given the law applying to himself, and where it was necessary the laws were amended and the amendments written down; and he decreed that justices should judge in accordance with what was written, and should not accept gifts, but that all men, whether rich or poor, should have justice in his kingdom. That year also an elephant was brought to Frankia.

AD 803   This year the emperor Charles celebrated Easter at the palace of Aix, and held an assembly at Mainz. And he acted without summoning the host throughout the year, except that he sent out his warriors on patrol wherever it was necessary.

II Capitularies

THE Capitularies are our most important source of information relating to law, government and society in the reign of Charles the Great. They are not simple documents to handle. F. L. Ganshof in his brilliant study, *Recherches sur les Capitulaires* (Paris 1958), demonstrates the complexity and variety of the capitularies, and further invaluable information is provided in the text and notes of his *Frankish Institutions under Charlemagne*, trs. S. Bryce and Mary Lyon (Providence, Rhode Island 1968) referred to below as Ganshof, *Recherches*, and Ganshof, *Frankish Institutions*. Many are still undated or dated only uncertainly, and their textual tradition is often equally uncertain. Some capitularies, for example **9** and **21**, were certainly kept in the royal archives, though it is a sad fact that not a single original text survives, nor one that can with certainty be taken as a first copy of an original. We have to rely on later collections of capitularies made either at the palace or by private individuals, that made by Ansegisus, abbot of St Wandrille, *c.* AD 827, proving particularly popular and effective.

We have selected only fifteen of more than a hundred documents presented by A. Boretius, enough we hope to illustrate the variety in substance and presentation. In some, the legislative element is important, in others minimal. In many the administrative element predominates and the capitulary is clearly intended to be a directive from the palace to royal agents, *missi dominici* or counts. Some are the work of a king or emperor anxious to reach all the Christian people under his command. Others have a more regional or limited approach. There are capitularies that are exclusively ecclesiastical in interest. Among documents of special importance should be mentioned the *Capitulare de villis* (**15**) and the *Brevium Exempla* (**23**), which are among the most important single documents to survive from this period, indispensable to the serious study of the development of western European society. The capitulary of Herstal (**9**), has a special interest as a document in which the compulsory exaction of tithes, first asserted by Pippin III, is re-affirmed and also as the first substantial document to which the term capitulary, a document broken up into *capita* or chapters, is precisely applied. The *encyclica de litteris colendis* (**14**) is fundamental to our understanding of the so-called Carolingian Renaissance.

Dr Percival has made his translations from the edition of A. Boretius, *MGH: Legum*, Sectio II, *Capitularia Regum Francorum* (Hanover 1883), and has checked variant readings from the earlier edition of G. H. Pertz, *MGH: Legum*, vol. I

(Hanover 1835, reprinted 1965), and from other recent editions where necessary. For convenience we give references to the number of the document in both principal editions (Boretius and Pertz) at the head of each capitulary. We have occasionally added short notes of guidance to modern authority. We have followed the chronological arrangement of Boretius, except where modern scholarship has shown it to be defective (**10** and **18**).

9 Herstal, 779

Herstal on the Meuse was one of the favourite residences of Charles during the early part of his reign. The *Capitulare Haristallense* presents a programme of reform in both ecclesiastical and secular affairs, which followed political set-backs in Spain and Saxony. The text below is the so-called *forma communis* applicable to the ancient Frankish Kingdom: the *forma langobardica* has longer entries under sections 5–14 and some other variants.

Source: Boretius 20; Pertz 21.

In the eleventh auspicious year of the reign of our lord and most glorious king, Charles, in the month of March, there was made a capitulary whereby, there being gathered together in one synod and council the bishops and abbots and illustrious counts, together with our most pious lord, decisions were agreed to concerning certain appropriate matters in accordance with God's will.

1 Concerning the metropolitans, that suffragan bishops should be placed under them in accordance with the canons, and that such things as they see needing correction in their ministry they should correct and improve with willing hearts.

2 Concerning bishops: where at present they are not consecrated they are to be consecrated without delay.

3 Concerning the monasteries that have been based on a rule, that they should live in accordance with that rule; and that convents should preserve their holy order, and each abbess reside in her convent without intermission.

4 That bishops should have authority over the priests and clerks within their dioceses, in accordance with the canons.

5 That bishops should have authority to impose correction on incestuous people, and should have the power of reproving widows within their dioceses.

6 That no one should be allowed to receive another's clerk, or to ordain him to any rank.

7 Concerning tithes, that each man should give his tithe, and that these should be disposed of according to the bishop's orders.

47

8   Concerning murderers and other guilty men who ought in law to die, if they take refuge in a church they are not to be let off, and no food is to be given to them there.

9   That robbers who are caught within an immunity area should be presented by the justices of that area at the count's court; and anyone who fails to comply with this is to lose his benefice and his office. Likewise a vassal of ours, if he does not carry this out, shall lose his benefice and his office; anyone who has no benefice must pay the fine.

10   Concerning a man who commits perjury, that he cannot redeem it except by losing his hand. But if an accuser wishes to press the charge of perjury they are both to go to the ordeal of the cross; and if the swearer wins, the accuser is to pay the equivalent of his wergeld. This procedure is to be observed in minor cases; in major cases, or in cases involving free status, they are to act in accordance with the law.

11   Concerning the judgement of, and punishment inflicted upon robbers, the synod have ruled that the testimony given by the bishops is probably equivalent to that of the count, provided there is no malice or ill will, and there is no intervention in the case except in the interests of seeing justice done. And if he [the judge] should maim a man through hatred or ill intent and not for the sake of justice, he is to lose his office and is to be subject to the laws under which he acted unjustly and to the penalty which he sought to inflict.

12   The heads of procedure which our father of happy memory decided upon for his hearings and for his synods: these we wish to preserve.

13   Concerning the properties of the churches from which the *census* now comes, the tithes and ninths should be paid along with that *census*; likewise tithes and ninths are to be given for those properties from which they have not so far come—from fifty *casati* one shilling, from thirty *casati* half a shilling, and from twenty a *tremissis* [*i.e.* fourpence]. And concerning precarial holdings, where they are now they are to be renewed, and where they are not they are to be recorded. And a distinction should be made between the precarial holdings established by our authority and those which they establish of their own volition from the property of the church itself.

14   Concerning the raising of an armed following, let no one dare to do it.

15   Concerning those who give tribute in candles, and those who are free by deed or charter, the long standing arrangements are to be observed.

16   Concerning oaths entered into by swearing together in a fraternity, that no one should dare to perform them. Moreover, concerning alms-giving, and fire and shipwreck, even though men enter into fraternities they are not to dare to swear to them.

17 Concerning travellers who are going to the palace or anywhere else, that no one should dare to assault them with an armed band. And let no one presume to take away another's crop when the fields are enclosed, unless he is going to the host or is acting as one of our *missi*; anyone who dares to do otherwise shall make amends for it.

18 Concerning the tolls that have before now been forbidden, let no one exact them except where they have existed from of old.

19 Concerning the sale of slaves, that it should take place in the presence of a bishop or count, or in the presence of an archdeacon or *centenarius*, or in that of a *vicedominus* or a count's justice, or before well-known witnesses; and let no one sell a slave beyond the march. Anyone who does so must pay the fine as many times over as the slaves he sold; and if he does not have the means to pay he must hand himself over in service to the count as a pledge, until such time as he can pay off the fine.

20 Concerning coats of mail, that no one should dare to sell them outside our kingdom.

21 If a count does not administer justice in his district he is to arrange for our *missus* to be provided for from his household until justice has been administered there; and if a vassal of ours does not administer justice, then the count and our *missus* are to stay at his house and live at his expense until he does so.

22 If anyone is unwilling to accept a payment instead of vengeance he is to be sent to us, and we will send him where he is likely to do least harm. Likewise, if anyone is unwilling to pay a sum instead of vengeance or to give legal satisfaction for it, it is our wish that he be sent to a place where he can do no further harm.

23 Concerning robbers, our instructions are that the following rules should be observed: for the first offence they are not to die but to lose an eye; for the second offence the robber's nose is to be cut off; for the third offence, if he does not mend his ways, he must die.

10 Mantua, 781

We include the *Capitulare Mantuanum* as an example of Charles's personal concern with Italian affairs, and also as an indication of the public and oral nature of government in Carolingian Europe. This capitulary is a memorandum based on the provisions made known to all at Mantua (*qualiter . . . omnibus notum facimus*).

Source: Boretius 90; Pertz 23.

Concerning the various provisions which we have made known to all men at the general assembly held at Mantua.

1 Concerning the administration of justice in God's Church, in the matter of widows and orphans, and others who need protection, it is our wish and our special instruction that all bishops, abbots and counts shall both give and accept full justice according to the law.

2 This we have decided, that everyone who has a claim shall make it three times to his count, and shall find suitable men to give truthful witness that he made the claim and was unable to secure justice as a result of it; and if anyone does otherwise, and brings his claim prematurely to the palace, he shall pay the legal penalty.

3 Further, the count shall declare before witnesses on their behalf that he was willing to give them justice, and he shall have his notary write everything down, namely, what claim they made and what justice they received; so that when the people have made their claim the counts can have no excuse unless it is abundantly clear that they were willing to give them justice; also, that the count himself or his advocate can testify by an oath that there was no negligence in giving them justice, and we can know through their report whether they made the claim to them or not.

4 Let this be known to all men, that if anyone makes a claim after the case has been legally closed, he must either receive 15 strokes of the rod or be made to pay 15 shillings.

5 Let no one receive another's priest and allow him to celebrate mass before he has been interviewed and examined by the local bishop.

6 When a bishop goes the round of his parishes, let the count or his agent [*sculdhais*] give him assistance, so that he can perform his ministry in full, according to the canons.

7 Let no one sell Christian or pagan slaves or arms of any kind or stallions outside our kingdom; anyone who does so must be made to pay our fine, and if he is unable to bring the slaves back he must pay their worth.

8 With regard to tolls: let no one presume to levy a toll except in accordance with ancient custom, and let it be levied only in places recognized by law from of old; anyone who levies it unlawfully must make payment according to the law, and in addition must pay our fine to our *missi*.

9 Concerning the coinage: after the first day of August let no one dare to give or receive the pennies now current; anyone who does so is to pay our fine.

10 Concerning brigands who rarely come before our *missi*: let the counts seek them out, and keep them on bail or in custody until the *missi* return to them.

11 Let no one receive a Lombard man in vassalage or in his house until he knows whence he comes or how he was born; anyone who does otherwise must pay our fine.

12 Concerning the guest-houses: it is our wish and our instruction that they be restored.

13 With regard to the royal vassals and their justice: let them give and receive justice before the count.

11 Paderborn, 785

The Capitulare Paderbrunnense (Capitulatio de partibus Saxoniae) and the following *Capitulare Saxonicum* demonstrate the strength and harshness of Frankish rule in Saxony, and show the intimate involvement of the Church in the conquest and settlement of Saxony. Paderborn became one of the chief Frankish centres, and the seat of an important bishopric. References to the law of the Saxons in both capitularies (**11**, clause 33 and **12** clauses 3 and 10, for example), remind us that each of the principal groups brought under the authority of Charles the Great enjoyed the protection of its own peculiar laws. Capitularies often represent the product of the legislative force of the Carolingian realm or empire, but the law that ensured a man's status and offered him protection under normal circumstances was his own law—the law of the Saxons, the *Alemanni*, the Bavarians, the Lombards or, most significant of all, the law of the Ripuarian or Salian Franks (*see also* **20**).

Source: Boretius 26; Pertz 27.

Capitulary concerning the
parts of Saxony

1 Decisions were taken first on the more important items. All were agreed that the churches of Christ which are now being built in Saxony and are consecrated to God should have no less honour than the temples of idols had, but rather a greater and more surpassing honour.

2 If anyone takes refuge in a church, let no one presume to drive him out of that church by force; rather let him be in peace until he is brought to plead his case, and in honour of God and in reverence for the saints of that church let his life and all his members be respected. But let him pay for his offence according to his means and according to what is decided; and after this let him be brought to the presence of our lord the king, who shall send him wherever in his mercy he shall decide.

3 If anyone makes forcible entry to a church, and steals anything from it by violence or stealth, or if he sets fire to the church, let him die.

4 If anyone in contempt of the Christian faith should spurn the holy Lenten fast and eat meat, let him die; but let the priest enquire into the matter, lest it should happen that someone is compelled by necessity to eat meat.

5 If anyone kills a bishop or a priest or a deacon, he shall likewise pay with his life.

6 If anyone is deceived by the devil, and believes after the manner of pagans that some man or some woman is a witch and eats people, and if because of this he burns her or gives her flesh to someone to eat or eats it himself, let him pay the penalty of death.

7 If anyone follows pagan rites and causes the body of a dead man to be consumed by fire, and reduces his bones to ashes, let him pay with his life.

8 If there is anyone of the Saxon people lurking among them unbaptized, and if he scorns to come to baptism and wishes to absent himself and stay a pagan, let him die.

9 If anyone sacrifices a man to the devil, and after the manner of pagans offers him as a victim to demons, let him die.

10 If anyone takes counsel with pagans against Christians, or wishes to persist with them in hostility to Christians, let him die; and anyone who treacherously approves of this against the king or against Christian people, let him die.

11 If anyone is shown to be unfaithful to our lord the king, let him suffer the penalty of death.

12 If anyone rapes the daughter of his lord, he shall die.

13 If anyone kills his lord or his lady, he shall be punished in the same way.

14 However, if anyone has committed these capital crimes and has gone undetected, and goes of his own accord to a priest and is willing to make his confession and undergo a penance, he shall be excused the death penalty on the priest's testimony.

15 On the lesser items all were agreed. For each and every church the people in the area who attend it are to provide a farmstead and two manses of land; and for every 120 men among them, be they noble or free or *lidi*, they are to give a male and a female slave to the church.

16 This too was decided, with Christ's blessing, that of any revenue which comes to the royal fisc, whether it be from infringement of the peace or a ban of any kind [*sive in frido sive in qualecumque banno*], or from any other payment due to the king, a tithe is to be given to the churches and the clergy.

17 Likewise, in accordance with God's command, we instruct all men to give a tithe of their substance and labour to their churches and clergy; and let nobles, free men and *lidi* alike make partial return to God for what he has given to each and every Christian.

18 On Sundays there are to be no assemblies or public gatherings, except in cases of great need or when an enemy is pressing; rather let all attend church to hear the word of God, and give their time to prayers and lawful occupations. Likewise on the greater feast days they should gather to serve God and his Church, and put off secular business.

19 Likewise it was decided to include in these enactments that all infants should be baptized within the year; we have decided further, that if anyone scorns to offer an infant for baptism before a year has gone by, and does not consult a priest or obtain his permission, he shall, if he is of noble birth, pay 120 shillings to the fisc, if he is a free man 60 shillings, and if he is a *lidus* 30.

20 If anyone contracts a forbidden or unlawful marriage, he shall pay 60 shillings if he is a noble, 30 if he is a free man, and 15 if he is a *lidus*.

21 If anyone offers prayers to springs or trees or groves, or makes an offering after the manner of the gentiles and consumes it in honour of demons, he shall pay 60 shillings if he is a noble, 30 if he is a free man, and 15 if he is a *lidus*. But if they do not have the means to pay at once, they are to be placed in the service of the church until such time as the shillings are paid.

22 It is our order that the bodies of Christian Saxons shall be taken to the church's cemeteries and not to the pagan burial mounds.

23 We have decided to hand over the diviners and sooth-sayers to the churches and the clergy.

24 With regard to robbers and other criminals who flee from one county to another, if anyone receives them into his power, and keeps them with him for seven nights for any purpose other than to bring them to justice, let him pay our fine. Likewise, if the count lets such a man abscond, and refuses to bring him to justice, and can give no reason for so doing, let him lose his office.

25 With regard to sureties, let no one, under any circumstances, dare to use another man as a surety; anyone who does this shall pay our fine.

26 Let no one take it upon himself to bar the way to any man coming to us to appeal for justice; if anyone tries to do this he shall pay our fine.

27 If any man is unable to find a surety, his property is to be placed in distraint until he provides one. But if he dares to enter his house in defiance of the ban, let him forfeit ten shillings or one ox in payment for the ban, and in addition pay in full his original debt. And if the surety does not keep to the appointed day, let him lose whatever he stood to lose in his capacity as surety; but let him who was debtor to the surety pay back double the loss that he caused his surety to suffer.

28 With regard to payments and rewards: let no one take reward against an innocent person [*cf.* Psalm 15.4]; if anyone dares to do this, he must pay our fine. And if, which God forbid, it should happen that a count does it, let him lose his office.

29 Let all the counts endeavour to be at peace and concord with one another: and if it should happen that some disagreement or quarrel should arise among them, they must not scorn our help in settling it.

30 If anyone kills a count or conspires to kill him, his inheritance shall be made over to the king and he shall be subject to his jurisdiction.

31 We have given authority to the counts, within the areas assigned to them, to impose a fine of up to 60 shillings for feuds or other major crimes; but for minor offences we have fixed the limit of the count's fine at 15 shillings.

32 If anyone has to give an oath to a man, let him swear that oath in church on the appointed day; and if he scorns to swear, let him give a pledge; and anyone who shows himself negligent must pay 15 shillings and afterwards give full satisfaction in the case.

33 With regard to perjury, the law of the Saxons is to apply.

34 We forbid the Saxons to come together as a body in public gatherings, except on those occasions when our *missus* assembles them on our instructions; rather, let each and every count hold court and administer justice in his own area. And the clergy are to see to it that this order is obeyed.

12 Concerning the Saxons, 797

The Latin title of this document is the *Capitulare Saxonicum*.

Source: Boretius 27; Pertz 35.

1 In the seven hundred and ninety-seventh year of the incarnation of Our Lord Jesus Christ, and in the thirtieth and twenty-fifth years respectively of the reign of our lord and most mighty king, Charles, there being assembled together at the palace at Aix at his bidding on the twenty-eighth day of October the reverend bishops and abbots and the illustrious counts, and there being also gathered together the Saxons from the several regions—from Westphalia, from Angaria and from Eastphalia—they did all with one mind agree and ordain that for those matters for which the Franks pay 60 shillings if they have offended against the king's ban, the Saxon shall likewise pay, if they have done something contrary to the ban. The matters in question are these: first that the Church, and then that widows, orphans and humble folk generally, should be left in rightful peace and quiet; that no one should dare to commit rape or violence or arson within his neighbourhood; and that no one should presume to hold back from military service in defiance of the king's ban.

2   Those who offend in any of the eight matters mentioned are to pay, Saxons and Franks alike, 60 shillings.

3   It was agreed by all the Saxons that, in all cases where Franks are bound by law to pay 15 shillings, the noble Saxons shall pay 12 shillings, free men 5, and *lidi* 3.

4   This also they decided, that when any case is settled within a district by the local authorities, the people of the district are to receive 12 shillings as a fine [*pro districtione*] in the usual way, and they are to have this concession also in payment of the wergeld which it was their custom to have. But if cases are settled in the presence of the royal *missi*, the people are to have these 12 shillings as wergeld and the royal *missus* is to receive another 12 on the king's behalf, on the grounds that he has been troubled with the matter. If, however, the case is carried through to the palace for a settlement in the king's presence, then both of the 12 shilling payments, that for wergeld and that owed to the local people, making 24 shillings in all, are to be paid to the king's account, on the grounds that the settlement was not arrived at within the district concerned. And if there is anyone who is unwilling to abide by what his neighbours have decided in his district, and who comes to the palace for this reason, and if it is there decided that the original decision was just, he must on the first occasion, as explained above, pay 24 shillings to the king's account; and if he then goes away and refuses to abide by it or to make a just settlement, and is again brought to the palace for this reason and judged, let him pay the 24 shillings twice over; and if, in spite of this, he is detained and brought to the palace for the same reason a third time, let him pay for it three times over to the king.

5   If any noble is summoned to court and refuses to come, let him pay four shillings; free men are to pay two shillings and *lidi* one.

6   In the matter of priests, it was decided that if anyone should presume to do harm to them or to their men, or should take anything from them unlawfully, he should pay back everything to them and make amends twice over.

7   Concerning the king's *missi*, it was decided that if a *missus* should happen to be killed by them [the Saxons], he who dared to do it should pay for him three times over. Likewise, for anything done to their men, they should see that threefold restoration is made and payment given according to their own law.

8   Concerning fire-raising, it was decided that no one should dare to do so in his district out of anger or enmity or for any other spiteful motive: there should, however, be an exception if a man is so rebellious that he refuses to accept a

court's decision and cannot be otherwise restrained; and if he refuses to come to us and be judged in our presence; in such a case a common hearing should be declared and all the people in the district must come, and if they are unanimous in this court the fine can be raised in order to restrain him. When at this hearing a common course of action is agreed upon, let it be carried out in accordance with their own law, and not through any anger or spiteful intent, but only in order to restrain a man for us. If anyone dares to raise a fire in any other circumstances, let him, as is said above, pay 60 shillings.

9   Likewise, seeing that our lord the king, for the sake of peace and for [preventing] feuds and for other important reasons, wishes to impose a stronger fine [*bannum*], it was decided, with the consent of the Franks and of his faithful Saxons, according to his decision, as the case demands and as opportunity allows, to double the 60 shilling payment; and if anyone goes against this order, let him pay 100 shillings, or even up to a thousand.

10   Concerning the criminals who should (according to the Saxon law code) incur the death penalty, it was decided by all that whoever of them seeks refuge in the royal prerogative it shall be part of that prerogative either to hand the criminal back for punishment, or with their consent to remove him and his wife and family and all his goods from the district, and settle them inside his kingdom or in the march or wherever he wishes, and to have possession of him as though dead.

11   Note should be taken of the proper equivalents of the Saxon shillings; a yearling calf of either sex, in autumn when it is put to byre, is to count for one shilling; likewise in spring, when it comes out of the byre; but afterwards, as it grows older, it should increase in value proportionately. Of oats, the Bortrini must give 40 bushels for a shilling, and of rye 20 bushels; those to the south, however, must give 30 bushels of oats for a shilling and 15 bushels of rye. Of honey, the Bortrini must give one and a half *siccli* for a shilling, while those of the south are to give two *siccli*. Likewise of winnowed barley they are to give the same amount as of rye for one shilling. In silver, 12 pennies make a shilling. And in other media of exchange the values shall be the equivalents in each case.

13 The Synod of Frankfurt, 794

The ecclesiastical nature of the assembly at Frankfurt is reflected in the contents of the *Synodus Franconofurtensis* (*Capitulare Franconofurtense*) which is mostly concerned with Church affairs. Laymen were however also present, and attention should be drawn to important statements on matters of general social concern, notably detailed regulations relating to prices (clause 4) and to coinage (clause 5).

Source: Boretius 28; Pertz 34.

1 A gathering, under God's blessing, in accordance with the apostolic authority and the order of our most pious lord king, Charles, in the twenty-sixth year of his reign, of all the bishops and priests of the kingdom of the Franks, of Italy, of Aquitaine and Provence in synod and council, among whom, in the holy assembly, was the most gentle king himself. Whereat, under the first and foremost head, there arose the matter of the impious and wicked heresy of Elipandus, bishop of the see of Toledo, and Felix, bishop of Urgel, and their followers, who in their erroneous belief concerning the Son of God assert adoption: this heresy did all the most holy fathers above mentioned repudiate and with one voice denounce, and it was their decision that it should be utterly eradicated from the Holy Church.

2 There was presented for discussion the matter of the new synod of the Greeks, organized at Constantinople on the subject of the adoration of images, in which it was stated that they regarded as anathema those images of the saints which did not have a bearing on the service or adoration of the Holy Trinity; our most holy fathers aforementioned repudiated and despised all such adoration and service, and agreed in condemning it.

3 After this had been dealt with a decision was reached concerning Tassilo, the cousin of our lord king, Charles, who had formerly been duke of Bavaria. He took his stand in the midst of the most holy council, asking pardon for the sins that he had committed, both for those which he had perpetrated in the time of our lord king, Pippin, against him and against the kingdom of the Franks, and for those later ones committed under our lord and most pious king, Charles, in which he had shown himself to be a breaker of his word. He begged to be thought worthy of indulgence from the king, and appeared to do so in all humility, since he wholeheartedly repudiated all anger and scandalous behaviour on his part and all things committed against the king to which he had been party. Moreover, all his rights and properties, everything that should lawfully belong to himself or his sons or daughters in the duchy of Bavaria, he disowned and renounced, and forswearing all claims to it for the future irrevocably surrendered it, and along with his sons and daughters commended it to the mercy of the king. Wherefore our lord [the king], moved with pity, both forgave the said Tassilo graciously for the sins he had committed, restored full favour to him, and with compassion received him in love and affection, so that from henceforth he might be secure in the mercy of God. And so he ordered three copies of this decision to be written to the one effect: one he ordered to be kept in the palace, another to be given to the said Tassilo for him to keep by him in the monastery, and the third to be deposited in the chapel of the sacred palace.

4 Our most pious lord the king, with the consent of the holy synod, gave instructions that no man, whether he be cleric or layman, should ever sell corn in time of abundance or in time of scarcity at a greater price than the public level

recently decided upon, that is, a *modius* of oats one penny, a *modius* of barley two pennies, a *modius* of rye three pennies, a *modius* of wheat four pennies. If he should wish to sell it in the form of bread, he should give 12 loaves of wheat bread, each weighing two pounds, for one penny, and for the same price 15 of equal weight of rye bread, 20 of barley bread of the same weight, and 25 of oat bread of the same weight. For the public corn of our lord the king, if it should be sold, the price is to be two *modii* of oats for a penny, one *modius* of barley for a penny, two pence for a *modius* of rye, and three for a *modius* of wheat. Anyone who holds a benefice of us should take the greatest possible care that, if God but provide, none of the slaves of the benefice should die of hunger; and anything that remains above what is necessary for the household he may freely sell in the manner laid down.

5 Concerning the pennies, you should be fully aware of our edict, that in every place, in every city and in every market these new pennies must be current and must be accepted by everyone. Provided they bear the imprint of our name and are of pure silver and of full weight, if anyone should refuse to allow them in any place, in any transaction of buying or selling, he shall, if he is a free man, pay 15 shillings to the king, and, if he is of servile status and the transaction is his own, shall lose the transaction or be flogged naked at the stake in the presence of the people; but if he has done it on his lord's orders, the lord, if it is proved against him, shall pay the 15 shillings.

6 It was ordained by our lord the king and by the holy synod that bishops should administer justice in their parishes. And if any person from among the abbots, priests, deacons, sub-deacons, monks and other clerics, or anyone else in the parish should refuse to obey his bishop, let them come to their metropolitan, and let him decide the case along with his suffragans. Our counts also are to come to the bishops' courts. And if there is anything which the metropolitan bishop cannot put right or settle, then let the accusers finally come to us, with the accused and with letters from the metropolitan, that we may know the truth of the matter.

7 It was ruled by our lord the king and by the holy synod that a bishop should not move from one city to another, but should stay and take care of his church; likewise a priest or a deacon should stay in his church according to the canons.

8 With regard to the dispute between Ursio, bishop of Vienne and the advocate of Elifantus, bishop of Arles, there were read letters of St Gregory, Zosimus, Leo and Symmachus, which made it clear that the church of Vienne should have four suffragan sees, with itself as the fifth over them, and that the church at Arles should have nine suffragan sees under its authority. As to the question of Tarantaise and Embrun and Aix, an embassy was arranged to the apostolic see; and whatever may be decided by the pontiff of the Church of Rome shall be adhered to.

9 It was ruled also by the same our lord the king and by the holy synod that Peter the bishop [of Verdun] should assert before God and his angels and, in the presence of two or three others, as though he were receiving consecration, or indeed in the presence of his archbishop, should swear that he had not conspired for the death of the king or against his kingdom nor been unfaithful to him. The said bishop, since he could find no one with whom he could swear, decided for himself that he would, as God's man, go before the judgement of God, and testify without relics and without the holy gospels and solely in the presence of God that he was innocent of these matters, and that in accordance with his innocence God should help this his man, who was bound to submit to his judgement and did so. Yet it was not by order of the king or by the decision of the holy synod but by his own free will that he submitted to God's judgement, and was acquitted by Our Lord and found innocent. Nevertheless, our king in his mercy bestowed his favour on the said bishop and endowed him with his former honours, and would not allow a man whom he perceived to merit nothing harmful to be without honour as a result of the charge alleged against him.

10 It was ruled by our lord the king and decided by the holy synod that Gaerbodus, who said he was a bishop but had no witnesses of his consecration, and yet had sought episcopal insignia from Magnardus the metropolitan bishop (who declared moreover that he was not ordained deacon or priest according to canonical prescription), should be deposed by the said metropolitan or by the other bishops of the province from that rank of bishop which he claimed to have.

11 That monks should not go out for secular business nor to engage in lawsuits, unless they do so in accordance with the precepts of the rule itself.

12 That men should not become recluses unless the bishop of the province and the abbot have previously approved of them, and they are to enter upon their place of retreat according to their arrangements.

13 That an abbot should sleep alongside his monks according to the rule of St Benedict.

14 That greedy men should not be chosen as cellarers in the monasteries, but that such men should be chosen as the rule of St Benedict instructs.

15 Concerning a monastery where there are bodies of saints; that it should have an oratory within its cloister where the peculiar and daily office may be done.

16 We have heard that certain abbots, led on by greed, require a payment on behalf of those entering their monastery. Therefore we and the holy synod have decided that under no circumstances shall money be required for receiving brothers into a holy order, but that they should be received in accordance with the rule of St Benedict.

17 That an abbot should not be chosen, when the king so orders, in the congregation, except by the consent of the local bishop.

18 That whatever sin is committed by the monks, we do not allow the abbots under any circumstances to blind them or inflict the mutilation of members upon them, unless the discipline of the rule provides for it.

19 That priests, deacons, monks and clerks should not go into taverns to drink.

20 That a bishop should not be permitted to be ignorant of the canons and the rule.

21 That the Lord's day should be observed from evening to evening.

22 That it should not be proper to consecrate bishops in small towns and villages.

23 Concerning other men's slaves, that they should not be taken in by anyone, and should not be ordained by bishops without their lords' permission.

24 Concerning clerks and monks, that they should remain steadfast in their chosen way of life.

25 That in general, tithes and ninths (or the *census*) should be paid by all who owe them, in respect of benefices and Church property, according to the earlier enactments of our lord the king; and every man should give the lawful tithe in respect of his property to the Church. For we have been informed that in that year when the severe famine broke out there was an abundance of empty corn eaten by demons, and voices of reproach were heard.

26 That the church buildings and their roofs should be repaired and restored by those who hold benefices dependent on them. And where, on the testimony of trustworthy men, it is found that they have in their own houses any wood or stone or tiles that were previously on the church buildings, they must restore to the church everything that has been taken from it.

27 Concerning clerks, that they should under no circumstances move from one church to another, nor be taken in without the knowledge of the bishop and letters of commendation from the diocese to which they belonged, lest it should happen that discord arise in the Church as a result. And wherever such men are found, they must all return to their own church; and let no one dare to keep such a man by him once his bishop or abbot has indicated his wish to have him back. And if it should happen that the lord does not know where he should look for his clerk, let the man with whom he is staying keep him in custody and not allow him to wander elsewhere, until such time as he is restored to his lord.

28   That men should not be ordained without restriction [*absolute*].

29   That each and every bishop should give good teaching and instruction to those placed in his charge, so that there will always in God's house be found men who are worthy to be chosen according to the canons.

30   Concerning clerks who quarrel among themselves or who act in opposition to their bishop, they are to take all the measures that the canons prescribe. And if it should happen that a quarrel arises between a clerk and a layman, the bishop and the count should meet together and should with one mind decide the case between them according to what is right.

31   Concerning plots and conspiracies, that they should not occur; and where they are discovered they are to be crushed.

32   That monasteries should be guarded according to the provisions of the canons.

33   That the catholic faith of the Holy Trinity, the Lord's Prayer and the Creed should be preached and handed on to all men.

34   Concerning the stamping out of greed and covetousness.

35   Concerning the practice of hospitality.

36   Concerning criminals, that they should not be allowed to accuse their superiors or their bishops.

37   Concerning absolution in time of emergency.

38   Concerning priests who have been disobedient towards their bishops: they must under no circumstances communicate with the clerks who live in the king's chapel, unless they have made their peace with their bishop, lest it should happen that excommunication according to the canons should come upon them as a result.

39   If a priest is caught in a criminal act, he should be brought before his bishop and be dealt with according to the ruling of the canons. And if it should happen that he wishes to deny the offence, and his accuser is unable to offer proof of it, and the matter cannot be settled before the bishop, then the decision should be referred to their whole council.

40   Concerning girls who have been deprived of their parents: they should, under the supervision of the bishops and priests, be entrusted to suitably sober women, in accordance with the teaching of canonical authority.

41   That no bishop should abandon his proper see by spending his time elsewhere, nor dare to stay on his own property for more than three weeks. And the relatives or heirs of a bishop should in no circumstances inherit after his death any property which was acquired by him after he was consecrated bishop, either by purchase or by gift; rather, it should go in full to his church. Such property as he had before then shall, unless he make a gift from it to the Church, pass to his heirs and relatives,

42 That no new saints should be revered or invoked in prayers, nor memorials of them erected by the wayside; only those are to be venerated in church which have been deservedly chosen on the basis of their passions or their lives.

43 Concerning the destruction of trees and groves, let the authority of the canons be observed.

44 That the chosen judges should not be rejected by either side in a dispute.

45 Concerning their witnesses, let the canons be observed. And small children should not be compelled to swear an oath, as the Guntbadingi do.

46 Concerning young girls, at what time they are to take the veil and what are to be their occupations before the age of 25, the writings of the canons should, if necessary, be consulted.

47 Concerning abbesses who do not live according to the canons or the monastic rule: the bishops are to make inquiries and give notice to the king, so that they may be deprived of their office.

48 Concerning offerings which are made to the Church or for the use of the poor, the provisions of the canons are to be observed; such funds are not to be dispensed except by those appointed by the bishop.

49 Concerning priests, and not ordaining them before their thirtieth year.

50 That when the sacred mysteries are accomplished all men should be peaceable towards one another during the rites of the mass.

51 Concerning not reciting names until an oblation is offered.

52 That no one should believe that God cannot be prayed to except in three languages only; since God can be prayed to, and man listened to if his prayers are just, in any language.

53 That no bishop or priest should be allowed to be ignorant of the sacred canons.

54 Concerning churches which are built by free men; it is allowed to bestow them as gifts, or to sell them, provided that no church is destroyed and the daily offices are observed.

55 Our lord the king informed the holy synod that he had permission of the holy see, that is of Pope Hadrian, to keep Angilramnus the archbishop permanently in his palace to deal with ecclesiastical matters. He asked the synod

that he might be allowed to have bishop Hildebald there on the same terms as he had Angilramnus, since for him also, as for Angilramnus, he had the apostolic permission. The whole synod agreed, and decided that he should be in the palace to deal with ecclesiastical matters.

56   He suggested also that the holy synod should think it right to accept Alcuin into its fellowship and prayers, since he was a man of learning in the doctrines of the Church. All the synod agreed to the suggestion of our lord the king, and accepted him into their fellowship and their prayers.

14 Charles the Great on the study of literature, end of the eighth century

The *Encyclica de litteris colendis* (*Karoli epistola de litteris colendis*) appears to have been issued in the form of a circular letter. This copy from Boretius was directed to Baugulf, abbot of Fulda. A new text of the *De litteris* was discovered by P. Lehmann in 1927, and edited by L. Wallach in his article 'Charlemagne's *De litteris colendis* and Alcuin', *Speculum* (1951), pp. 289–92. See also Ganshof's *Recherches*, p. 45, *n.* 173, and *Frankish Institutions*, p. 54 and *n.* 406.

Source: Boretius 29; Pertz 29.

We, Charles, by the grace of God king of the Franks and Lombards and patrician of the Romans, to Abbot Baugulf and all your congregation and our faithful teachers [*oratoribus*] entrusted to your charge, send affectionate greeting in the name of Almighty God. Be it known to your devotion, most pleasing in the sight of God, that we, along with our faithful advisers, have deemed it useful that the bishoprics and monasteries which through the favour of Christ have been entrusted to us to govern should, in addition to the way of life prescribed by their rule and their practice of holy religion, devote their efforts to the study of literature and to the teaching of it, each according to his ability, to those on whom God has bestowed the capacity to learn; that, just as the observance of a rule gives soundness to their conduct, so also an attention to teaching and learning may give order and adornment to their words, and that those who seek to please God by living aright may not fail to please him also by rightness in their speaking. For it is written: 'Either by your words shall you be justified, or by your words shall you be condemned [Matthew 12.37].' For although it is better to do what is right than to know it, yet knowledge comes before action. Thus each man must first learn what he wishes to carry out, so that he will know in his heart all the more fully what he needs to do, in order that his tongue may run on without stumbling into falsehood in the praise of Almighty God. For since falsehood is to be shunned by all men, how much more should it be avoided, as far as they are able, by those who have been chosen for this one purpose, that they should give special service to truth. Letters have often been sent to us in these last years from certain monasteries, in which was set out what the brothers there living were striving to do for us in their holy and pious prayers; and we found that in most of these writings their sentiments were sound but their speech uncouth. Inwardly their pious devotions gave them a message of truth, but because of their neglect of learning their unskilled tongues could not express it without fault. And so it came about that we began to fear that their lack of knowledge of writing might be matched by a more serious lack of wisdom in the understanding of holy scripture. We all know well that, dangerous as are the errors of words, yet much more dangerous are the errors of doctrine. Wherefore we urge you, not merely to avoid the neglect of the study of literature, but with a devotion that is humble and pleasing to God to strive to learn it, so that you may be able more easily and more rightly to penetrate the mysteries of the holy scriptures. For since there are figures of speech, metaphors and the like to be found on the sacred pages, there can be no doubt that each man who reads them will understand their spiritual meaning more quickly if he is first of all given full instruction in the study of literature. Let men be chosen for this work who have the will and ability to learn and also the desire to instruct others; and let it be pursued with an eagerness equal to my devotion in prescribing it. For we want you, as befits the soldiers of the Church, to be inwardly devout and outwardly learned, pure in good living and scholarly in speech; so that whoever comes to see you in the name of God and for the inspiration of your holy converse, just as he is strengthened by the sight of you, so he may be instructed also by your wisdom, both in reading and chanting, and return rejoicing, giving thanks to Almighty God. Therefore, if you wish to keep our favour, do not neglect to send copies of this letter to all your suffragans and fellow bishops, and to all the monasteries.

15 'De Villis', end of the eighth century

The *Capitulare de Villis vel Curtis Imperialibus* appears in a manuscript of the early ninth century. It contains no date and makes no explicit reference to any historical event: its date, authorship and purpose have consequently been matters for considerable discussion. Most authorities place it in the reign of Charlemagne on stylistic and general historical grounds, but some would attribute it to Charlemagne's son, Louis the Pious, who from 794 to 813 was ruler of Aquitaine and is known from other sources to have carried out a reform of estates in this area. The question of its date is not of major importance, as the attribution to Louis implies that it was written in AD 794 (the date of estate reforms) and if Charlemagne is the author a date before 800 is also suggested by references in four of the sections to the queen (Charlemagne's fourth and last wife having died in that year). There is little hope of resolving the authorship beyond doubt, but the following points are relevant: first, it has been argued that a number of words in the document are paralleled only, or mainly, in Aquitaine; but this may merely reveal the origin of the person drafting the document. Secondly, it has been pointed out that the list of plants with which the document ends is more appropriate in a southern than a northern context; but it is not entirely so (for example, there is no mention of olives). Thirdly, there are signs, particularly towards the end of the document, of later additions and alterations (section 63, for example, is arguably a more appropriate conclusion than section 70), and this should warn us against pressing the words used too closely. It has also been discovered that in this, as in other documents of the period, those responsible for drafting were apt to use much older material, including such things as later Roman glossaries. The case for Louis as the author is thus unproven, and there is little positive evidence to justify the attribution to Charlemagne. The purpose of the enactment was not to establish a new system, but rather to improve an existing one. The document reflects the situation of the royal estates, as long as one assumes that a rather lower level of neatness and efficiency actually existed than is here implied.

The most famous commentary on the *Capitulare de Villis* is that of B. Guérard, *Explication du 'Capitulaire de Villis'* (Paris 1853), but perhaps the most useful introduction in English is that of R. Latouche, *The Birth of Western Economy* (London 1961), ch. III. Learned commentaries of great interest and importance of the last generation include K. Verhein, 'Studien zu den Quellen zum Reichsgut der Karolingerzeit: Das *Capitulare de Villis*', *Deutsches Archiv* X (1954), and Th. Mayer, 'Das *Capitulare de Villis*', *Zeitschrift der Savigny Stiftung f. Rechtsgeschichte, Germanische Abteilung* 79, 1962, both of which give extensive references to the work of earlier scholars, notably to the seminal work of A. Dopsch.

Source: Boretius 32; Pertz 102.

1   It is our wish that those of our estates which we have established to minister to our needs shall serve our purposes entirely and not those of other men.

2   That all our people shall be well looked after, and shall not be reduced to penury by anyone.

3   That the stewards shall not presume to put our people to their own service, and shall not compel them to give their labour or to cut wood or to do any other work for them; and they shall accept no gifts from them, neither a horse nor an ox, nor a cow, nor a pig, nor a sheep, nor a piglet, nor a lamb, nor anything other than bottles of wine, vegetables, fruit, chickens and eggs.

4   If anyone of our people does harm to our interests through theft or any other neglect of duty, let him make good the damage in full, and in addition let him be punished by whipping according to the law, except in the case of murder or arson, for which a fine may be exacted. As far as concerns other men, let the stewards be careful to give them the justice to which they have a right, as the law directs. Our people, as we have said, are to be whipped in preference to being fined. Free men, however, who live on our crown lands [*fiscis*] and estates shall be careful to pay for any wrong they may have done, according to their law; and whatever they may give as their fine, whether it be cattle or any other form of payment, shall be assigned to our use.

5 Whenever it falls to our stewards to see that our work is done, whether it be sowing or ploughing, harvesting, haymaking or the gathering of grapes, let each one of them, at the appropriate time and place, supervise the work and give instructions as to how it should be done, so that everything may be successfully carried out. If a steward is not in his district, or cannot get to a particular place, let him send a good messenger from among our people, or some other man who can be trusted, to look after our affairs and settle them satisfactorily; and the steward shall be especially careful to send a reliable man to deal with this matter.

6 It is our wish that our stewards shall pay a full tithe of all produce to the churches that are on our estates, and that no tithe of ours shall be paid to the church of another lord except in places where this is an ancient custom. And no clerics shall hold these churches except our own or those from our people or from our chapel.

7 That each steward shall perform his service in full, according to his instructions. And if the necessity should arise for his service to be increased, let him decide whether he should add to the manpower or to the days spent in performing it [*si servitium debeat multiplicare vel noctes*].

8 That our stewards shall take charge of our vineyards in their districts, and see that they are properly worked; and let them put the wine into good vessels, and take particular care that no loss is incurred in shipping it. They are to have purchased other, more special, wine to supply the royal estates. And if they should buy more of this wine than is necessary for supplying our estates they should inform us of this, so that we can tell them what we wish to be done with it. They shall also have slips from our vineyards sent for our use. Such rents from our estates as are paid in wine they shall send to our cellars.

9 It is our wish that each steward shall keep in his district measures for *modii* and *sextaria*, and vessels containing eight *sextaria*, and also baskets of the same capacity as we have in our palace.

10 That our mayors and foresters, our stablemen, cellarers, deans, toll-collectors and other officials shall perform regular services, and shall give pigs in return for their holdings: in place of manual labour, let them perform their official duties well. And any mayor who has a benefice, let him arrange to send a substitute, whose task it will be to carry out the manual labour and other services on his behalf.

11 That no steward, under any circumstances, shall take lodgings for his own use or for his dogs, either among our men or among those living outside our estates.

12 That no steward shall commend a hostage of ours on our estates.

13 That they shall take good care of the stallions, and under no circumstances

allow them to stay for long in the same pasture, lest it should be spoiled. And if any of them is unhealthy, or too old, or is likely to die, the stewards are to see that we are informed at the proper time, before the season comes for sending them in among the mares.

14 That they shall look after our mares well, and segregate the colts at the proper time. And if the fillies increase in number, let them be separated so that they can form a new herd by themselves.

15 That they shall take care to have our foals sent to the winter palace at the feast of St Martin.

16 It is our wish that whatever we or the queen may order any steward, or whatever our officials, the seneschal or the butler, may order them in our name or in the name of the queen, they shall carry out in full as they are instructed. And whoever falls short in this through negligence, let him abstain from drinking from the moment he is told to do so until he comes into our presence or the presence of the queen and seeks forgiveness from us. And if a steward is in the army, or on guard duty, or on a mission, or is away elsewhere, and gives an order to his subordinates and they do not carry it out, let them come on foot to the palace, and let them abstain from food and drink until they have given reasons for failing in their duty in this way; and then let them receive their punishment, either in the form of a beating or in any other way that we or the queen shall decide.

17 A steward shall appoint as many men as he has estates in his district, whose task it will be to keep bees for our use.

18 At our mills they are to keep chickens and geese, according to the mill's importance—or as many as is possible.

19 In the barns on our chief estates they are to keep not less than 100 chickens and not less than 30 geese. At the smaller farms they are to keep not less than 50 chickens and not less than 12 geese.

20 Every steward is to see that the produce is brought to the court in plentiful supply throughout the year; also, let them make their visitations for this purpose at least three or four times.

21 Every steward is to keep fishponds on our estates where they have existed in the past, and if possible he is to enlarge them. They are also to be established in places where they have not so far existed but where they are now practicable.

22 Those who have vines shall keep not less than three or four crowns of grapes.

23 On each of our estates the stewards are to have as many byres, pigsties, sheepfolds and goat-pens as possible, and under no circumstances are they to be

without them. They are also to have cows provided by our serfs for the performance of their service, so that the byres and plough-teams are in no way weakened by service on our demesne. And when they have to provide meat, let them have lame but healthy oxen, cows or horses which are not mangy, and other healthy animals; and, as we have said, our byres and plough-teams must not suffer as a result of this.

24 Every steward is to take pains over anything he has to provide for our table, so that everything he gives is good and of the best quality, and as carefully and cleanly prepared as possible. And each of them, when he comes to serve at our table, is to have corn for two meals a day for his service; and any other provisions, whether in flour or in meat, are similarly to be of good quality.

25 They are to report on the first of September whether or not there will be food for the pigs.

26 The mayors are not to have more land in their districts than they can ride through and inspect in a single day.

27 Our houses are to have continuous watch-fires and guards to keep them safe. And when our *missi* and their retinues are on their way to or from the palace, they shall under no circumstances take lodging in the royal manor houses, except on our express orders or those of the queen. And the count in his district, or the men whose traditional custom it has been to look after our *missi* and their retinues, shall continue, as they have done in the past, to provide them with pack-horses and other necessities, so that they may travel to and from the palace with ease and dignity.

28 It is our wish that each year in Lent on Palm Sunday, which is also called Hosanna Sunday, the stewards shall take care to pay in the money part of our revenue according to our instructions, after we have determined the amount of our revenue for the year in question.

29 With regard to those of our men who have cases to plead, every steward is to see to it that they are not compelled to come into our presence to make their plea; and he shall not allow a man to lose, through negligence, the days on which he owes service. And if a serf of ours is involved in a lawsuit outside our estates, his master is to do all he can to see that he obtains justice. And if in a given place the serf has difficulty in obtaining it, his master shall not allow him to suffer as a result, but shall make it his business to inform us of the matter, either in person or through his messenger.

30 It is our wish that from all the revenue they shall set aside what is needed for our purposes; and in the same way they are to set aside the produce with which they load the carts that are needed for the army, both those of the householders and those of the shepherds, and they shall keep a record of how much they are sending for this purpose.

31 That in the same way each year they shall set aside what is necessary for the household workers and for the women's workshops; and at the appropriate time they are to supply it in full measure, and must be in a position to tell us how they have disposed of it and where it came from.

32 That every steward shall make it his business always to have good seed of the best quality, whether bought or otherwise acquired.

33 After all these parts of our revenue have been set aside or sown or otherwise dealt with, anything that is left over is to be kept to await our instructions, so that it can be sold or held in reserve as we shall decide.

34 They are to take particular care that anything which they do or make with their hands—that is, lard, smoked meat, sausage, newly-salted meat, wine, vinegar, mulberry wine, boiled wine, garum, mustard, cheese, butter, malt, beer, mead, honey, wax and flour—that all these are made or prepared with the greatest attention to cleanliness.

35 It is our wish that tallow shall be made from fat sheep and also from pigs; in addition, they are to keep on each estate not less than two fattened oxen, which can either be used for making tallow there or can be sent to us.

36 That our woods and forests shall be well protected; if there is an area to be cleared, the stewards are to have it cleared, and shall not allow fields to become overgrown with woodland. Where woods are supposed to exist they shall not allow them to be excessively cut and damaged. Inside the forests they are to take good care of our game; likewise, they shall keep our hawks and falcons in readiness for our use, and shall diligently collect our dues there. And the stewards, or our mayors or their men, if they send their pigs into our woods to be fattened, shall be the first to pay the tithe for this, so as to set a good example and encourage other men to pay their tithe in full in the future.

37 That they shall keep our fields and arable land in good order, and shall guard our meadows at the appropriate time.

38 That they shall always keep fattened geese and chickens sufficient for our use if needed, or for sending to us.

39 It is our wish that the stewards shall be responsible for collecting the chickens and eggs which the serfs and manse-holders contribute each year; and when they are not able to use them they are to sell them.

40 That every steward, on each of our estates, shall always have swans, peacocks, pheasants, ducks, pigeons, partridges and turtle doves, for the sake of ornament.

41 That the buildings inside our demesnes, together with the fences around them, shall be well looked-after, and that the stables and kitchens, bakeries and wine-presses, shall be carefully constructed, so that our servants who work in them can carry out their tasks properly and cleanly.

42   That each estate shall have in its store-room beds, mattresses, pillows, bed-linen, table-cloths, seat-covers, vessels of bronze, lead, iron and wood, fire-dogs, chains, pot-hangers, adzes, axes, augers, knives and all sorts of tools, so that there is no need to seek them elsewhere or to borrow them. As to the iron tools which they provide for the army, the stewards are to make it their business to see that these are good, and that when they are returned they are put back into the storeroom.

43   They are to supply the women's workshops with materials at the appropriate times, according to their instructions—that is, linen, wool, woad, vermilion, madder, wool-combs, teazles, soap, oil, vessels and the other small things that are needed there.

44   Two thirds of the Lenten food shall be sent each year for our use—that is, of the vegetables, fish, cheese, butter, honey, mustard, vinegar, millet, panic, dry or green herbs, radishes, turnips, and wax or soap and other small items; and as we have said earlier, they are to inform us by letter of what is left over, and shall under no circumstances omit to do this, as they have done in the past, because it is through those two thirds that we wish to know about the one third that remains.

45   That every steward shall have in his district good workmen—that is, blacksmiths, gold- and silver-smiths, shoemakers, turners, carpenters, shield-makers, fishermen, falconers, soap-makers, brewers (that is, people who know how to make beer, cider, perry or any other suitable beverage), bakers to make bread for our use, net-makers who can make good nets for hunting or fishing or fowling, and all the other workmen too numerous to mention.

46   That the stewards shall take good care of our walled parks, which the people call *brogili*, and always repair them in good time, and not delay so long that it becomes necessary to rebuild them completely. This should apply to all buildings.

47   That our hunters and falconers, and the other servants who are in permanent attendance on us at the palace, shall throughout our estates be given such assistance as we or the queen may command in our letters, on occasions when we send them out on an errand or when the seneschal or butler gives them some task to do in our name.

48   That the wine-presses on our estates shall be kept in good order. And the stewards are to see to it that no one dares to crush the grapes with his feet, but that everything is clean and decent.

49   That our women's quarters shall be properly arranged—that is, with houses, heated rooms and living rooms; and let them have good fences all round, and strong doors, so that they can do our work well.

50 That each steward shall determine how many horses there should be in a single stable, and how many grooms with them. Those grooms who are free men, and have benefices in the district, shall live off those benefices. Similarly the men of the fisc, who hold manses, shall live off them. And those who have no holding shall receive their food from the demesne.

51 Every steward is to take care that dishonest men do not conceal our seed from us, either under the ground or elsewhere, thus making the harvest less plentiful. Similarly, with the other kinds of mischief, let them see to it that they never happen.

52 It is our wish that the men of the fisc, our serfs, and the free men who live on our crown lands and estates shall be required to give to all men the full and complete justice to which they are entitled.

53 That every steward shall take pains to prevent our people in his district from becoming robbers and criminals.

54 That every steward shall see to it that our people work well at their tasks, and do not go wasting time at markets.

55 It is our wish that the stewards should record, in one document, any goods or services they have provided, or anything they have appropriated for our use, and, in another document, what payments they have made; and they shall notify us by letter of anything that is left over.

56 That every steward in his district shall hold frequent hearings and dispense justice, and see to it that our people live a law-abiding life.

57 If any of our serfs should wish to say something to us about his master in connection with our affairs, he is not to be prevented from coming to us. And if a steward should learn that his subordinates wish to come to the palace to lodge a complaint against him, then that steward shall present his arguments against them at the palace, and give reason why we should not be displeased at hearing their complaint. In this way we wish to find out whether they come from necessity or merely on some pretext.

58 When our puppies are entrusted to the stewards they are to feed them at their own expense, or else entrust them to their subordinates, that is, the mayors and deans, or cellarers, so that they in their turn can feed them from their own resources—unless there should be an order from ourselves or the queen that they are to be fed on our estate at our own expense. In this case the steward is to send a man to them, to see to their feeding, and is to set aside food for them; and there will be no need for the man to go to the kennels every day.

59 Every steward shall, when he is on service, give three pounds of wax and eight *sextaria* of soap each day; in addition, he shall be sure to give six pounds of wax on St Andrew's Day, wherever we may be with our people, and a similar amount in mid-Lent.

60 Mayors are never to be chosen from among powerful men, but from men of more modest station who are likely to be loyal.

61 That each steward, when he is on service, shall have his malt brought to the palace; and with him shall come master-brewers who can make good beer there.

62 That each steward shall make an annual statement of all our income, from the oxen which our ploughmen keep, from the holdings which owe ploughing services, from the pigs, from rents, judgement-fees and fines, from the fines for taking game in our forests without our permission and from the various other payments; from the mills, forests, fields, bridges and ships; from the free men and the hundreds which are attached to our fisc; from the markets; from the vineyards, and those who pay their dues in wine; from hay, firewood and torches, from planks and other timber; from waste land; from vegetables, millet and panic; from wool, linen and hemp; from the fruits of trees; from larger and smaller nuts; from the graftings of various trees; from gardens, turnips, fishponds; from hides, skins and horns; from honey and wax; from oil, tallow and soap; from mulberry wine, boiled wine, mead and vinegar; from beer and from new and old wine; from new and old grain; from chickens and eggs and geese; from the fishermen, smiths, shield-makers and cobblers; from kneading troughs, bins or boxes; from the turners and saddlers; from forges and from mines, that is, from iron- or lead-workings and from workings of any other kind; from people paying tribute; and from colts and fillies. All these things they shall set out in order under separate headings, and shall send the information to us at Christmas time, so that we may know the character and amount of our income from the various sources.

63 With regard to all the things mentioned so far, our stewards should not think it hard of us to make these demands, since it is our wish that they likewise should be able to make demands of their subordinates without giving offence. And all the things that a man ought to have in his house or on his estates, our stewards shall have on our estates.

64 That our carts which go to the army as war-carts shall be well constructed; their coverings shall be well-made of skins, and sewn together in such a way that, should the necessity arise to cross water, they can get across rivers with the provisions inside and without any water being able to get in—and, as we have said, our belongings can get across safely. It is also our wish that flour—12 *modii* of it—should be placed in each cart for our use; and in those carts which carry wine they are to place 12 *modii* according to our measurement, and they are also to provide for each cart a shield, a lance, a quiver and a bow.

65 That the fish from our fishponds shall be sold, and others put in their place,

so that there is always a supply of fish; however, when we do not visit the estates they are to be sold, and our stewards are to get a profit from them for our benefit.

66 They are to give an account to us of the male and female goats, and of their horns and skins; and each year they are to bring to us the newly-salted meat of the fattened goats.

67 With regard to vacant manses and newly acquired slaves, if they have any surplus which they cannot dispose of, they are to let us know.

68 It is our wish that the various stewards should always have by them good barrels bound with iron, which they can send to the army or to the palace, and that they should not make bottles of leather.

69 They shall at all times keep us informed about wolves, how many each of them has caught, and shall have the skins delivered to us. And in the month of May they are to seek out the wolf cubs and catch them, with poison and hooks as well as with pits and dogs.

70 It is our wish that they shall have in their gardens all kinds of plants: lily, roses, fenugreek, costmary, sage, rue, southernwood, cucumbers, pumpkins, gourds, kidney-bean, cumin, rosemary, caraway, chick-pea, squill, gladiolus, tarragon, anise, colocynth, chicory, ammi, sesili, lettuces, spider's foot, rocket salad, garden cress, burdock, penny-royal, hemlock, parsley, celery, lovage, juniper, dill, sweet fennel, endive, dittany, white mustard, summer savory, water mint, garden mint, wild mint, tansy, catnip, centaury, garden poppy, beets, hazelwort, marshmallows, mallows, carrots, parsnip, orach, spinach, kohlrabi, cabbages, onions, chives, leeks, radishes, shallots, cibols, garlic, madder, teazles, broad beans, peas, coriander, chervil, capers, clary. And the gardener shall have house-leeks growing on his house. As for trees, it is our wish that they shall have various kinds of apple, pear, plum, sorb, medlar, chestnut and peach; quince, hazel, almond, mulberry, laurel, pine, fig, nut and cherry trees of various kinds. The names of apples are: *gozmaringa, geroldinga, crevedella, spirauca*; there are sweet ones, bitter ones, those that keep well, those that are to be eaten straightaway, and early ones. Of pears they are to have three or four kinds, those that keep well, sweet ones, cooking pears and the late-ripening ones.

16 General Capitulary for the *missi*, spring 802

An important concise discussion of the *Capitulare missorum Generale (Capitulare Aquisgranense)* appears in Ganshof, *Frankish Institutions*, pp. 56–7 and *nn.* 14–20. Ganshof interprets it essentially as a formulation of a programme of *imperial* reform for Church and State. It should be read in conjunction with the following document **(17)** which sets out the instructions to the *missi* whose duty it was to publish and to see to the implementation of this capitulary. Ganshof supports the view that the title given by Boretius is inadequate, and refers to it instead as the 'Programmatic capitulary' (*Ce grand capitulaire programmatique: Recherches* (1958), p. 52, *n*. 207). We have omitted the purely ecclesiastical clauses, 10–24.

Source: Boretius 33; Pertz 43.

1 Concerning the commission despatched by our lord the emperor. Our most serene and most Christian lord and emperor, Charles, has selected the most prudent and wise from among his leading men, archbishops and bishops, together with venerable abbots and devout laymen, and has sent them out into all his kingdom, and bestowed through them on all his subjects the right to live in accordance with a right rule of law. Wherever there is any provision in the law that is other than right or just he has ordered them to inquire most diligently into it and bring it to his notice, it being his desire, with God's help, to rectify it. And let no one dare or be allowed to use his wit and cunning, as many do, to subvert the law as it is laid down or the emperor's justice, whether it concerns God's churches, or poor people and widows and orphans, or any Christian person. Rather should all men live a good and just life in accordance with God's commands, and should with one mind remain and abide each in his appointed place or profession: the clergy should live a life in full accord with the canons without concern for base gain, the monastic orders should keep their life under diligent control, the laity and secular people should make proper use of their laws, refraining from ill-will and deceit, and all should live together in perfect love and peace. And the *missi* themselves, as they wish to have the favour of Almighty God and to preserve it through the loyalty they have promised, are to make diligent inquiry wherever a man claims that someone has done him an injustice; so everywhere, and amongst all men, in God's holy churches, among poor people, orphans and widows, and throughout the whole people they may administer law and justice in full accordance with the will and the fear of God. And if there be anything which they themselves, together with the counts of the provinces, cannot correct or bring to a just settlement, they should refer it without any hesitation to the emperor's judgement along with their reports. And in no way, whether by some man's flattery or bribery, or by the excuse of blood relationship with someone, or through fear of someone more powerful, should anyone hinder the right and proper course of justice.

2 Concerning the promise of fealty to our lord the emperor. He has given instructions that in all his kingdom all men, both clergy and laity, and each according to his vows and way of life, who before have promised fealty to him as king, should now make the same promise to him as Caesar; and those who until now have not made the promise are all to do so from 12 years old and upwards. And that all should be publicly informed, so that each man may

understand how many important matters are contained in that oath—not only, as many have thought until now, the profession of loyalty to our lord the emperor throughout his life, and the undertaking not to bring any enemy into his kingdom for hostile reasons, nor to consent to or be silent about anyone's infidelity towards him, but also that all men may know that the oath has in addition the following meaning within it.

3 First, that everyone on his own behalf should strive to maintain himself in God's holy service, in accordance with God's command and his own pledge, to the best of his ability and intelligence, since our lord the emperor himself is unable to provide the necessary care and discipline to all men individually.

4 Second, that no man, through perjury or any other craft or deceit, or through anyone's flattery or bribery, should in any way withhold or take away or conceal our lord the emperor's serf, or his landmark, or his land, or anything that is his by right of possession; and that no one should conceal the men of his fisc who run away and unlawfully and deceitfully claim to be free men, nor take them away by perjury or any other craft.

5 That no one should presume to commit fraud or theft or any other criminal act against God's holy churches or against widows or orphans or pilgrims; for the lord emperor himself, after God and his saints, has been appointed their protector and defender.

6 That no one should dare neglect a benefice held of our lord the emperor, and build up his own property from it.

7 That no one should presume to ignore a summons to the host from our lord the emperor, and that no count should be so presumptuous as to dare to excuse any of those who ought to go with the host, either on the pretext of kinship or through the enticement of any gift.

8 That no one should presume to subvert in any way any edict or any order of our lord the emperor, nor trifle with his affairs nor hinder nor weaken them, nor act in any other way contrary to his will and his instructions. And that no one should dare to be obstructive about any debt or payment that he owes.

9 That no one in court should make a practice of defending another man in an unlawful manner, by arguing the case weakly through a desire for gain, by hampering a lawful judgement by showing off his skill in pleading, or by presenting a weak case in an attempt to do his client harm. Rather should each man plead for himself, be it a question of tax or debt or some other case, unless he is infirm or unacquainted with pleading; for such men the *missi* or the chief men who are in the court or a judge who knows the case can plead it before the court, or if necessary a man can be provided to plead, who is approved by all parties and has a good knowledge of the case at issue; this, however, should only be done at the convenience of the chief men or *missi* who are present. At all events, it must be done in accordance with justice and the law; and no one should be allowed to impede the course of justice by offering a reward or a fee, by skilful and ill-intentioned flattery, or by the excuse of kinship. And let no one make an unlawful agreement with anyone, but let all men be seriously and willingly prepared to see that justice is done.

10–24 [These sections are all on ecclesiastical matters, dealing with the duties and conduct of clergy, monks, etc.]

25 That the counts and *centenarii* should strive to see that justice is done, and should have as assistants in their duties men in whom they can have full confidence, who will faithfully observe justice and the law, will in no wise oppress the poor, and will not dare, for flattery or a bribe, to conceal in any manner of concealment any thieves, robbers or murderers, adulterers, evil-doers and performers of incantations and auguries, and all other sacrilegious people, but rather will bring them to light, that they may receive correction and punishment according to the law, and that with God's indulgence all these evils may be removed from among our Christian people.

26 That the justices should give right judgement according to the written law, and not according to their private opinions.

27 We ordain that no one in all our kingdom, whether rich or poor, should dare to deny hospitality to pilgrims: that is, no one should refuse a roof, a hearth and water to any pilgrims who are travelling the country in the service of God, or to anyone who is journeying for love of God or for the salvation of his soul. And if a man should be willing to offer any further benefit to such people, let him know that God will give him the best reward, as he himself said: 'Whoso shall receive one such little child in my name receiveth me'; and in another place, 'I was a stranger, and ye took me in [Matthew 18.5; 25.35].'

28 Concerning the commissions coming from our lord the emperor. The counts and the *centenarii* should, as they are desirous of the favour of our lord the emperor, provide for the *missi* who are sent upon them with all possible attention, that they may go about their duties without any delay; and he has given instructions to all men that it is their duty to make such provision, that they suffer no delay to occur anywhere, and that they help them to go upon their way with all haste, and make such provision for this as our *missi* may require.

29 Concerning those poor men who owe payment of the royal fine and to whom the lord emperor in his mercy has given remission; the counts or *missi* are not to have the right for their part to bring constraint upon people so excused.

30 Concerning those whom the lord emperor wishes, with Christ's blessing, to have peace and protection in his kingdom, that is, those who have thrown themselves upon his mercy, those who, whether Christians or pagans, have desired to offer any information, or who from poverty or hunger have sought his intervention: let no one dare to bind them in servitude or take possession of them or dispose of them or sell them, but rather let them stay where they themselves choose, and live there under the lord emperor's protection and in his mercy. If anyone should presume to transgress this instruction, let him know that a man so presumptuous as to despise the lord emperor's orders must pay for it with the loss of his life.

31 For those who administer the justice of our lord the emperor let no one dare to devise harm or injury, nor bring any hostility to bear upon them. Anyone who presumes to do so must pay the royal fine; and if he is guilty of a greater offence, the orders are that he be brought to the king's presence.

32 Murder, by which a great multitude of our Christian people perish, we ordain should be shunned and avoided by every possible means; Our Lord himself forbade hatred and enmity among his faithful, and murder even more. How can a man feel confident that he will be at peace with God, when he has killed the son most close to himself? Or who can believe that Christ Our Lord is on his side, when he has murdered his brother? It is, moreover a great and unacceptable risk with God the Father and Christ the ruler of heaven and earth to arouse the hostility of men. With men, we can escape for a time by hiding, but even so by some chance of fortune we fall into our enemy's hands; but where can a man escape from God, from whom no secrets are hid? What rashness to think to escape his anger! For this reason we have sought, by every kind of precept, to prevent the people entrusted to us for ruling from perishing as a result of this evil; for he who feels no dread at the anger of God should not receive mild and benevolent treatment from us; rather would we wish a man who had dared to commit the evil act of murder to receive the severest of punishments. Nevertheless, in order that the crime should not increase further, and in order that serious enmity should not arise among Christians when they resort to murders at the persuasion of the devil, the guilty person should immediately set about making amends, and should with all possible speed pay the appropriate recompense to the relatives of the dead man for the evil he has done to them. And this we firmly forbid, that the parents of the dead man should dare in any way to increase the enmity arising from the crime committed, or refuse to allow peace when the request is made; rather, they should accept the word given to them and the compensation offered, and allow perpetual peace, so long as the guilty man does not delay payment of the compensation. And when a man sinks to such a depth of crime as to kill his brother or a relative, he must betake himself immediately to the penance devised for him, and do so as his bishop instructs him and without any compromising. He should strive with God's help to make full amends, and should pay compensation for the dead man according to the law and make his peace in full with his kinsmen; and once the parties have given their word let no one dare to arouse further enmity on the matter. And anyone who scorns to pay the appropriate compensation is to be deprived of his inheritance pending our judgement.

33 We forbid absolutely the crime of incest. If anyone is stained by wicked fornication he must in no circumstances be let off without severe penalty, but rather should be punished for it in such a way that others will be deterred from committing the same offence, that filthiness may be utterly removed from our Christian people, and that the guilty person himself may be fully freed from it through the penance that is prescribed for him by his bishop. The woman concerned should be kept under her parents' supervision subject to our judgement. And if such people are unwilling to agree to the bishop's judgement concerning their improvement they are to be brought to our presence, mindful of that exemplary punishment for incest imposed by Fricco upon a certain nun.

34 That all should be fully and well prepared for whenever our order or announcement may come. And if anyone then maintains that he is not ready and disregards our instructions he is to be brought to the palace—and not he alone, but all those who presume to go against our edict or our orders.

35 That all bishops and their priests should be accorded all honour and respect in their service of God's will. They should not dare to stain themselves or others with incestuous unions. They should not presume to solemnize marriages until the bishops and priests, together with the elders of the people, have carefully inquired to see if there be any blood relationship between the parties, and should only then give their blessing to the marriage. They should avoid drunkenness, shun greediness, and not commit theft; disputes and quarrels and blasphemies, whether in normal company or in a legal sense, should be entirely avoided; rather, they should live in love and unity.

36 That all men should contribute to the full administration of justice by giving their agreement to our *missi*. They should not in any way give their approval to the practice of perjury, which is a most evil crime and must be removed from among our Christian people. And if anyone after this is convicted of perjury he should know that he will lose his right hand; but he is also to be deprived of his inheritance subject to our judgement.

37 That those who commit patricide or fratricide, or who kill an uncle or a father-in-law or any of their kinsmen, and who refuse to obey and consent to the judgement of the bishops, priests, and other justices, are for the salvation of their souls and for the carrying out of the lawful judgement to be confined by our *missi* and counts in such custody that they will be safe, and will not pollute the rest of the people, until such time as they are brought to our presence. And in the meantime they are not to have any of their property.

38 The same is to be done with those who are arraigned and punished for unlawful and incestuous unions, and who refuse to mend their ways or submit to their bishops and priests, and who presume to disregard our edict.

39 That no one should dare to steal our beasts in our forests; this we have forbidden already on many occasions, and we now firmly ban it again, that no one should do it any more and should take care to keep the faith which everyone has promised to us and desires to keep. And if any count or *centenarius* or vassal of ours or any of our officials should steal our game he must at all costs be brought to our presence to account for it. As for the rest of the people, anyone who steals the game in this way should in every case pay the appropriate penalty, and under no circumstances should anyone be let off in this matter. And if anyone knows that it has been done by someone else, in accordance with the faith he has promised to us to keep and has now to promise again he should not dare to conceal this.

40 Finally, therefore, from all our decrees we desire it to be known in all our kingdom through our *missi* now sent out: among the clergy, the bishops, abbots, priests, deacons, clerks, and all monks and nuns, that each one in his ministry or profession should keep our edict or decree, and when it is right should of his good will offer thanks to the people, give them help, of if need be correct them in some way. Similarly for the laity, in all places everywhere, if a plea is entered concerning the protection of the holy churches, or of widows or orphans or less powerful people, or concerning the host, and is argued on these cases, we wish them to know that they should be obedient to our order and our will, that they maintain observance of our edict, and that in all these matters each man strive to keep himself in God's holy service. This in order that everything should be good and well-ordered for the praise of Almighty God, and that we should give thanks where it is due; that where we believe anything to have gone unpunished we should so strive with all earnestness and willingness to correct it that with God's help we may bring it to correction, to the eternal reward both of ourselves and of all our faithful people. Similarly concerning the counts and *centenarii*, our officers (*ministerialibus*), we wish all the things above mentioned in our deliberations to be known. So be it.

17 Special Capitularies for the *missi*, 802

The *Capitularia missorum Specialia* (*Capitula missis dominicis data*) give a precious insight into the actual working of Carolingian administration at the highest level. They consist essentially of memoranda of instructions given to the *missi* who had been sent throughout the empire after the framing of the 'Programmatic Capitulary' of spring, 802 (**16**). An important modern edition of this capitulary was published by W. A. Eckhardt, 'Die capitularia missorum specialia von 802', *Deutsches Archiv*, XII (1956).

Source: Boretius 34; Pertz 44.

<table>
<tr><td>

Capitulary for the missi *for Paris and Rouen*

In Paris, Meaux, Melun, Provins, Estampes, Chartres and Poissy: Fardulfus and Stephanus. In Le Mans, Exmes, Lisieux, Bayeux, Coutances, Avranches, Evreux and Merey, and for that part of the Seine and Rouen: Bishop Magenardus and Madelgaudus.

</td><td>

Capitulary for the missi *for Orleans*

First, for the city of Orleans on the Seine, by the direct route, then to Troyes, with the whole of its region, then to Langres, from Langres to the town of Besançon in Burgundy, from there to Autun, and afterwards to the Loire as far as Orleans: those sent are Archbishop Magnus and Count Godefredus.

</td></tr>
</table>

1 Concerning the oath of fealty, that all should reaffirm it.

2 Concerning bishops and the clergy, whether they are living according to the canons, and whether they are well acquainted with them and are carrying them out.

3 Concerning abbots, whether they are living according to a rule or according to the canons, and whether they are well acquainted with that rule or those canons.

4 Concerning the monasteries where there are monks, whether they live according to the rule in cases where it is part of their vows.

5 Concerning convents, whether the nuns live according to a rule or to the canons, and concerning their cloisters.

6 Concerning secular laws.

7 Concerning perjury.

8 Concerning murder.

9 Concerning adultery and other unlawful acts, whether committed in bishoprics and monasteries and convents or among laymen.

10 Concerning those men who have plundered our benefices and made up their private holdings. Likewise concerning the property of the churches.

11 Concerning those Saxons who have our benefices in Frankia, in what way they cultivate them, and with what degree of care.

12 Concerning the oppressions of poor free men, who owe military service and are oppressed by the justices.

13 That all men be well prepared for whatever order may come from us.

13a Concerning the preparation of ships around the coast.

13b Concerning the free men who live around the coastal regions; if a message should come to them instructing them to come and give assistance, and they refuse to obey it, each of them must pay twenty shillings, a half to his lord and a half to the people. If one of them is a *lidus* he must pay fifteen shillings to the people and give his back to be flogged. If he is a serf he must pay ten shillings to the people and receive the flogging.

14 Concerning the commissions coming to us and the *missi* sent out by us.

15 Concerning those whom we wish to have peace and protection throughout the kingdoms which by the favour of Christ belong to us.

16 Concerning those men who have been killed in administering our justice.

17 Concerning tithes and ninths and the dues to God's churches, that they should be at pains to pay them and to make good what is wanting.

18 Concerning the ban of our lord the emperor and king, and those things for which it has been his wont to exact a fine, that is, violence offered to churches, to widows or orphans or those unable to defend themselves, and rape, and failure to observe a decree concerning the host, that those who offend against the king in these respects should make full reparation.

18a That they make careful enquiries among the bishops, abbots, counts, abbesses and all our vassals, to see what degree of mutual harmony and friendship they have in their various districts, or whether there appears to be any discord among them; and that they be careful to report to us the whole truth of these matters, confirmed by their oath. That all of them should have good administrators [*vicedomos*] and advocates.

19 In addition, they are to enquire into and settle any matter that may be necessary, whether in our jurisdiction or in that of the churches, concerning widows, orphans, minors, and all other persons. And whatever they find that needs correcting, let them take pains to correct it to the best of their ability; what they cannot correct on their own they must have referred to our presence.

The oath whereby I reaffirm that from this day forth, being of sound mind and with no evil intent from my part to his, I am a faithful subject of our lord and most pious emperor, Charles, son of King Pippin and Queen Berthana, for the honour of his kingdom, as a man ought lawfully to be towards his lord; so help me God, and these relics of the saints here situated, for all the days of my life with all my will and with what intelligence God has given me, I will so attend and consent.

Again: the oath whereby I affirm. I am a faithful servant of our lord and most pious emperor, Charles, son of King Pippin and Queen Berthana, as a man lawfully ought to be towards his lord, for his kingdom and for his right. And this oath which I have sworn I shall willingly keep to the best of my knowledge and ability, from this day forth, so help me God, who created heaven and earth, and these relics of saints.

18   Aix, 802–3 (Boretius, 801–13)

The *Capitulare Aquisgranense* should be read in conjunction with the two preceding documents as one of the *capitula legibus addenda* published probably early in 803 at Aix in consequence of the reforming activity of the preceding twelvemonth.

Source: Boretius 77; Pertz 103.

Charles, most serene and august emperor crowned by God, mighty and peaceable, together with the bishops, abbots, counts, dukes, and all the faithful of the Church of Christ in common consent and counsel, took decisions in the palace at Aix under the following heads, in accordance with the Salic, Roman and Burgundian laws, that each of his faithful subjects should do justice in the manner prescribed: these decisions he confirmed with his own hand, that all his subjects might strive to reinforce them with their hand also.

1   That the bishops should go the rounds of the parishes committed to their charge, and should there take pains to inquire concerning incest, patricide fratricide, adultery, vainglory, and the other evils which are contrary to the will of God, and which it is written in holy scripture that Christians ought to avoid. They should take care where necessary to improve the churches in their parishes; likewise those belonging to us which we have given in benefice, and those of others where there are relics of saints. The monks should live well ordered lives in accordance with the instructions of their bishop and the rule of their abbot and following their good examples, according to their several situations. The administrators [*praepositi*] and those who are outside the monasteries should not have huntsmen, since we have often ordained before now that monks should not live outside a monastery.

2   That churches, widows and orphans should be left in peace according to the king's ban. If they are not the matter should, if possible, be brought to our presence; but if this is not possible our *missi* are to inquire into how it came about.

3   That draught animals are likewise to be left in peace according to the king's decree.

4   That those who hold a benefice of us should strive in all things to improve it; and that our *missi* should take note of this.

5   That our *vicarii* and *centenarii* should not buy slaves from the king's servant.

And that these same *vicarii* should receive for our use any inheritance for which heirs are lacking, lest there should be any misuse of it.

6 Concerning those who are free by written charter, if they should die without formal bequest their inheritance is to be taken over for our use; nor should a count or *vicarius* appropriate it for himself, but rather it should be called in for our use. Likewise it is our wish that when our ban brings us revenue, this revenue should come to our use or to anywhere that we may instruct.

7 Concerning an inheritance to be divided among heirs, if they should quarrel over it and the king should send one of his *missi* to make the division, a tithe of the slaves and of the land in the inheritance should be given to the king's fisc.

8 That the *vicarii* should have wolf-hounds, each of them having two in his district; and they are not to attend at the gathering of the host or the courts of the count or *vicarius*, unless a complaint should arise concerning them. And let them take particular trouble to obtain some profit from this, and hand over the skins of the wolves for our use. Everyone of those who attend the court in that district is to be given one *modius* of corn.

9 Concerning the host, that each count in his county should be responsible for commanding every man to go to join the host in answer to the summons on pain of a fine of 60 shillings, and that they should come at the time announced to the place to which they were ordered. And the count is to see to it that they are properly equipped, that is, with a lance, a shield, a bow and two bowstrings, and 12 arrows. Between them two men are to have these things. The bishops, counts and abbots are to have men specially appointed to take good care of this, to come on the day announced for the gathering, and to see to it that they are properly equipped. They are to have breastplates and helmets, and are to have their army ready at the proper time, that is, for the summer.

10 That the provisions for the king should be transported in carts, together with those for the bishops, counts, abbots, and high officials of the king: flour, wine, sides of bacon and other food in abundance, hand querns, adzes, axes, augers, slings, and men who can use them properly. And the king's marshals are to bring stones for them, on 20 pack-horses if need be. Let each man be fully equipped for military duty, and have all his equipment in sufficient quantity. Each count is to keep two thirds of the fodder in the county for the use of the host, and must have good bridges and good boats.

11 That the counts, each in his county, should keep a prison; and the judges and the *vicarii* are to have gallows.

12 That men of good birth who behave unfairly or unjustly within the county should be brought into the presence of the king; and the king is to impose restraint upon them by imprisonment or exile until such time as they are prepared to mend their ways.

13 That the *vicarii* should not accept gifts in respect of those criminals who are condemned to death before the count; if they do so they are to suffer the same penalty as the criminal was condemned to suffer; for when the magistrates have passed judgement upon a man it is not permissible for a count or a *vicarius* to grant him his life. But if a fine [*bannus*] has been decided upon in his case, even when the fine has been paid, he must remain subject to it until the count or the man who had a complaint or case against him is satisfied, and shall then be free of the fine.

14 That the bishops and abbots should have advocates, and that these should have their own property in the county concerned; and that they should be good and upright men, and should make it their purpose to deal with cases in a just and rightful manner.

15 That the *vicarii* should not give their consent to those who wish to give themselves into servitude as recompense for theft; rather, the matter should be dealt with as the law directs.

16 That no one should abandon his lord once he has received a one shilling payment from him, except if the lord wishes to kill him or beat him with a staff or dishonour his wife or daughter or take away his inheritance.

17 That no one in the host should have a staff, but rather a bow.

18 Concerning the forests, that the foresters should look after them well, and also take good care of the beasts and fishes. And if the king has given one or more beasts to anyone within the forest he should not take more than was allowed to him.

19 That a good, intelligent and careful bailiff should be chosen for our property, a man who knows how to render an account to our *missus* and to perform his service: to improve the buildings in the various places, to feed the pigs, cattle and other animals, to tend the gardens, bees, geese, chickens, fishponds, fish weirs, mills and clearings, and to see to the manuring of the ploughlands. There should be a royal lodge in the forest, with fishponds, and men living there. They are to plant vines, establish orchards, and wherever they can find able-bodied men they are to give them woodland to clear, so that our service may be improved. That our women, who are in service on our property, should be given wool and flax on our behalf, and should make woollen and linen cloth, and should come to our estate-office to render account through our bailiffs or the messengers sent by them.

20 And if any of our faithful subjects should wish to engage in a battle or any other contest with his enemy, and should call one of his peers to give him assistance, and if this man should refuse and should persist in neglecting his duty in this matter, then the benefice that he had is to be taken from him and is to be given to him who remained steadfast and loyal.

19 Additions to the *Lex Ribuaria* (Boretius, 803)

We have included the *Capitulare legi Ribuariae additum* as an example of the use to which capitularies could be put in relation to the national laws. Capitularies *legibus addita* indicate the strength of Charles's authority over his entire realm despite the variation in law among the peoples under his control. Modifications similar in type to those made here to the laws of the Ripuarian Franks were made also to the laws of the Salian Franks (see particularly Boretius, 142: Louis the Pious, 819, or a little later). A similar result was achieved for the Saxons and Frisians (**11**, and **12**) and also in Italy (see Boretius, 91, 95 and 214). See Ganshof *Recherches*, pp. 89–96, on the relationship between the capitularies and the national laws. The best exposition in English of the problems concerning Salic law appears in J. M. Wallace-Hadrill's 'Archbishop Hincmar and the *Lex Salica*', in *The Long-haired Kings* (London 1962), especially pp. 117–18.

Source: Boretius 41; Pertz 55.

Here begins a new enactment of law of the emperor Charles, to be added to the 'Lex Ribuaria'

1   *Chapter I* If any free man strikes a blow against another free man, he shall pay 15 shillings.

2   *Chapter X* The death of a king's man, that is a man of the fisc, or of a churchman or *lidus* shall be paid for by 100 shillings.

3   *Chapter XII* A free man who is unable to pay some charge, and has no sureties, shall be allowed to give himself in pledge to the man whose debtor he is until such time as he can pay the charge which he owes.

4   *The same chapter* In the matter of the herd [*de sonesti*], a man must either pay 600 shillings or swear an oath with 12 others; and if he who brings the case is unwilling to accept the oath of the 12 men he must contest it with him either by the cross or by shield and staff.

5   *Chapter XX* No one shall be allowed to send away his slave because of injury caused by him to anyone; rather, according to the nature of the injury, the lord should be responsible on his behalf or offer him in payment or for punishment by the plaintiff. If, however, the slave takes flight after committing the offence, so that he cannot at all be found by his lord, then his lord should take pains to clear himself of any suspicion that it was at his wish or with his knowledge that his slave did such a deed.

6   *Chapter XXXIII* If anyone is lawfully summoned to court and does not come, he shall, if he has no legitimate excuse for staying away, be judged liable to a fine of 15 shillings; likewise for the second and third summons. But if he

scorns to come the fourth time, his property is to be forfeit until he comes and gives justice in the matter for which he was summoned. If he fails to come within the year, inquiry shall be made of the king concerning his property which was placed in forfeit, and whatever the king decides about it shall be done. The first summons shall be for 7 days, the second for 14, the third for 21 and the fourth for 42. Similarly, if it should happen that he has no property of his own, let the amount be placed in forfeit from his benefice until inquiry has been made of the king.

7   *Chapter XXXV*   If the owner comes and refuses to take back a sequestrated property, he should contest it by combat or by the cross.

8   *Chapter XLVIII*   A man who has no sons and wishes to make some other person his heir must make his bequest in the presence of the king, or of the count and the *scabini*, or of the royal *missi* who have been at the time appointed to administer justice in the province.

9   *Chapter LVII*   A man who has been freed by penny-throw cannot bequeath to his descendants until the third generation is reached.

10   *Chapter LXIV*   Likewise a man who has been freed by charter.

11   *Chapter LXVII*   All oaths should be sworn in church or over relics; those which are to be sworn in church should be in the presence of six chosen people or, if there must be twelve people, such as can be found. In this way God, and the saints whose relics they are, will help a man to speak the truth.

12   *Chapter LXXII*   If an item of sequestrated property is removed by theft it shall be possible for him to whose care it was entrusted to clear himself of the theft on oath, that the theft was not committed with his approval or knowledge. And he should merely make good the value of it without additional charge.

20   Double Capitulary of Thionville for the *missi*, 805

Thionville on the Moselle was another of the favourite residences of Charles (see **9**). The *Capitulare Duplex in Theodonis Villa promulgata (Duplex Capitulare missorum in Theodonis Villa datum)*, the last of the great general capitularies to be published, was like Herstal a 'capitulary of reform' (Ganshof, *Frankish Institutions*, p. 7). It concerns both ecclesiastical and secular affairs, and points of general interest are its references to the control of feuds (clause 5) and to the insistence that the obligation of suit of court (earlier limited to three times a year at fixed dates) should not weigh too oppressively on poor freemen (clause 16). As with **17**, this capitulary has the force of a memorandum to the *missi*, since their terms of reference for active implementation of orders were given orally.

Source: Boretius 43; Pertz 71.

Within the church

1   Readings.

2   Singing.

3   Scribes, that they should not write badly.

4   Notaries.

5   Other disciplines.

6   Calculation.

7   The art of medicine.

8   Concerning churches that are left without land and without appointments or lighting; and concerning those people who exact tithes and do not take proper care of the churches; and concerning altars, that there should not be an over-abundance of them in the churches.

9   Concerning laymen recently converted, that they should not be sent out on other business before they have learned their law fully by living according to it.

10   Concerning those who withdraw from the world rather than perform some service for their lord, and then do neither: let them choose one of two courses—either they must live fully in accordance with the canons or they must follow a monastic rule.

11   Concerning male and female slaves belonging to the king, that they should not receive the tonsure or the veil except in moderation, and only where there are enough of them and the estates will not be deserted.

12   Concerning excessively large gatherings, that they should in no circumstances take place; only so many people should be gathered together as can take proper counsel.

13   Concerning those who have not been submitted to probation according to the rule, that they should straightway make amends and be submitted as the rule directs.

14   That young girls of the age of infancy should not take the veil before they know how to choose what they want, so preserving the authority of the canons.

15   That laymen should not be put in charge of monks within the monasteries, nor be made archdeacons.

16   Concerning incestuous persons, that they should be examined according to the canons, nor through anyone's friendship should some be let off lightly and others punished.

To all and sundry

1 Concerning the peace, that all who as the result of some crime are rebels against it should be brought to justice.

2 Concerning the administration of justice in cases affecting God's churches, widows, orphans and minors, that they should not be looked down upon when they appear as plaintiffs in the public courts, but should be given a careful hearing.

3 Concerning the administration of the royal justice, that it be fully inquired into.

4 Concerning the occasions when famine occurs, or plague, or pestilence, or unseasonable weather, or any such tribulation, that men should not wait for our edict but should straightway pray to God for his mercy. As to the scarcity of food in this present year, let each man help his own people as best he can, and not sell his corn at too high a price; and let no foodstuffs be sold outside our empire.

5 Concerning arms, and the prohibition on carrying them within the country—that is, shields and lances and coats of mail. And if there is a private feud, an inquiry is to be made as to which of the two parties is in the wrong, with a view to pacifying them, even if it means doing so against their will; and if there is no other way of pacifying them, let them be brought to our presence. And if, after they are appeased, one of them should kill the other, he must make a payment for him and must lose the hand by which he was forsworn, and in addition pay the royal fine.

6 Concerning the provision of arms for the army, the arrangements which we commended in an earlier capitulary are to be observed, and in addition every man with 12 manses is to have a coat of mail; anyone who has a coat of mail and does not bring it with him is to lose all his benefice along with it.

7 Concerning traders who travel in the territories of the Slavs and Avars, and how far they ought to go on their business; in the region of Saxony as far as Bardowiek, where Hredi is to be in charge; to Schesel, where Madelgaudus is to be in charge; to Magdeburg, with Aito in charge; to Erfurt, with Madelgaudus; to Halazstadt, with Madelgaudus again; to Forcheim, to Pfreimt and to Regensburg, with Audulfus; and to Lorsch, with Warnarius. They must not take arms and coats of mail with them to sell; and if they are caught while carrying them their entire stock is to be confiscated, one half being given to the palace, the other being divided between the *missi* already mentioned and the man who discovered them.

8 Concerning plaintiffs and counsel who will neither submit to the judgement of the magistrate nor make a formal renunciation of it, the old custom is to be observed, that is, they are to be kept in custody until they do one thing or the

other. And if they appeal to the palace concerning the matter and bring letters they are not to be believed, but they should not be put in prison; rather, they should be sent to our palace together with their guard and the letters themselves, so that they can be examined there as is fitting.

9 Concerning the swearing of oaths, that fealty should not be sworn to anyone except to us, and by each man to his [own] lord with a view to our interest and that of the lord himself; excepted from this are those oaths which are rightly owed by one man to another in accordance with the law. Infants, who were formerly unable to swear because of their tender age, should now swear fealty to us.

10 Concerning conspiracies, those who dare to undertake them and who seal any conspiracy with an oath are to be judged in one of three ways. First, whenever any harm has been done as a result of it, the authors of the deed are to be put to death, and their helpers are to be flogged by one another and made to cut off one another's noses. Where no harm has been done, they are again to be flogged by one another, and must take turns to shave one another's hair. If a conspiracy has been sealed by the clasping of hands those responsible, if they are free men, are to swear before suitable witnesses that they had no evil intention in so doing, or, if they cannot swear this, are to compound according to their law; if they are slaves they are to be flogged. And for the future let there be no conspiracy of this kind in our kingdom, with or without the swearing of oaths.

11 Concerning perjuries, that they should be guarded against, and that witnesses should not be brought to oath before they have been examined; and if they cannot be examined otherwise they should be separated and questioned individually. And it should not be allowed for the accuser alone to choose witnesses in the absence of his opponent. And under no circumstances should anyone who has not fasted be brought to oath or allowed to give testimony. And if anyone is brought to give testimony and is refuted, let him who would refute him and prove him wrong say why he refuses to accept his word. And witnesses should be chosen from the district in question and not from another one, lest it become necessary to inquire into the case too far outside the county. And if anyone is convicted of perjury he must lose his hand or else make payment to redeem it.

12 Concerning advocates: that is, that corrupt advocates, and bad *vicedomini*, *vicarii* and *centenarii* should be removed from office, and only those chosen who are both able and willing to examine and deal with cases justly. And if a bad count is discovered he is to be reported to us.

13 Concerning tolls, it is our wish that the old established and lawful tolls should be exacted from traders on bridges, on water crossings and on sales; and that the new and unlawful ones—when ropes are slung across or when people go under bridges in boats or for similar situations, in which no assistance is being

provided for the traveller—are not to be exacted; nor should they be exacted from people who are moving their property for reasons other than trade, from one of their houses to another or to the palace or to the army. If any doubtful case should arise it is to be looked into at the next court hearing which we are due to hold along with our *missi*.

14 Concerning runaway clerks or laymen, and also women, the instructions which we have given in another capitulary are to be observed.

15 Concerning free men who wish to devote themselves to the service of God, that they should not do so before they have asked permission of us. The reason for this is that we have heard that some of them do so not so much from devotion as from a desire to escape the army or some other royal service, while others do so because of someone's greed, when they are at the mercy of people who want to acquire their property; it is for these reasons that we have made the restriction.

16 Concerning the oppression of poor free men, that they should not be unjustly oppressed by men more powerful than themselves for any evil purpose, to the point of being compelled to sell or hand over their property. The reason for our previous statements about free men, and for this present one, is that their relatives should not be unjustly dispossessed so that their service to the king is lessened, and that their heirs should not, as a result of their poverty, be reduced to beggars or robbers or criminals. Also, poor men should not be summoned too often to court, and our instructions in an earlier capitulary to this effect are to be observed.

17 Concerning churches, and saints which have been recently adopted without authority, that they should not be venerated without the bishop's approval: in this, and in all the churches, canonical authority is to be maintained.

18 Concerning false mints, because they are appearing unlawfully and against our edict in many places it is our wish that the only place for a mint shall be in our palace, unless other instructions are given by us; however, those pennies which have now been minted are to be used, provided they are of good weight and pure metal.

19 Concerning the payment for the host, it is our wish that our *missi* should this year exact it faithfully, without showing favour to anyone or succumbing to blandishments or threats, in accordance with our orders; that is, from a man who owns six pounds worth of gold, silver, coats of mail, bronze vessels, clothes, horses, oxen, cows or other livestock (and the wives and children are not to be deprived of their garments for this purpose) they are to take the lawful payment, that is, three pounds. From those who own no more than three pounds worth of the above-mentioned items 30 shillings are to be exacted; from anyone who has not more than two pounds worth 10 shillings; and if he has one pound they are to take five shillings, so that he can prepare himself again for the service of God and

for employment by us. And our *missi* should take care and make diligent inquiry, that they do not with any ill intent subvert our justice by giving it or commending it to another.

20 It is our wish that the royal *census* should be paid wherever it has been lawfully due, whether on a man's own person or on his property.

21 Concerning robbers, our instructions in an earlier capitulary are to hold good.

22 Concerning free men who have married wives belonging to the royal fisc, and women who have husbands of similar status, that they should not as a result of this be debarred from inheriting of their parents, from pleading their case, or from giving testimony; rather, the same honour should be shown to us in this matter as we know was shown to our ancestors, whether kings or emperors.

21 The division of the kingdoms, 806

The *Divisio Regnorum* (*Divisio Imperii*), an immensely important constitutional document, is traditionally included among the capitularies but has many of the attributes of a diploma. See Ganshof, *Recherches* p. 44, who justifies the traditional attribution, arguing that Charles wished to embody this vital statement in the most solemn form open to him.

Source: Boretius 45; Pertz 75.

In the name of the Father and of the Son and of the Holy Ghost. Charles, most serene Augustus, great and peaceable emperor crowned by God, ruler of the Roman empire, by mercy of God king of the Franks and Lombards, to all the faithful subjects of us and of the Holy Church of God, both present and future.
You are all aware, and there is no one, we believe, who does not know, how the divine mercy, at whose bidding the passing ages move through succeeding generations to their close, has enriched us with a great token of his compassion and blessing by giving us three sons, and through them has confirmed our own prayers and hopes concerning the kingdom, and has lightened our fears of being forgotten by a hostile posterity. This being so, it is our wish that this also should be known to you, that we desire to have these our sons, by the grace of God, as co-rulers of the kingdom granted to us by God so long as we remain alive, and after we have left this mortal life to leave them, if God in his majesty so allows, as heirs to our empire and kingdom, which has been and is to remain under God's protection. We shall not, by granting it in a confused and disorganized manner, or by a general reference to the kingdom as a whole, bequeath to them a cause of strife and disagreement; rather, we have divided the whole extent of the kingdom into three portions, and have described each portion and stated which

of them is to protect and rule it, in such a way that each of them shall be content with his portion as we have assigned it, and shall with God's help strive to defend the boundaries of his kingdom which border on foreign lands, and to remain at peace and in charity with his brother.

1 The divisions of our empire and kingdom, which has been and is to remain under God's protection, which we have decided upon, are as follows: the whole of Aquitaine and Gascony, except for Touraine, and all the land westwards from them towards Spain, parts of the region of Nevers, which is situated on the River Loire, namely the Nivernais itself, the districts of Avallon and Auxois, Chalon, Mâcon, Lyon, Savoy, Maurienne, Tarantaise, Mont-Cenis, the valley of Susa as far as the passes, and then along the edge of the Italian mountains as far as the sea, these districts, together with their cities and whatever is included between them and the sea to the south or Spain to the west, in other words the part of Burgundy already specified, Provence, Septimania and Gothia, we have assigned to our beloved son Louis.

2 Italy, which is called Lombardy; and Bavaria, as held by Tassilo (except for the two towns called Ingolstadt and Lauterhofen, which we once gave in benefice to Tassilo and which belong to the district called Nordgau); and of Alamania, the part which is on the south side of the Danube; and from the source of the Danube along the river as far as the Rhine (on the boundary between the districts of Kletgau and Hegau, at the place called Engen), then up-river along the Rhine towards the Alps: whatever is within these boundaries and faces towards the south or the east, along with the duchy of Cur and the district of Thurgau, is to belong to our beloved son Pippin.

3 Whatever of our kingdom lies outside these boundaries, that is to say Frankia and Burgundy (with the exception of that part which we have assigned to Louis), and Alamania (with the exception of that portion which we have assigned to Pippin), Austria, Neustria, Thuringia, Saxony, Frisia, and the part of Bavaria called Nordgau, we have granted to our beloved son Charles: and this in such a way that Charles and Louis may each have a route into Italy to bring aid to their brother if the necessity arises, Charles through the Val d'Aosta, which belongs to his kingdom, and Louis through the valley of Susa; and Pippin will have a way in and out through the Norican Alps and Cur.

4 These things we have so ordered that, if Charles, who is the eldest, should die before his brothers, the part of the kingdom which he has is to be divided between Pippin and Louis as it was once divided between ourselves and our brother Carloman, in such a way that Pippin should have that portion which our brother Carloman had, and Louis should take over that part which we ourselves took as our share.

If however Pippin should come to the end of his allotted days while Charles and Louis are still alive, then Charles and Louis are to divide the kingdom which he held between themselves, and the division is to be made as follows: starting from the entrance to Italy at Aosta, Charles is to have Ivrea, Vercelli, and Pavia, and then, using the River Po as a boundary as far as the borders of Reggio, he is to have Reggio itself, Eraclea, and Modena as far as the boundaries of St Peter. These cities, together with their immediate neighbourhoods and territories and the counties pertaining to them, and everything from Pippin's kingdom which lies on the left of the route to Rome, with the addition of the duchy of Spoleto, this portion Charles, as we have said, is to take over. And whatever of this kingdom (starting from the cities and counties already mentioned) lies on the right of the route to Rome—that is, the remaining portion of the Transpadane region together with the duchy of Tuscany southwards as far as the sea and northwards to Provence—is to fall to Louis as an addition to his kingdom.

But if Louis should die and the others remain alive, Pippin is to have that part of Burgundy which we included in his kingdom, along with Provence and Septimania or Gothia as far as Spain, while Charles is to have Aquitaine and Gascony.

5 And if a son should be born to any of these three brothers, and the people should wish to choose him to succeed his father as ruler of the kingdom, it is our wish that the boy's uncles should agree to this, and should allow their brother's son to rule in that portion of the kingdom which his father, their brother, held.

6 Following this arrangement authorized by us, and in order to achieve our desire of a lasting peace between them, we have decided to give instructions and orders to these our sons, that none of them should take it upon himself to invade the territory or boundaries of his brother's kingdom, nor enter that kingdom with evil intent to disturb it or to diminish its boundaries; rather, each of them should help his brother and give him aid against his enemies as far as is reasonable and possible, be it inside his kingdom or against peoples outside it.

7 Nor should any of them receive a man of his brother's for whatever reasons and with whatever complaints he may seek refuge with him; nor should he make intercession on behalf of such a man, because it is our wish that any man who does wrong and is in need of intercession should seek refuge inside the kingdom of his lord, either at the holy places or with the men in office and should obtain his lawful intercession from them.

8 We likewise ordain that if any free man should leave his lord against his wishes and travel from one kingdom to another, the king must not receive him himself, nor should he allow his men to receive such a man or to take it upon themselves to keep him unlawfully by them.

9 Wherefore it seems good to us to ordain that after our departure from this mortal life the men of each of them shall receive benefices each in the kingdom of his lord and not in another's, lest it should happen that if things are done

differently some scandal should arise. As for his own property, let each of these men have it without opposition, in whatever kingdom it lawfully falls for him to have it.

10 And each free man, after the death of his lord, shall have the right to commend himself to whomsoever he wishes throughout these three kingdoms; likewise he who has not yet been commended to anyone.

11 Concerning gifts and sales which normally take place between one part and another, it is our instruction that none of these three brothers should accept from another's kingdom, from any man, a gift or a sale of immovable property, that is, lands, vineyards and woods, slaves [*servorum*] who are already housed, or any other property that is counted as part of an inheritance, with the exception of gold, silver and gems, arms and clothing, slaves [*mancipiis*] who are not housed, and those items of exchange which are recognized as properly belonging to merchants. For other free men, however, we do not consider it right to forbid this.

12 If, as normally happens, there are women who are lawfully asked for in marriage from one part or kingdom to another, they are not to be denied to those who ask for them justly, but rather it should be possible to give and receive them in turn and for the peoples to be joined together by such alliances. The women themselves are to have control of their property in the kingdom from which they come, even though they have to live in another kingdom because of their marriage.

13 Concerning hostages who are given as surety and are sent by us to various places for guarding, it is our wish that the king in whose kingdom they are should not allow them to return to their own country without the permission of the brother from whose kingdom they were removed; rather, each of them should give mutual assistance to the others for the future in the matter of receiving hostages, if one brother should make a reasonable request to another to do so. Our orders are the same for those who are sent into exile for their misdeeds, or who are due to be sent.

14 If a lawsuit or a quarrel or other such dispute should arise between the parties over the boundaries or confines of their kingdoms, which cannot be cleared up or settled by human testimony, it is our wish that the doubt should be removed by a willing and truthful inquiry under the judgement of the cross of God, and that no case of this kind should ever be settled by a struggle of any kind or on the field of battle. If a man of one kingdom should come to his lord and accuse a man of another kingdom of treachery against that lord's brother, let the lord send him to his brother, so that he can substantiate before him what he said about his man.

15 Above all else, it is our order and our instruction that these three brothers

should together undertake the care and protection of the church of St Peter, just as it was once undertaken by our grandfather Charles, and by our father King Pippin of happy memory, and later by ourselves, that they should strive with the help of God to defend it from its enemies, and should ensure that, as far as concerns themselves and as far as reason demands, it enjoys its proper rights. Likewise concerning other churches that are under their control, it is our instruction that these should enjoy their proper rights and honour, and that the dignitaries and officials of the holy places should have control over matters relating to those places, in whichever of the kingdoms the possessions of those churches may be.

16 But if, as we pray may not happen, a part of these ordinances and agreements should by some chance or through ignorance be broken, it is our instruction that they should take pains to correct it as quickly as possible in accordance with justice, lest a greater damage should come about as a result of the delay.

17 Concerning our daughters—that is, the sisters of the aforementioned sons—it is our order that after our departure from this life they should have, each of them, the freedom to choose the brother to whose care and protection they wish to entrust themselves. If one of them should choose the monastic life, it should be possible for her to live honourably under the protection of the brother in whose kingdom she wishes to spend her time. If, on the other hand, she is lawfully and reasonably sought in marriage by a worthy suitor, and if the married state is what she desires, it should not be denied to her by her brothers, so long as the man himself as suitor and the woman herself in consenting are acting in accord with their honest and reasoned wishes.

18 As to our grandchildren—that is, the children of our aforementioned sons, both those already born and those who are still to be born—we have decided to ordain that our sons should not in any circumstances either kill or maim or blind or compel to accept the tonsure any of them who may be accused in their presence, without a proper inquiry and examination. Rather, it is our wish that they should be honoured by their fathers and uncles, and should be obedient to them with all the deference that is fitting in those who are so related to one another.

19 Finally, we have decided to ordain that any matter or decision pertaining to their profit or use which we may wish to add to these our decrees and ordinances should be observed and obeyed by our beloved sons aforementioned in just the same way as the matters here decreed and described are to be observed and obeyed.

20 All these things we have so arranged, and have so set out and confirmed, that so long as it may please the Divine Majesty that we should live this mortal

life the control of this kingdom and empire under the protection of God should be ours, as it has hitherto been in the matter of government and administration and in the royal and imperial overlordship as a whole, and that we should enjoy the obedience of our beloved sons aforementioned and of our people beloved of God, with all the deference shown to sons by their fathers and by people to their emperor and king. Amen.

22 Concerning the mobilization of the army, 808

The *Capitulare missorum de exercitu promovendo* was prompted by the partial failure of a mobilization order. Clause 8 is exceptionally important because of the insight it gives into the publication and use of capitularies.

Source: Boretius 50; Pertz 56.

Summary of enactments which the royal missi *must have for mobilizing the army*

1   That every free man who has four occupied manses of his own or in benefice from another should equip himself and go on his own behalf to join the host, either with his lord (if his lord goes) or with his count. A man who has three manses of his own should be joined by someone who has one and who can give him assistance so that he can go on behalf of both. A man who has only two manses of his own should be joined by someone who also has two, and one of them should go to join the host, with the other giving him assistance. A man who has only one manse of his own should be joined by three others in a similar situation who can give him assistance: he should go alone, and the three who give him assistance should remain at home.

2   It is our wish and our command that these our *missi* should make careful enquiry concerning those who in the previous year stayed away from the host in defiance of the order which was made earlier, in conjunction with our instruction concerning children and poor men; and if there is anyone discovered who has not given assistance to his fellows in joining the host in accordance with our orders, nor gone to join it himself, he should pay our fine [*haribannum*] in full and should give his pledge to pay it according to the law.

3   But if it should happen that a man is found who maintains that, on the order of a count or a *vicarius* or *centenarius*, he gave to the said count or *vicarius* or *centenarius* those things with which he should have prepared himself, and that for this reason he failed to make the journey—if our *missi* can establish that this is true, then the man on whose instructions he stayed away shall be liable to our fine and shall pay it, whether he be a count or a *vicarius* or the advocate of a bishop or abbot.

4 With regard to the tenants of the counts, the following are to be excepted from the rule and should not be made to pay the fine, namely, two who are left behind with his wife, and another two who are ordered to stay behind to look after his official responsibilities and to carry out his duties to us. In such circumstances our instructions are that for every official post the count has he should leave at home two men to look after it, in addition to the two who are with his wife; all the rest he should have with him, or, if he himself stays at home, should send with whoever it is who goes to the host on his behalf. Bishops and abbots should have at home two only of their tenants or lay men.

5 With regard to our men, and those of the bishops and abbots, who have benefices or such holdings as to make them liable to go to the host according to our instruction, with the exception of those whom we have allowed to stay at home, if there are any discovered who have paid money to have themselves excused or have stayed at home with their lords' permission, they must pay our fine as set out above, and must give their word concerning it. Their lords, moreover, who allowed them to remain at home, or their lords' servants who took payment from them, must likewise pay our fine and give a pledge until such time as we are informed of it.

6 It is our wish that our *missi* should make careful enquiries concerning something that has been brought to our notice as being done in some places, namely that some men, after giving assistance out of their own pocket to their fellows who have gone to join the host, have, on the orders of a count or of his servants, made a payment to be allowed to stay at home, even though they were not bound to go to the host since they had given the assistance appointed by us to their fellows: this is to be looked into and reported to us.

7 It is our wish that those of our *missi* whose duty it is to carry out this function should obtain a fine from those men who should have gone with the host and who did not go; likewise they should obtain a fine from the count or the *vicarius* or the *centenarius* who agreed to their staying at home, and also from all those who in the past year allowed the instructions about a military expedition issued by us to go unobeyed.

8 It is our wish that four copies of this capitulary be made out: one copy is to be held by our *missi*, a second by the count in whose district these things are to be done (so that both our *missus* and our count will act precisely in accordance with what is set out in our enactment), the third by those of our *missi* who are to be set over our army, and the fourth by our chancellor.

9 It is our wish that the men of our faithful followers whom we have ordered to stay at home with us or on our service should not be compelled to go with the army, but should themselves remain at home or in the service of their lord. Nor should those who were with us in the past year be ordered to pay the fine.

23 The *Brevium Exempla*

K. Verhein has published two important articles on the *Beneficiorum fiscorcumque Regalium Describendorum Formulae* and its relationship to the *Capitulare de villis*: 'Studien zu den Quellen zum Reichsgut der Karolingerzeit', *Deutsches Archiv* X and XI (1954 and 1955). The first cited above discusses **15**; the second is specifically on *Die 'Brevium Exempla'*. The title *Brevium exempla ad describendas res ecclesiasticas et fiscales* has no manuscript authority but is a convenient description, used by nineteenth-century editors to identify a manuscript imperfect in its early stages. The document itself survives in the same early ninth-century Wolfenbüttel manuscript that contains the *Capitulare de Villis*, and in fact it immediately precedes the *Capitulare de Villis*. The *Brevium Exempla* consists of three separate items, and was assembled in its present form during the last fourteen years of Charlemagne's reign or very early in the reign of his son and successor, Louis the Pious. The three separate items are:

1 Extracts from surveys relating to the lands belonging to the bishopric of Augsburg. After a concluding fragment from a survey of an unknown villa, a full inventory is given of the monastery in Staffelsee (on the island now known as Worth). This section concludes with a short compressed summary of the properties owned by the bishopric.

2 An account of benefactions made to the monastery of Wissembourg in Alsace together with a list of those who held their former property from the abbey by precarial tenure, and a list of those who held benefices from the abbey. The last sentence, 'et sic cetera de talibus rebus breviare debes', indicates that this was intended as a model, and gives a clue to the official character of the *Brevium Exempla*. This part of the *Brevium* is similar in form and content to the great polyptychs of ninth-century Frankia.

3 A survey of five royal estates in the north of France. This is a model survey of estates contributing to the maintenance of the king and his servants. The first four are typical rural estates, closely resembling the pattern of rural holding suggested in the *Capitulare de Villis*. The fifth relates to a wine-bearing district which may be Triel (département Seine-et-Oise). The description of Asnapius is especially interesting as it has been identified with certainty as the modern Annappes (département Nord). Other estates in the modern districts of Nord and Pas-de-Calais have also been identified with near certainty with the *fisci* of the *Brevium* (P. Grierson, 'The identity of the unnamed fiscs in the *Brevium Exempla ad describendas res ecclesiasticas et fiscales*', *Rev. Belge de philologie et d'histoire*, Vol. XVIII, 1939)—Cysoing (probably *Grisio*), Somain-en-Ostrevant (both département Nord), and Vitry-en-Artois (département Pas-de-Calais).

Attention should be drawn to Hans Reinhardt, *Der St Galler Klosterplan [vom Jahr 820]*, (St Gallen 1952), and to 'Studien zum St Galler Klosterplan' *Mitteilungen zur Vaterländische Geschichte*, vol. XLII (Berne 1962).

Source: Boretius 128; Pertz 101.

. . . does not go, he gives for two years a ram of best quality, and in the third year four *modii* of corn.

The same

We found in the island called Staffelsee a church built in honour of St Michael, in which we found one altar adorned with gold and silver; five reliquaries, gilded and adorned with gems of glass and crystal, and one other of copper, partly gilded; one small cross for relics, gilded, with a key and silver plating; one other small cross for relics, made of gold and glass; one other cross, larger, of gold and silver with glass gems. There hangs above the altar one crown of silver partly gilded, weighing two pounds, and in the middle of this hang one small cross of gilded copper and one crystal globe; and all around the crown hang 35 rows of pearls of various colours. There is coined silver to the value of three shillings. There are four gold ear-rings, weighing 17 *denarii*. There are two silver chalices, one of them engraved on the outside and gilded and weighing 30 *solidi* along with its paten, the other also engraved on the outside and gilded and weighing 15 *solidi* along with its paten; one silver offertory-box, weighing six *solidi*. One silver box with lid, for carrying incense, weighing six *solidi*; another silver box, weighing five *solidi*.

We found there one silver thurible, partly gilded, weighing 30 *solidi*; one other thurible of copper, antique; one copper flask, one other flask of pewter; one copper ewer, with basin; one large glass jar; two small glass flasks with balsam. Above this same church hang two good bells, which have two copper-gilt circlets on their ropes. We found there two chasubles, brown in colour, one made of wool and dyed; one surplice, one other of silk; seven albs; four amices; thirteen linen cloths embroidered with silk, for offering at the altar; eight cloths for dressing the altars; two cloths for dressing an altar, made of wool and dyed; two cloths of dyed linen; 20 linen cloths embroidered with silk for dressing the altars; four silk maniples, adorned with gold and pearls, and four others of silk; four corporals; two stoles; one cushion covered in silk. Books: a book of the Heptateuch of Moses, the book of Joshua, the book of Judges, of Ruth, four books of the Kings, and two books of the Chronicles in one volume; a book of the Psalms of David, the book of the Proverbs of Solomon, the book Ecclesiastes, the book of the Song of Songs, the book of Wisdom, the book of Jesus Ben Sirach, the book of Job, the book of Tobit, the book of Judith, the book of Esther, two books of Maccabees in one volume; 12 books of prophets and two books of Esdras in one volume; a book of the Acts of the Apostles, a book of the letters of Paul, seven books of canonical literature and a book of the Apocalypse, all in one volume; one lectionary, with a binding adorned with leaves of copper gilt, one book of sermons by various authors, a book of forty sermons of St Gregory, three books of sacraments, two lectionaries, one book of excerpts from the canons, one book of expositions of the Psalms (no author), one old book of the four Gospels, two books of antiphons, one book of St Jerome's commentary on St Matthew, one book of the rule of St Benedict. There are two barrels full of glass there; three sheets and one lump of lead, and 170 reed pens; one faldstool.

As above. We found in this same place, and associated with the church already mentioned, a homestead (*curtis*) with a demesne house and other buildings. Attached to this homestead are 740 *jornales* of arable land, and enough meadow to yield 670 loads of hay. Of grain we found none, except 30 loads which we gave to the workers on the home farm, who are 72 in number and are given their keep until the feast of St John. Of malt, 12 *modii*, one saddle horse, 26 oxen, 20 cows, one bull, 61 younger beasts, five calves, 87 wethers, 14 lambs, 17 he-goats, 58 she-goats, 12 kids, 40 pigs, 50 piglets, 63 geese, 50 chickens, 17 beehives, 20 sides of bacon with the offal, 27 [measures of] lard, one boar killed and hung, 40 cheeses. Half a *sicclus* of honey, two *siccli* of butter, five *modii* of salt, three *siccli* of soap, five feather beds with pillows, three bronze cauldrons and six iron ones, five pot-hooks, one iron lamp, 17 barrels bound in iron, 10 scythes, 17 sickles, seven adzes, seven axes, 10 goatskins, 20 sheepskins, one fishing net. There is a women's workshop there, with 24 women in it; we found in it five pieces of woollen cloth, along with four bandages and five pieces of linen. There is one mill there: each year it pays 12 *modii* [of grain].

Associated with this homestead are 23 free manses, all occupied. Of these there are six, each of which gives 14 *modii* of grain each year, four sucking pigs, one *seiga* in weight of flax, two chickens, 10 eggs, one *sextarius* of flax seed, one *sextarius* of lentils. Each one does service for five weeks each year, ploughs three *jornales*, cuts one load of hay in the demesne meadow and brings it in, and does carrying service. Of the rest there are six, each of which ploughs two *jornales* each year and sows and harvests them, cuts three loads of hay in the lord's meadow and brings them in, and does labour service for two weeks; these men give one ox between two for the army. When one of them does not go to the army, he rides to wherever he is told. There are five manses which give two oxen each year; each man rides to wherever he is told. There are four manses, each of which ploughs nine *jornales* each year and sows and harvests them, and cuts three loads of hay in the lord's meadow and brings it in. Each of them does labour service for six weeks in the year, does carrying service, takes a share in bringing in the wine, manures one *jornalis* of the demesne, and gives 10 loads of wood. There is one manse which ploughs nine *jornales* each year and sows and harvests them; it cuts three loads of hay in the lord's meadow and brings them in, does carrying service and gives a pack-horse. It does labour service for five weeks in the year. There are also 19 servile manses, all occupied. Each of these gives one sucking pig each year, five chickens and 10 eggs, feeds four of the lord's pigs, ploughs half a plough-land, does labour service for three days a week, does carrying service, and gives a pack-horse. The wife makes one piece of linen and one piece of woollen cloth, prepares malt and bakes bread.

There remain seven homesteads of that diocese of which no record is here given: they are contained in the full survey. The diocese of Augsburg has in all 1,006 free manses which are occupied and 35 which are vacant, also 421 servile ones which are occupied and 45 which are vacant. Adding free and servile ones together the totals are 1,427 occupied, 80 vacant.

[Concerning those] clerics and laymen who have given their properties to the monastery called Wissembourg, and in return have received the usufruct of them.

Hartwic the priest has given to the monastery mentioned above a half share of the church built in the village of Hessiheim in the district of Worms, together with a demesne house, four servile manses (all occupied), and five *picturae* of vineyard. In return he has received the church in the village of Unkenstein, along with a demesne house, six servile manses (all occupied), five *picturae* of vineyard, and meadows yielding 20 loads of hay, on condition that he shall hold what he gave in precarial tenure for the rest of his life.

Motwinus and his wife have likewise given to the monastery a demesne house in the village of Hessiheim in the same district, along with six servile manses (all occupied), five *picturae* of vineyard, and meadows yielding 12 loads of hay. In return they have received a demesne house in the same village, with six servile manses (all occupied), seven *picturae* of vineyard, and meadows yielding 15 loads of hay.

Unroh likewise has in precarial tenure for the rest of his life, in the same village and district, one manse which is occupied and two servile ones which are vacant, one *pictura* of vineyard, and meadows yielding 20 loads of hay.

Birniho the priest has given to the monastery a church in the village of *Franconadal* in the same district, along with a demesne house, seven servile manses (all occupied), three *picturae* of vineyard, and meadows yielding 20 loads of hay. In return he has received three servile manses (all vacant) in the village of *Marisga* in the same district, with one *pictura* of vineyard and meadows yielding 20 loads of hay.

Likewise Gomoaldus has given to the monastery a demesne house in the village called *Wisa* in the same district, along with five servile manses (all occupied), three *picturae* of vineyard, and meadows yielding 20 loads of hay. In return he has received a demesne house in the same village, with four servile manses (all occupied), and two *picturae* of vineyard.

Graolfus the clerk has given to the monastery a demesne house in the same village and district, with five servile manses (all occupied), and four *picturae* of vineyard. In return he has received a demesne house in the same village and district, with five servile manses (all occupied), and five *picturae* of vineyard.

This is how you should record the other items also.

Concerning the holders of benefices of this same monastery

Humbertus holds as a benefice a demesne house in the village called Wanesheim in the district of Worms, along with six servile manses (all occupied), two free manses which are occupied and four which are vacant, meadows yielding 20 loads of hay, six *picturae* of vineyard, and woodland held in common.

Fridericus also has a benefice in this village.

Baldrich holds as a benefice a demesne house in the same village and district, with five servile manses which are occupied and four which are vacant, meadows yielding 30 loads of hay, five *picturae* of vineyard, one mill, and woodland held in common.

Gerbertus holds as a benefice a demesne house in the same village and district, with five servile manses (all vacant), and five *picturae* of vineyard.

Meginhartus holds as a benefice a demesne house in the village of *Alasenza* in the same district, with two servile manses which are occupied and three which are vacant, meadows yielding 15 loads of hay, one *pictura* of vineyard, one mill, and woodland held in common.

Herigis holds as a benefice in the same village and district four servile manses which are occupied and one which is vacant, and two *picturae* of vineyard.

Waltheri holds as a benefice in the same village and district a demesne house with six servile manses (all occupied), six *picturae* of vineyard, and meadows yielding six loads of hay; he also holds two servile manses which are occupied and two which are vacant between *Lorenzenvillare* and Hepfanheim and Winolfesheim. This same Waltheri holds one church and a demesne house in the village of Danstat in the district of Speyer, with four free manses and 10 servile ones (all occupied), and one servile manse which is vacant, five *picturae* of vineyard, and meadows yielding 20 loads of hay.

And this is how you should record the other items of this kind.

Here should follow a record of livestock.

Concerning the district of this or that mayor

We found on the crown estate of *Asnapius* a royal house, well built of stone, with three chambers; the whole house surrounded by galleries, with 11 rooms for women; underneath, one cellar; two porches; 17 other houses inside the courtyard, built of wood, with as many rooms and with the other amenities all in good order; one stable, one kitchen, one bakehouse, two barns, three haylofts. A courtyard with a strong palisade and a stone gateway with a gallery above from which to make distributions. A smaller courtyard similarly enclosed with a palisade, well ordered and planted with various kinds of trees. Household linen: one set of bedding, one tablecloth, one towel. Equipment: two bronze bowls, two cups, two bronze cauldrons and one of iron, one cooking pan, one pot-hook, one fire-dog, one lamp, two axes, one adze, two augers, one hatchet, one chisel, one scraper, one plane, two scythes, two sickles, two iron-tipped spades. Wooden equipment: a sufficient quantity. Produce: nine baskets of old spelt from the previous year, which will yield 450 measures of flour; 100 *modii* of barley. In the present year there were 110 baskets of spelt: of these 60 baskets have been sown, and we found the rest [in store]; 100 *modii* of wheat: 60 have been sown, and we found the rest. [———]¹ *modii* of rye, all of which has been sown; 1,800 *modii* of barley: 1,100 have been sown, and we found the rest; 430 *modii* of oats, one *modius* of beans, 12 *modii* of peas. From the five mills, 800 smaller *modii*: 200 *modii* were given to the workers on the home farm, and we found the rest. From the four brewhouses, 650 smaller *modii*. From the two bridges, 60 *modii* of salt and two shillings. From the four gardens, 11 shillings, two *modii* of honey, one *modius* of butter in payment of dues; 10 sides of bacon from the previous year, 200 sides of new bacon, along with the offal and lard; 43 measures of cheeses from the present year. Livestock: 51 head of older horses, five three-year-olds, seven two-year-olds, seven yearlings, 10 two-year-old colts, eight yearlings, three stallions, 16 oxen, two donkeys, 50 cows with calves, 20 bullocks, 38 yearling calves, three bulls, 260 older pigs, 100 piglets, five boars, 150 ewes with lambs, 200 yearling lambs, 120 rams, 30 she-goats with kids, 30 yearling goats, three he-goats, 30 geese, 80 chickens, 22 peacocks.

The same as above. Concerning the dependent manses of the above demesne. In the village of *Grisio* we found demesne manses, with three haylofts and a courtyard enclosed with a hedge. There is a garden with trees, 10 geese, eight ducks and 30 chickens.

In another village we found demesne manses, with a courtyard enclosed with a hedge and three haylofts inside it; one *aripennis* of vineyard, a garden with trees, 15 geese and 20 chickens.

In the village of ——, demesne manses, with two haylofts, one barn, one garden, a courtyard with a good hedge.

As above. We found that the measures for *modii* and *sextaria* were the same there as at the palace. We found no workmen, no goldsmiths, silversmiths or blacksmiths, no huntsmen or men for other duties. Garden plants: we found lily, costmary, garden mint, parsley, rue, celery, lovage, sage, summer savory, juniper, leek, garlic, tansy, wild mint, coriander, shallots, onions, cabbages, kohlrabi, betony. Trees: pears, apples, medlars, peaches, hazels, walnuts, mulberries, quinces.

We found on the crown estate of —— a royal house, well-built of stone outside and wood inside, with two chambers and two galleries; eight other houses inside the courtyard, built of wood; a well-built women's workshop with a store room; one stable; a kitchen and bakehouse combined; five barns, three granaries. A courtyard enclosed with a palisade and added spikes, with a wooden gateway. The gateway has a gallery above it. A smaller courtyard, likewise enclosed with a palisade. An orchard adjoining it, full of trees of various kinds. Inside, one fishpond stocked with fish; one garden, in good order. Household linen: one set of bedding, one table-cloth, one napkin. Equipment:

¹ The number is missing in the MS.

two bronze bowls, one mug, one basin, two bronze cauldrons and one of iron, one frying pan, one pot-hook, one fire-dog, one lamp, one axe, one adze, two augers, one chisel, one hatchet, one scraper, one plane, two scythes, three sickles, two mattocks, two shovels tipped with iron, and wooden equipment in sufficient quantity. Produce: 80 baskets of old spelt from the previous year, which would yield 400 measures of flour; 90 baskets of spelt from the present year, which would yield 450 measures; 700 *modii* of new barley for the staff, and 600 *modii* for sowing; 80 sides of old bacon from the previous year, 100 sides from this year, along with the offal and lard, and 150 sides in payment of dues, along with the offal and lard—making 330 sides in all; 24 measures of cheeses.

Livestock: 79 head of older horses, 24 three-year-old fillies, 12 two-year-olds, 13 yearlings, six two-year-old colts and 12 yearlings. Four stallions or mules, 20 oxen, two donkeys, 30 cows with calves, three bulls, 10 other animals, 150 large pigs and 100 smaller ones, 80 ewes with lambs, 58 yearling lambs, 82 rams, 15 she-goats with kids, six yearling goats, six he-goats, 50 hives of bees, 40 geese, six ducks, 100 chickens, eight peacocks.

We found on the crown estate of —— a royal house with two chambers and two fireplaces, one cellar, two porches. A small enclosed courtyard with a strong palisade; inside it, two chambers, along with two women's workshops and three women's houses; a chapel, well-built of stone; two other houses in the courtyard, built of wood, and four granaries, two barns, one stable, one kitchen, one bakehouse; a second courtyard with a hedge and two wooden gates with galleries above them. One set of bedding, one table-cloth, one napkin. Equipment: two bronze bowls, two mugs, two bronze cauldrons and one of iron; one salt-pan, one axe, one adze, one auger, one chisel, one plane; wooden equipment for their needs. Produce: 20 baskets of old spelt from last year, which will yield 100 measures of flour. This year there were 20 baskets of spelt; 10 of these were sown, and we found the rest. 160 *modii* of rye: 100 *modii* were sown, and we found the rest. 450 *modii* of barley: 300 *modii* were sown, and we found the rest. 200 *modii* of oats, all sown. 60 sides of old bacon from last year; 50 sides from this year, along with the offal and lard; 15 sides in payment of dues, along with the offal and lard; making ——[2] sides in all.

Livestock: 44 head of older horses, 10 three-year-old fillies, 12 two-year-olds and 15 yearlings, seven two-year-old colts, two stallions or mules, 24 oxen, six cows with calves, five other animals, 90 large pigs and 70 small ones, 150 ewes with lambs, 200 yearling lambs, eight rams, 20 she-goats with kids, 16 yearling goats, five he-goats, 10 geese.

We found on the crown estate of—— a royal house, well-built of wood with one chamber, one cellar, one stable, three living rooms, two barns, one kitchen, one bakehouse, three hay-lofts. A courtyard enclosed with a palisade and strengthened with a hedge. A garden planted with trees of various kinds. Two

[2] From this point on several numbers are missing in the MS.

wooden gateways. Three fishponds stocked with fish. Equipment: two bronze bowls, two bronze mugs, one pot-hook, one fire-dog, one plate, one axe, one adze, one auger, one chisel, and a shovel tipped with iron. Wooden equipment in sufficient quantity. Household linen: one set of bedding, one mattress, one pillow, two linen sheets, one towel, one cloth, one napkin. Produce: 20 baskets of old spelt from last year, which will yield 100 measures of flour; this year there were 30 baskets of spelt—one basket was sown, and we found the rest. Eight hundred *modii* of barley, 400 *modii* were sown, and we found the rest. 200 sides of old bacon from last year; 50 sides from this year, together with the offal and lard; 80 sides in payment of dues, with the offal and lard.

Livestock: —— head of older horses; —— three-year-old fillies, 10 two-year-olds and 11 yearlings; —— three-year-old colts, 10 two-year-olds and five yearlings; two stallions, —— oxen, —— cows with calves; eight bullocks, three yearling calves, one bull, 150 large pigs and 100 small ones, 150 ewes with lambs, 200 yearling lambs, 100 rams, 30 she-goats with kids, 90 yearling goats, 10 he-goats, 20 geese, four ducks.

We found on the crown estate of *Treola* a demesne house, very well built of stone: two chambers with two fireplaces, one porch, one cellar, one wine-press, three living-quarters for men, built of wood, one gallery with a women's workshop; three other buildings of wood, one barn, two hay-lofts; a courtyard enclosed by a wall, with a stone built gateway. Household-linen: one mattress, one pillow, one bed, one linen cloth, one blanket, one seat-cover. Equipment: one iron-bound cask, one lead plate. From the demesne vineyards, 730 *modii* of wine; 500 *modii* from payment of dues, two pounds of hemp.

Garden plants: costmary, garden mint, lovage, celery, beet, lily, southernwood, tansy, sage, summer savory, catnip, juniper, clary, chicory, wild-mint, betony, agrimony, mallows, marshmallows, cabbages, chervil, coriander, leek, cibols, shallots, chives, garlic.

Trees: pears of various kinds, apples of various kinds, medlars, peaches, nuts, plums, hazels, mulberries, quinces, cherries.

This is the total of the above villas.

There are in all: —— baskets of old spelt of last year, which will yield —— measures of flour; old wheat —— and so on for all the other items, you will give figures for past and present amounts, and for amounts still remaining.

III Letters

THE two chief collections of letters written in the age of Charlemagne are the letters of Alcuin, the Northumbrian scholar, preserved by contemporaries and by succeeding generations as copy-book models of how letters should be written, and the collection of papal letters, assembled in 791 and known as the *Codex Carolinus*, many of which refer to the period before the accession of Charles. We have drawn comparatively heavily on the Alcuin collection, partly because of its intrinsic interest, partly because of its special interest to an English-speaking audience. We have taken some of our selection of Alcuin's letters from Professor Dorothy Whitelock's translations in volume I of *English Historical Documents* (referred to as *EHD* below). Dr Percival has translated the remainder of the Alcuin selection from the standard edition by E. Duemmler, *Alcuini Epistolae, MGH Epistolae IV, Karolini Aevi*, vol. II (Berlin 1895) (referred to as Duemmler below). Translations from the *Codex Carolinus* (ed. W. Gundlach) are based on the text in *MGH, Epp. III*, ed. E. Duemmler *et al.*, *Merovingici et Karolini Aevi*, vol. I (Berlin 1892), and the last letter in our selection (**40**) is also taken from the same volume. It was the custom in the Carolingian court for the scholars to take on biblical or classical nicknames. Charles was known as David, Alcuin as Albinus or Flaccus, Angilbert as Homer.

Letters of Alcuin

The first six letters in this selection refer to the English situation, to the feeling of horror that followed the sack of Lindisfarne by the Vikings in 793, to the difficulties arising from the presence of exiles in Carolingian Europe, and to the disputes or possible reasons for dispute, commercial as well as religious, that existed between Charles the Great and Offa of Mercia, the most powerful king in eighth-century England. The English situation is handled with diplomatic caution and one notes how careful Charles is to explain that he had harboured the exile Hringstan and his followers 'for the sake of reconciliation and not for enmity' (**26**) and how careful again the Franks are to ensure that the Scottish priest was returned home for fair trial (**27**). The references to false pilgrims, that is to say presumably merchants in disguise, and to dissatisfaction over the size of cloaks (**28**; *cf. also* p. 22 above) mirror English complaints over imported black stones and represent elements in what appears to have been our first clearly recorded trade dispute with France (*see* Sir Frank Stenton, *Anglo-Saxon England*, 3rd edn. (London 1971), p. 221). The letters to Offa are included as good examples of influential thought concerning Christian kingship at the Carolingian court in the decade before the imperial coronation.

The remaining letters consist of a short note which conveys written instructions to envoys in service outside the realm, two letters, one in Charles's own name, written to Pope Leo III on the occasion of his accession, two which show the concern of Alcuin and the Carolingian world with missionary enterprise, and finally two which strike a more personal note, giving us a clearer glimpse of Alcuin himself, the fine scholar, product of the English school at York, who from 782 to the time of his death in 804, was one of the chief figures in the active intellectual life of Carolingian Europe. The letter of Charles to the pope (**31**) gives an illuminating insight into the royal attitude to the duty of the pope: 'to raise your hands to God, with Moses, to aid our armies'. Alcuin's essential humanity and awareness of royal responsibility come out in his warnings (**33** and **34**) against exploitation and excessive severity in teaching newly converted peoples. He writes that it is better to lose tithes than to forfeit faith and that it would be more helpful if the 'easy yoke and light burden of Christ were preached to the tough Saxons as forcefully as the payment of tithes and the legal rigour of the edict . . . are exacted [**34**].'

24 Alcuin to Ethelred, king of Northumbria, 793, after 8 June

Source: Duemmler, 16; *EHD* I, 193, pp. 775–7.

To the most beloved lord king, Ethelred, and all his chief men, Alcuin the humble deacon, sends greeting.

Mindful of your most sweet love, O men my brothers and fathers, also esteemed in Christ the Lord; desiring the divine mercy to conserve for us in long-lasting prosperity our land, which it once with its grace conferred on us with free generosity; I do not cease to warn you very often, my dearest fellow-soldiers, either with words, when present, if God should grant it, or by letters when absent, by the inspiration of the divine spirit, and by frequent iteration to pour forth to your ears, as we are citizens of the same country, the things known to belong to the welfare of an earthly kingdom and to the beatitude of an eternal kingdom; that the things often heard may be implanted in your minds for your good. For what is love in a friend, if it is silent on matters profitable to the friend? To what does a man owe fidelity, if not to his fatherland? To whom does he owe prosperity, if not to its citizens? We are fellow-citizens by a two-fold relationship: sons of one city in Christ, that is, of Mother Church, and natives of one country. Thus let not your kindness shrink from accepting benignly what my devotion is eager to offer for the welfare of our country. Do not think that I impute faults to you; but understand that I wish to avert penalties.

Lo, it is nearly 350 years that we and our fathers have inhabited this most lovely land, and never before has such terror appeared in Britain as we have now suffered from a pagan race, nor was it thought that such an inroad from the sea could be made. Behold, the church of St Cuthbert spattered with the blood of the priests of God, despoiled of all its ornaments; a place more venerable than all in Britain is given as a prey to pagan peoples. And where first, after the departure of St Paulinus from York, the Christian religion in our race took its rise, there misery and calamity have begun. Who does not fear this? Who does not lament this as if his country were captured? Foxes pillage the chosen vine, the heritage of the Lord has been given to a people not his own; and where there was the praise of God, are now the games of the Gentiles; the holy festivity has been turned to mourning [*cf.* Amos 8.10].

Consider carefully, brothers, and examine diligently, lest perchance this unaccustomed and unheard-of evil was merited by some unheard-of evil practice. I do not say that formerly there were no sins of fornication among the people. But from the days of King Ælfwold fornications, adulteries and incest have poured over the land, so that these sins have been committed without any shame and even against the handmaids dedicated to God. What may I say about avarice, robbery, violent judgements?—when it is clearer than day how much these crimes have increased everywhere, and a despoiled people testifies to it. Whoever reads the holy scriptures and ponders ancient histories and considers the fortune of the world will find that for sins of this kind kings lost kingdoms and peoples their country; and while the strong unjustly seized the goods of others, they justly lost their own.

Truly signs of this misery preceded it, some through unaccustomed things, some through unwonted practices. What portends the bloody rain, which in the time of Lent in the church of St Peter, prince of the apostles, in the city of York, which is the head of the whole kingdom, we saw fall menacingly on the north side from the summit of the roof, though the sky was serene? Can it not be expected that from the north there will come upon our nation retribution of blood, which can be seen to have started with this attack which has lately befallen the house of God?

Consider the dress, the way of wearing the hair, the luxurious habits of the princes and people. Look at your trimming of beard and hair, in which you have wished to resemble the pagans. Are you not menaced by terror of them whose fashion you wished to follow? What also of the immoderate use of clothing beyond the needs of human nature, beyond the custom of our predecessors? The princes' superfluity is poverty for the people. Such customs once injured the people of God, and made it a reproach to the pagan races, as the prophet says: 'Woe to you, who have sold the poor for a pair of shoes [Amos 2.6], that is, the souls of men for ornaments for the feet. Some labour under an enormity of clothes, others perish with cold; some are inundated with delicacies and feastings like Dives clothed in purple, and Lazarus dies of hunger at the gate [*cf.* Luke 16.19 ff.]. Where is brotherly love? Where the pity which we are admonished to have for the wretched? The satiety of the rich is the hunger of the poor. That saying of Our Lord is to be feared: 'For judgement without mercy to him that hath not done mercy [James 2.13].' Also we read in the words of the blessed Peter: 'The time is that judgement should begin at the house of God [I Peter 4.17].'

Behold, judgement has begun, with great terror, at the house of God, in which rest such lights of the whole of Britain. What should be expected for other places, when the divine judgement has not spared this holy place? I do not think this sin is theirs alone who dwell in that place. Would that their correction would be the amendment of others, and that many would fear what a few have suffered, and each say in his heart, groaning and trembling: 'If such great men and fathers so holy did not defend their habitation and the place of their repose, who will defend mine?' Defend your country by assiduous prayers to God, by acts of justice and mercy to men. Let your use of clothes and food be moderate. Nothing defends a country better than the equity and godliness of princes and the intercessions of the servants of God. Remember that Hezekiah, that just and pious king, procured from God by a single prayer that 185,000 of the enemy were destroyed by an angel in one night [Isaiah 37.36; II Kings 20.3 ff]. Likewise with profuse tears he averted from him death when it threatened him, and deserved of God that 15 years were added to his life by this prayer [II Kings 20.3 ff; Isaiah 38.1 ff.].

Have decent habits, pleasing to God and laudable to men. Be rulers of the people, not robbers; shepherds, not plunderers. You have received honours by God's gift; give heed to the keeping of his commands, that you may have him as a preserver whom you had as a benefactor. Obey the priests of God; for they have an account to make to God, how they admonish you; and you, how you obey them. Let one peace and love be between you; they as interceders for you, you as defenders of them. But, above all, have the love of God in your hearts, and show that love by keeping his commandments. Love him as a father, that he may defend you as sons. Whether you will or not, you will have him as a judge. Pay heed to good works, that he may be propitious to you. 'For the fashion of this world passeth away [I Corinthians 7.31]'; and all things are fleeting which are seen or possessed here. This alone from his labour can a man take with him, what he did in alms-giving and good works. We must all stand before the judgement seat of Christ, and each must show all that he did, whether good or evil. Beware of the torments of hell, while they can be avoided; and acquire for yourselves the kingdom of God and eternal beatitude with Christ and his saints in eternal ages.

May God both make you happy in this earthly kingdom and grant to you an eternal country with his saints, O lords, my dearest fathers, brothers and sons.

25 The sack of Lindisfarne, 793, after 8 June

Source: Duemmler, 17; *EHD* I, 194, pp. 778–9.

To the best sons in Christ of the most blessed father, St Cuthbert the bishop, Bishop Higbald and all the congregation of the church of Lindisfarne, Alcuin the deacon sends greeting with celestial benediction in Christ.

The intimacy of your love used to rejoice me greatly when I was with you; but conversely, the calamity of your tribulation saddens me greatly every day, though I am absent; when the pagans desecrated the sanctuaries of God, and poured out the blood of saints around the altar, laid waste the house of our hope, trampled on the bodies of saints in the temple of God, like dung in the street [*cf.* Isaiah 5.25]. What can we say except lament in our soul with you before Christ's altar, and say: 'Spare, O Lord, spare thy people, and give not thine inheritance to the gentiles, lest the pagan say, "Where is the God of the Christians?" [*cf.* Joel II.17].' What assurance is there for the churches of Britain, if St Cuthbert, with so great a number of saints, defends not his own? Either this is the beginning of greater tribulation, or else the sins of the inhabitants have called it upon them. Truly it has not happened by chance, but is a sign that it was well merited by someone. But now, you who are left, stand manfully, fight bravely, defend the camp of God. Remember Judas Maccabaeus, how he cleansed the temple of God, and set free the people from foreign servitude [II Maccabees 10.2–4]. If anything ought to be corrected in your grace's habits, correct it quickly. Call back to you your patrons who have left you for a time. They lacked not power with God's mercy; but, we know not why, they kept silence. Do not glory in the vanity of raiment; this is not a glory to priests and servants of God, but a disgrace. Do not in drunkenness blot out the words of your prayers. Do not go out after luxuries of the flesh and worldly avarice, but continue steadfastly in the service of God and in the discipline of the regular life, that the most holy fathers, who begot you, may not cease to be your protectors. Treading in their footsteps, you may remain secure by their prayers. Be not degenerate sons of such great fathers. In no wise will they cease from defending you if they see you follow their example.

Yet be not dismayed in mind by this calamity. God chastiseth every son whom he receiveth [*cf.* Hebrews 12.6]; and thus he perhaps chastised you more harshly, because he loved you more. Jerusalem, the city loved by God, perished with the temple of God in the flames of the Chaldeans. Rome, encircled by a crown of holy apostles and innumerable martyrs, was shattered by the ravages of pagans, but by the pity of God soon recovered. Almost the whole of Europe was laid desolate by the fire and sword of the Goths and Huns; but now, by God's mercy, it shines adorned with churches, as the sky with stars, and in them the offices of the Christian religion flourish and increase. Exhort yourselves in turn, saying: 'Let us return to the Lord Our God, for he is bountiful to forgive [Isaiah 50.7], and never deserts them that hope in Him [cf. Judith 13.17].'

And you, holy father, leader of the people of God, shepherd of the holy flock, physician of souls, light set upon a candlestick, be the pattern of all goodness to all who see you; be the herald of salvation to all who hear you. Let your company be of decent behaviour, an example to others unto life, not unto perdition. Let your banquets be in soberness, not in drunkenness. Let your garments be suitable to your order. Do not adapt yourself to the men of the world in any vain thing. Empty adornment of clothing, and useless elegance, is to you a reproach before men and a sin before God. It is better to adorn with good habits the soul which will live for ever, than to deck in choice garments the body which will soon decay in the dust. Let Christ be clothed and fed in the person of the poor man, that doing this you may reign with Christ. The redemption of man is true riches [cf. Proverbs 13.8]. If we love gold, let us send it before us to heaven, where it will be kept for us, and we have that which we love. Let us love what is eternal, and not what is perishable. Let us esteem true riches, not fleeting ones, eternal, not transitory. Let us acquire praise from God, and not from men. Let us do what the saints did whom we praise. Let us follow their footsteps on earth, that we may deserve to be partakers of their glory in the heavens. May the protection of the divine pity guard you from all adversity, and set you with your fathers in the glory of the celestial kingdom, O dearest brothers.

When our lord king Charles returns home, having by the mercy of God subdued his enemies, we plan, God helping us, to go to him; and if we can then be of any profit to your holiness, regarding either the youths who have been led into captivity by the pagans or any other of your needs, we will take diligent care to bring it about. Farewell in Christ, most beloved, and ever advancing, be strengthened.

26 Charles the Great to Æthelheard, archbishop of Canterbury, and Ceolwulf, bishop of Lindsey, 793–6

Source: Duemmler, 85; *EHD* I, 196, p. 780.

Charles, by the grace of God, king of the Franks and Lombards and patrician of the Romans, to Archbishop Æthelheard and his fellow-bishop Ceolwulf, sends greeting of eternal beatitude.

By no means do we think it right that the vast distance by land and the breadth of the stormy sea should sever the bonds of a friendship joined in Christ. But the longer the distance dividing human intercourse, with so much firmer faith should be maintained the pact of loyalty between friends. Since in his presence fear or shame often reveals outwardly in a man's face what he does not hold in his heart, holy fidelity is laudable in those absent and admirable in those present.

Hence, relying on that friendship which once, when we were together, we established in loyal words, we have sent to your kindness these miserable exiles from their country, praying that you may deign to intercede for them with my dearest brother King Offa, that they may be allowed to return to their native land in peace and without unjust oppression of any kind, and to serve anyone whatever. For their lord, Hringstan,[1] has died. It seemed to us that he would have been faithful to his lord, if he had been allowed to remain in his own country. But to shun the danger of death, as he was wont to say, he fled to us; and was ever ready to purge himself with oath from all disloyalty. We kept him with us for some little time, for the sake of reconciliation, not out of enmity.

If indeed you can obtain peace by your prayer for these fellow-countrymen of his, let them remain in their own land. But if my brother reply more harshly concerning them, send them back to us uninjured. It is better to live in exile than to perish, to serve in a foreign land than to die in one's own. I have confidence in my brother's goodness, if you intercede earnestly for them, that he will receive them kindly, for our affection and still more for the love of Christ, who said: 'Forgive, and you shall be forgiven [Luke 6.37].'

May the divine goodness keep your holiness, interceding for us, safe into eternity.

27 Charles the Great to Offa, king of Mercia, 793–6

Source: Duemmler, 87.

Charles, by the grace of God king of the Franks and defender of God's holy Church, to his beloved brother and friend King Offa, greeting.

Your Scottish priest has been staying with us for some time in the diocese of Hildebald, bishop of Cologne, but has, it is said, been called to task by an accuser for having eaten meat in the season of Lent. Our clergy, however, were unwilling to judge him because they were unable to find a full testimony of accusation against him. Nevertheless, they could not allow him to stay any longer in his usual place of residence because of the disgrace, lest the priestly office should be cheapened in the eyes of the ignorant masses or rumour and gossip be used by some to encourage the breaking of the holy fast. It seemed to our clergy that he should be sent for judgement to his own bishop, to the district in which he made his vows to God.

---

[1] Professor Whitelock points out that the manuscript has *Umhringstan,* an impossible name, and suspects that the *um-* had been repeated in error from the previous word, *illorum.*

Wherefore we ask that you in your providence should order him to return to his country as soon as time and a suitable passage allow, so that he may be judged in the place from which he came. For the purity in custom, firmness in faith and honour in converse of God's Holy Church should in all places be diligently observed in accordance with the precepts of canon law, like one perfect and immaculate dove, whose wings are of silver and whose hinder parts should shine with the appearance of gold [*cf.* Psalm 68.13].

May the Lord Christ give life, health and prosperity to you and your faithful subjects for ever.

28 Charles the Great to Offa, king of Mercia, 796

Source: Duemmler, 100; *EHD* I, 197, pp. 781–2.

Charles, by the grace of God, king of the Franks and Lombards and patrician of the Romans, to the revered man his dearest brother, Offa, king of the Mercians, sends greeting of present prosperity and eternal blessedness in Christ.

Between royal dignities and exalted personages of the world, the keeping of the laws of friendship joined in the unity of peace, and of the concord of holy love, with the deepest affection of heart, is wont to be of profit to many. And if we are commanded by Our Lord's precept to untie the knots of enmity, how much more ought we to take care to secure the links of love? Hence, most beloved brother, mindful of the ancient pact between us, we have sent these letters to your reverence, that the treaty established in the root of faith may flourish in the fruit of love. Having perused your brotherly letters, which have at divers times been brought to us by the hands of your messengers, and endeavouring to reply adequately to the several suggestions of your authority, we first give thanks to the Almighty God for the sincerity of the Catholic faith which we found laudably set down in your pages; recognizing you to be not only a most strong protector of your earthly country, but also a most devout defender of the holy faith.

Concerning pilgrims, who for the love of God and the salvation of their souls desire to reach the thresholds of the blessed apostles, as we granted formerly, they may go in peace free from all molestation, bearing with them the necessities for their journey. But we have discovered that certain persons fraudulently mingle with them for the sake of commerce, seeking gain, not serving religion. If such are found among them, they are to pay the established toll at the proper places; the others may go in peace, immune from toll.

You have written to us also about merchants, and by our mandate we allow that they shall have protection and support in our kingdom, lawfully, according to the ancient custom of trading. And if in any place they are afflicted by wrongful oppression, they may appeal to us or to our judges, and we will then order true justice to be done. Similarly our men, if they suffer any injustice in your dominion, are to appeal to the judgement of your equity, lest any disturbance should arise anywhere between our men.

Regarding the priest Odberht, who desires on his return from Rome to live abroad for the love of God, as he often says, and did not come to accuse you, I inform you, dear brother, that we have sent him to Rome with the other exiles who in fear of death have taken refuge under the wings of our protection; so that in the presence of the apostolic lord and your archbishop—since, as your letters have informed us, they had bound themselves by a vow—their cause may be heard and judged, that equitable judgement may be effective where pious intercession failed. What could be safer for us than that the opinion of the apostolic authority should determine a case in which the views of others disagree?

As for the black stones which your reverence begged to be sent to you, let a messenger come and consider what kind you have in mind, and we will willingly order them to be given, wherever they are to be found, and will help with their transport. But as you have intimated your wishes concerning the length of the stones, so our people make a demand about the size of the cloaks, that you may order them to be such as used to come to us in former times.

Moreover, we make known to your love that we have sent a gift from our dalmatics and palls to the various episcopal sees of your kingdom and of Ethelred's, in alms for the apostolic lord, Hadrian, our father and your friend; beseeching you to order diligent intercession for his soul, not having any doubt that his blessed soul is at rest, but to show our trust and love towards a friend most dear to us. So, also, the blessed Augustine has taught, that intercessions of ecclesiastical piety ought to be made for all; asserting that to intercede for a good man profits him who does it. Also from the treasure of earthly riches, which the Lord Jesus Christ has granted us with freely bestowed kindness, we have sent something to each of the metropolitan cities; also to your love, for joy and thanksgiving to Almighty God, we have sent a belt, and a Hunnish sword and two silk palls.

To the end that everywhere among Christian people the divine clemency may be preached and the name of Our Lord Jesus Christ be glorified in eternity, we pray that you cause assiduous intercessions to be made for us and for our faithful subjects, nay more, for all Christian people; that the most merciful goodness of the heavenly king may deign to protect, exalt and extend the kingdom of the Holy Church. May Almighty God deign to preserve in long-lasting prosperity the excellence of your dignity unimpaired for the protection of his Holy Church, most longed-for brother.

29 Alcuin to Offa, king of Mercia, 796, after 18 April

Source: Duemmler, 101; *EHD* I, 198, pp. 782–4.

To the most excellent man and to us most dear, Offa, king of the Mercians, his humble friend Alcuin sends greeting.

Be it known to your reverend love that the lord king, Charles, has often spoken to me of you in a most loving and loyal way, and in him you certainly have a most faithful friend. Thus he is sending envoys to Rome for the judgement of the apostolic pope and of Archbishop Æthelheard. He is also sending fitting gifts to you. Moreover, he is sending presents to all the episcopal sees in alms for himself and for the apostolic pope, that you should order prayers to be offered for them. Do you act faithfully, as you are always wont to act towards your friends.

Similarly, he had sent gifts both to King Ethelred and to his episcopal sees. But alas, the pity! When the gifts and letters had been given into the messengers' hands, the sad news came to us by the messengers who had returned from Ireland by way of you, of the treachery of the people and of his murder. King Charles withdrew his generous gifts, and was so greatly enraged against that nation, holding 'that perfidious and perverse race, murderers of their lords', as he called them, worse than pagans, that whatever benefit he could have taken away from them, or whatever evil he could have contrived, he would have put into effect, if I had not interceded for them.

I was prepared to come to you with the gifts of King Charles and return to my country. But it seemed better, for the sake of the peace of my people, for me to remain abroad; for I do not know what I could do among them, where no one can be safe or prevail with any wholesome counsel. Look at the most holy places laid waste by the pagans, altars defiled by perjuries, monasteries profaned by adulteries, the earth polluted with the blood of kings and princes. What can I do other than groan with the prophet: 'Woe to the sinful nation, a people laden with iniquity, a wicked seed, ungracious children; they have forsaken the Lord; they have blasphemed the holy Saviour of the world in their wickedness [Isaiah 1.4].' And if what was read in your highness's letter be true, that the iniquity started from the elders of the people, where then is safety and fidelity to be hoped for, if the turbulent torrent of iniquity flowed from the place where the purest fountain of truth and faith was wont to spring?

You, most wise ruler of the people of God, correct very diligently your people from perverse habits and instruct it in the precepts of God, that the land given to us by God may not be destroyed for the sins of the people. Be a father to the Church of Christ, a brother to the priests of God, and kind and just to all the people, moderate and peaceful in all your bearing and speech, and ever devout in the praise of God; that the divine clemency may preserve you in long-lasting prosperity, and may deign by the grace of his goodness to exalt, enlarge and crown in eternity with the benefits of everlasting piety, your kingdom, nay more, that of all the English.

I implore you that you order the several churches of your reverence to intercede for me, your servant and fellow-worker for your honour. The charge of the church of St Martin has come into my keeping, all unworthy as I am, not by my wishes but to a certain measure by necessity and from the advice of many.

Yet know that I am free faithfully to offer prayers for you there, and wherever I can.

Be with all love and care a friend of God and fill your days with His commands. Endeavour that an eternal reward may follow you and the heavenly blessing your descendants. Again and again I implore you for the love of God to take thought for the country, lest it perish; and for the churches of God, lest they be destroyed; and that truth with mercy may increase in it. For by the true saying of Solomon, the throne of the kingdom shall be strengthened in truth and mercy [*cf.* Proverbs 20.28]; these things may confirm you and your throne for ever, that you may rule happily in this world and live in glory with Christ in the heavenly kingdom.

May you flourish, by the favour of the Lord Christ, in all felicity, and may you advance in all goodness, for the consolation of the Holy Church of God, and the joy of Christian people, O lord most excellent and to us most dear.

I pray you, greet with my love that most noble youth [*i.e.* Ecgferth, Offa's son] and instruct him diligently in the fear of God; and may the hope of many not come to naught in him. Remember the proverb of Solomon: 'For in what way a boy is reared, when he is old he will not depart from it [*cf.* Proverbs 22.6].' Greet also the queen [*i.e.* Cynethrith] and lady of the royal household. May she live happy, rejoicing in an offspring of a happy father. And also I pray that you greet in my name all your highness's children. May the right hand of Almighty God ever protect, direct and guard you all.

I pray you to receive with your accustomed goodness the pupils we have trained and taught, and the messengers of the royal dignity. They indeed bear a peaceful message in their mouth and hands. Through them you can demand of me what you wish.

30 Charles the Great to Angilbert, abbot of St Riquier, 796

Source: Duemmler, 92.

Charles, by the grace of God king and defender of God's Holy Church, to Homer his counsellor, greeting.

When the divine mercy has guided your journey and brought you successfully to our lord and father the pope, you should be careful to remind him of all that is honourable in his life, and especially of the observance of the holy canons, and of the pious governance of God's Holy Church—this according to the opportunity for talk between you and his own readiness to hear. You should impress upon him as often as you can how few are the years of the office which he at present holds but how many are those of the eternal reward which is given to him who labours well in it; you should urge him most earnestly to root out the heresy of simony, which in many places is a mark of sickness upon the whole body of the Church; and you should mention anything else that you recall being complained of in our discussions. But you should on no account fail to inform him of the talk I had with the blessed pope Hadrian, his predecessor, concerning the construction of a monastery to St Paul, so that when, God willing, you return you will have some definite reply to bring to me.

May the Lord God lead you and bring you back with all success. May the Lord God rule and guide his heart in all goodness, that his deeds may redound to the profit of his Holy Church, and that he may be to us a dutiful father and a notable intercessor on our behalf; that the same God and Our Lord Jesus Christ may make us to prosper in his good will; and that he will deign to direct the course of our life, as much of it as is now left to us, towards the peace of everlasting stability. Go in prosperity, setting out in truth to return in joy, you son of Homer.

31 Charles the Great to Pope Leo III, 796

Source: Duemmler, 93.

Charles, by the grace of God king of the Franks and Lombards and patrician of the Romans, to Leo, pope of perpetual blessedness in Christ, greeting.

Having read your excellence's letters and having heard the contents of your written decree we have, I declare, rejoiced greatly at the unanimity of your election, at your modesty and humility, and at the loyalty of your promise to us; in all of which matters we offer manifold thanks from the bottom of our hearts to the divine goodness, in that, after the lamentable wound of grief which he inflicted upon us in the death of a friend so faithful and a father so dear to our heart, he saw fit, in his customary providence and mercy, to give us in you our consolation.

Wherefore in return we entrust to your holiness, as a token of our joy through the mercy of the same God and of Our Lord Jesus Christ, who has made provision for his Holy Church by the exaltation of your blessedness, our own prosperity and that of all our faithful subjects, and would inform you of the peacable conformity to the will of God throughout our whole kingdom, that you may rejoice in the security of our devotion as much as we delight in the succession of your holiness.

But of this also we would inform your most holy benevolence, that when I had prepared to send gifts as tokens of affection to my most dear father your predecessor, that I might show by the extent of my generosity the greatness of the love I had for him and that the trust and most sweet affection between us might be shown to the eyes of the many, lo! suddenly (I cannot speak of it without grief or think of it without tears for sadness) his death cut short my embassy, and the mournful observances of grief overwhelmed me just when I was preparing the tokens of joyfulness. And though the apostle forbids us to mourn for the dead, yet our love for him continues to call forth our tears, though we do not weep for him as dead but are mindful rather of his living a better life with Christ [*cf.* I Thessalonians 4.13]. If he is lost to us in his bodily presence, yet we believe that we have not lost his spiritual intervention on our behalf.

But it was a great consolation that the divine grace provided for us when he called you, O venerable lord, to take his place, that there might be someone who would daily intercede with St Peter, chief of the apostles, for the stability of the whole Church, for the safety of ourself and of our faithful subjects, and for the prosperity of the whole kingdom granted to us by God, and who with a father's goodness would adopt us as his son in love.

To confirm the peacable harmony of this most sweet affection we send to your holiness Angilbert, our servant and intimate counsellor. Whom before (as we promised through the devout men Campolus and Anastasius) we were prepared to send to our most blessed father your predecessor, but, as we have said, when all the gifts had been made ready his journey was suddenly delayed by the mournful news of our father's death. But now, being made more joyful by the succession of your holiness, we are eager to accomplish in you what we desired to do in that pious man, our father. Upon him [that is to say, Angilbert] we have enjoined everything that seemed appropriate to our wishes or to your needs, that from your discussions together you may take what measures you feel to be needful for the exaltation of God's Holy Church, for the stability of your office, or for the security of our patriciate.

For just as I entered upon a pact of holy fatherhood with our most blessed father your predecessor, so with your blessedness I desire to establish an inviolable treaty of the same trust and affection, to the end that by the divine favour of your apostolic holiness invoked in prayer the apostolic blessing may follow me wherever I may go, and that the holy see of the Church of Rome may with God's grace be defended always by our devotion. It is for us, in accordance with the help of divine goodness, outwardly to defend by force of arms the Holy Church of Christ in all places from the incursions of pagans and the ravages of infidels, and inwardly to fortify her with our confession of the Catholic faith. It is for you, most holy father, raising your hands to God with Moses, to aid our armies, to the end that with you as intercessors and with God as guide and giver our Christian people may in all places have the victory over the enemies of its holy name, and that the name of Our Lord Jesus Christ may be renowned throughout all the world.

May the wisdom of your authority abide always by the provisions of the canons and follow always the statutes of the holy fathers, that examples of complete holiness may shine in your converse for all men to see and from your mouth be heard the inspiration of holy admonition, and that 'your light so shine before men that they may see your good works, and glorify your Father which is in heaven [Matthew 5.16].'

May it please Almighty God to preserve in safety the blessedness of your authority, for the exaltation of his Holy Church, while many years shall run.

32 Alcuin to Pope Leo III, 796

Source: Duemmler, 94.

To the lord pope, Leo, most blessed and worthy of every name of honour, Albinus, a humble deacon of everlasting glory in Christ, sends greeting.

I beseech you, illustrious father, that your most holy piety will receive with indulgence this letter from my humble self, and that you will acknowledge me as the devoted servant of your affection. I have at all times and with all my heart shown love for the most blessed princes and shepherds of the holy see of Rome, being desirous through their most holy intercession to be numbered among the flock of Christ, which Christ our God himself, after his glorious Resurrection, entrusted for feeding to St Peter the chief of the apostles. And this I acknowledge to be right, that the whole multitude of that flock, even though it dwell in pastures which are scattered over the earth, should be subject to its shepherd in a single bond of loyalty and affection; and for him, as a good shepherd, it is fitting that he should take great care of the flock entrusted to him and with constant pious exhortation and holy intercession should see to it that none of them begin to wander through the steep places of error away from the path of truth and the pastures of everlasting life. The health of the flock is the glory of the shepherd, and its increase his eternal reward.

Behold yourself, most holy father, pontiff chosen by God, vicar of the apostles, heir to the holy fathers, prince of the Church and provider for the one immaculate dove. May faith in you be resplendent, may devotion shine forth, may love abound. In a spirit of fatherly compassion gather us, the sons of the Holy Church of God, with your most holy prayers and the sweetest of exhortations from holy scripture into that most firm and solid fold which is the Church, that none of us may be found wandering abroad, a prey to ravening wolves.

For the shining columns of the heavenly host, at the birth of Our Lord Jesus Christ, came to announce the glad tidings first of all to the shepherds, who were keeping faithful watch over their flocks. And lo! at your most holy watches, most worthy archimandrite, spent in pastoral cares, we doubt not that angel visitors from the seats above will attend; and with their aid you will be able, we believe, to obtain whatever you ask of the divine goodness.

Wherefore I, the least of the lowly ones in your most holy fold, a poor sheep ridden with sin, but raised up by the hope of your everlasting goodness, prostrate myself in spirit before the most holy feet of your fatherhood, and in supplication beg that by the ecclesiastical power of your apostolic authority you will deign to loose the terrible fetters of my sins, and with the prayers of your fatherly goodness will strive to direct the course of what life remains to me towards the gates of the everlasting city. What I ask is great indeed, but love can give great things. Christ in his mercy did not spurn the widow who asked for her son, but said: 'O woman, great is thy faith: be it unto thee even as thou wilt [Luke 7.12; Matthew 15.28].' Faith it is that bids me ask it; hope that strengthens my request; and love, I believe, that will not think to refuse it. Christ did not shrink from dying for us, though we were his enemies: how much more should we believe that you, holy father, will be willing to pray for your friends.

With you as its shepherd may Christ's flock increase. You are the comfort of them that mourn, the help of them that labour, the hope of them that cry to you, the light of life and glory of our faith. In the eyes of all men the place in which you stand makes you worthy of honour, the nobility of your conduct makes you worthy of praise, and the devotion of your piety makes you worthy of love. Seeing that the seat you hold is that of the holy fathers may you abide always by their examples, that with them you may as a manifold reward for your labours be thought worthy to enter the joys of the Lord your God.

My beloved son Angilbert can tell you of the devotion felt by our humble selves to the apostolic see, and also of the petition we wish to present. I know him to be faithful and true to your fatherhood, and it is for this reason that we have entrusted to him the task of pleading our needs, that the ears of your holiness may hear through his mouth the beseechings of my heart.

33 Alcuin to Charles the Great, 796

Source: Duemmler, 110.

To the lord Charles, most excellent and most devoted in every service of Christ, king of Germany, Gaul and Italy, and to the holy preachers of the word of God in the humble and Holy Mother Church, their son Albinus of everlasting glory in Christ sends greeting.

Glory and praise be to God our father and to our Lord Jesus Christ, in that by the grace of the Holy Spirit—through your devotion and ministry of the holy faith and good will—he has spread abroad the rule of Christianity and the acknowledgement of the true God, and has led numerous peoples far and wide from the errors of impiety into the way of truth. How great will be your glory, most blessed king, on the day of eternal judgement, when all those who through your good care have been turned from the cult of idolatry to the knowledge of the true God shall follow you as you stand in happy state before the judgement seat of Our Lord Jesus Christ, and because of them all the reward of everlasting bliss is bestowed upon you.

See with what devotion and kindness you toiled for the spreading of Christ's name to soften, by means of the counsel of true salvation, the hard nature of the unhappy Saxon people. But because the divine election seems not yet to have come among them, there are many of them even now who remain in the squalor of evil custom and are to be damned along with the devil.

And yet, O lover of truth and of the salvation of many, it pleased Christ to reward your good will with greater glory and praise. The races and peoples of the Huns, formidable in their ancient fierceness and courage, he subdued to his service through your campaigning sceptres; and with his grace preventing you he bound to the holy faith as with a yoke necks long proud, and poured the light of truth into minds that had been blind from of old.

But now your devotion, so wise and so pleasing to God, must provide devout preachers for the new people, men who are honourable in their ways, well trained in the knowledge of the holy faith, imbued with the teaching of the gospel, and in their preaching of the word of God close followers of the example of the holy apostles. They, in the early days of the faith, had milk (by which they meant their sweet teachings) to offer to their hearers: in the words of St Paul, 'And I, brethren, could not speak unto you as unto spiritual, but as unto carnal, even as unto babes in Christ. I have fed you with milk, and not with meat: for hitherto ye were not able to bear it, neither yet now are ye able [I Corinthians 3.1–2].' By this the preacher to the whole world (Christ speaking in him) meant to show that peoples newly converted to the faith should be fed on softer teachings, like the milk that is given in infancy, lest by taking sterner teaching the fragile mind should vomit out what it took in. Wherefore Our Lord Christ himself in the gospel, when asked why his disciples did not fast, replied saying: 'Neither do men put new wine into old bottles: else the bottles break, and the wine runneth out, and the bottles perish [Matthew 9.17].' For as St Jerome says, 'One kind of purity is that of a soul which is unspotted and has not been corrupted by contact with past vice, and another that of one which has been subjected to the filthiness and lust of many people.'

Having therefore considered these things, let your holy piety give thought to wise counsel, whether it would be good to impose the yoke of tithes on uncultured peoples in the early days of their faith, with a view to exacting them in full from the individual houses. You should consider whether the apostles for their part, who were taught by Christ the Lord himself and sent out to preach to the world, would have demanded the exaction of tithes or insisted on payments in any other way. We know that the tithing of our substance is a truly good thing; but it is better to lose it than to forfeit the faith. We indeed, who have been born, nurtured and trained in the Catholic faith, can only with difficulty endure that our substance be fully tithed; how much more will a still frail faith, a childish mind and a greedy mentality be reluctant to agree to such payments? When their faith is strengthened and they are confirmed in the practice of Christianity, then as to perfect men more rigorous teaching is to be given, which a mind that is well founded in the Christian religion is not likely to reject.

This also should be very carefully looked into, that the office of preaching and the sacrament of baptism be properly ordered, lest it should happen that the washing of the body in holy baptism is of no benefit, since there is no acknowledgement of the Catholic faith to accompany it in a mind capable of reason. So said the apostle: 'Let all things be done decently, and in order [I Corinthians 14.40]'. And Our Lord himself in the gospel, when teaching his disciples, said: 'Go ye therefore, and teach all nations, baptizing them in the name of the Father, and of the Son, and of the Holy Ghost [Matthew 28.19].' In the commentary which he wrote on the gospel of St Matthew, St Jerome explained the order of this instruction as follows: 'First, they teach all nations, and then when they are taught they sprinkle them with water. For it is not possible for the body properly to receive the sacrament of baptism unless the soul has previously received the truth of the faith into itself. They are baptized in the name of the Father and of the Son and of the Holy Spirit so that where there is one divinity there shall be one bounty, and the name of the Trinity is one single god. "Teaching them to observe all things whatsoever I have commanded you"—the order is all-important. He instructed the apostles, first, to teach all nations, and then to sprinkle them with the sacrament of their faith, and finally, after the instruction in the faith and the baptism, to tell them what things they should observe. And lest we should think that the instructions he gave them were unimportant he added a few words more—"all things whatsoever I have commanded you"—so that those who believed and were baptized in the name of the Trinity should do all the things they were instructed to do.'

Thus infants, who have no reasoning ability and are subject to the sins of others, can be saved through the sacrament of baptism by others' confession of faith, provided that, when they reach the appropriate age, they preserve the integrity of the faith confessed on their behalf. As the apostle said: 'With the heart man believeth unto righteousness; and with the mouth confession is made unto salvation [Romans 10.10].' This confession from the mouth leads to salvation only if it is firmly backed by belief from the heart.

Therefore, in teaching a man of mature age, that order should I think be carefully adhered to which St Augustine prescribed in the book to which he gave the title, 'On Catechizing the Unlettered'. First, the man is to be instructed in the immortality of the soul, in the life to come, in the rewards of good and evil, and in the eternity of each. After this he should be told for what sins and crimes he will suffer eternal punishment with the devil, and for what good deeds and benefits he will enjoy eternal glory with Christ. Then he should be taught most carefully the faith of the Holy Trinity, and should have expounded to him the coming of Our Lord Jesus Christ the Son of God into the world for the salvation of human kind. Soon, as we have said already, the newly opened mind should be strengthened with teaching of the mystery of his Passion, the truth of his Resurrection and the glory of his Ascension into heaven and of his future coming to judge all nations, and the resurrection of our bodies and the eternity of punishment for the wicked and of reward for the good. And when a man is strengthened and prepared with this faith he is to be baptized. And so, at the appropriate time, the teachings of the gospel can be given to him more frequently through the office of assiduous preaching, until he grows into perfect manhood and becomes a worthy habitation for the Holy Spirit and a perfect son of God in the works of mercy, just as Our Father in heaven is perfect, who liveth and reigneth in perfect Trinity and blessed unity, God and Lord for ever and ever, Amen.

May the grace of Our Lord Jesus Christ be with you always.

34 Alcuin to Meginfried, 796

Source: Duemmler, 111.

To Meginfried, most beloved friend in the love of Christ and treasurer of the royal palace, Flaccus Albinus of everlasting salvation gives greeting.

It is the custom for letters written with an affectionate pen to pass between friends in order that they may reveal the warmth of the heart in silent brotherly words, and that what lies hidden in the mind may appear openly in the writing. And so, mindful of you my most dear friend, I have taken the trouble to send you these words of advice, which are for your salvation and indeed for the salvation of many. Nor should you think me excessive in this my letter, but rather devoted: what I desire is your prosperity, both in the present life and in the life to come, that in this temporal life you may live in happiness and in that eternal one you may reign in bliss with Christ.

Now every man must give most serious thought to the question of what he should pursue and what he should avoid. The psalmist showed both of these things in one short verse when he said: 'Depart from evil, and do good [Psalm 34.14].' For him who desires to achieve eternal glory it is not enough simply to avoid evil if he does not also do good. Wherefore the fount of truth himself in the gospel replied to a questioner: 'If thou wilt enter into life, keep the commandments [Matthew 19.17].'

But each man should give thought to the rank in which God has placed him and to the talent with which he has endowed him. For it is not only to bishops and priests that the Lord entrusted his wealth to be multiplied: rather, he gave talents for good works to men of every rank and station, that they should take care to administer faithfully the favour given to them and strive to pass it on to their fellow servants. One man receives the talent of preaching, another of wisdom, another of riches, another of some position of responsibility, another perhaps of some craftsman's art—all by the gift of God, the giver of all these good gifts. And in all of these one must look to a man's loyalty and devotion, to see that he labours faithfully and does his best as a man should to increase the property of his lord, so that he may deserve to hear the longed-for words: 'Well done, good and faithful servant; thou has been faithful over a few things, I will make thee ruler over many things: enter thou into the joy of thy lord [Matthew 25.21].'

Now those who receive the talent for preaching should consider very carefully what is appropriate to a given age or a given person, what is fitting for a particular place or time, and even in what order the preaching of Christianity should be begun and carried through. For Our Lord Jesus Christ, when he returned in triumph and glory to his father's throne, instructed his disciples saying: 'Go ye therefore, and teach all nations, baptizing them in the name of the Father, and of the Son, and of the Holy Ghost: teaching them to observe all things whatsoever I have commanded you [Matthew 28.19–20].' First the faith should be taught; after this the sacraments of baptism are to be fully explained; and finally the teachings of the gospels should be conveyed to them. And if any of these three things is lacking the hearer will not be able to obtain salvation for his soul. Faith too, as St Augustine says, is a voluntary thing and not a matter for compulsion. A man can be drawn into faith, not forced into it. He can be forced into baptism, but this is no profit to him in the matter of faith, except that infancy, since it is subject to the sins of others, can obtain salvation through others' confession. A man of mature age should reply for himself, what he believes or what he desires; and if he professes his faith falsely he cannot truly obtain salvation.

Wherefore those who preach to the pagans should teach the faith to the people with prudent and peaceable words. The Lord knows who are his, and opens the hearts of those whose hearts he desires, that they may understand what is told them by their teachers. But even after they have received the faith and baptism their relatively weak minds should be presented with relatively gentle instructions. For the apostle Paul also, when writing to the newly-won people of the Galatians, said: 'I have fed you with milk, and not with meat [I Corinthians 3.2].' Meat is for strong men: that is to say, the more serious teachings are for those whose minds have long been exercised in the law of the Lord. And just as milk is appropriate for those of tender years, so more gentle teaching should be given to an uncultured people in the early days of its faith. And so we read also in the Acts of the Apostles that Paul and Barnabas went up to Jerusalem to ask James and the other apostles this question: how should they preach to the nations? And they wrote and with one mind decided that no burden of law should be laid upon their shoulders, but only that they should abstain 'from fornication, from blood, and from things strangled, and from idols

[Acts 15.28–9].' Indeed, St Paul himself, the preacher to the nations, gloried that he lived by the labour of his hands. For in one of his letters he said this: 'Ye yourselves know, that these hands have ministered unto my necessities, and to them that were with me . . . , that we might not be chargeable to any of you [Acts 20.34 and II Thessalonians 3.8].' And again; 'It were better for me to die, than that any man should make my glorying void. . . . What is my reward, then? Verily, that when I preach the gospel, I may make the gospel of Christ without charge [I Corinthians 9.15, 18].'

This then he did, this great preacher to the nations specially chosen by God, that he might utterly eradicate all occasion for avarice from among preachers, to the end that no one should preach the word of God ensnared by any covetousness, but rather being strengthened by the charity of Christ alone; as he himself said in the gospel, when preaching to his disciples: 'Freely ye have received, freely give [Matthew 10.9].'

If the easy yoke and the light burden of Christ were preached to the tough Saxon people as forcefully as the payment of tithes and the legal rigour of the edict for even the smallest of crimes are exacted, it may be that they would not shrink from the sacrament of baptism.

In short, let the teachers of the faith be well versed in the apostolic examples: let them be preachers, not poachers. Let them put their trust in the goodness of Him who said: 'Carry neither purse, nor scrip . . . (and so on) [Luke 10.4]', and of whom the prophet said: 'Who saveth them that trust in him [Susanna 60].'

These things I have written to please you, my venerable friend, that those who desire to hear your counsel may profit from your advice. May the best beloved David [*i.e.* Charles the Great himself] be made aware of all these things, to whom God has given both wisdom and good will, that he may convert many people to the love and praise of God. To him belong goodness and power sufficient to bestow benefits, save for one thing only which comes from the perilous times in which we live, namely, that he has fewer helpers in the Lord's work than is needful. Yet no one in the world, I believe, has better helpers than he. Let him teach them, advise them, train them in accordance with the wisdom given to him by God. And do you, the faithful administrator of his treasury, keeper of his counsels and his devoted helper, give him stout encouragement. Be gentle in counsel, energetic in action; peaceable at home, prudent on missions; show goodness to the poor and wretched, justice in your judgements, generosity in your alms-giving, that as a result of your earthly riches you may earn the everlasting riches of Christ in heaven.

Thus far my love for my dear David and my concern for the salvation of many has led me to recommend to you what I know to be useful in the sight of God and honourable in this our age.

For there are some priests of Christ who have parishes and positions of honour in our time and who do not wish to have offices of ministry. To me it would seem better that they should have full blessing and full reward with God. But as it is, another works for everlasting reward and they work for secular honour. They are, if I may be allowed to say it, deprived of the power of binding and loosing, which is the finest gift in Christ's Church that Christ gave to his apostles and through them to their successors. And for the churches, too, which have no shepherds, it is dangerous for Christ's flock to remain for long without a shepherd. 'Grievous wolves enter in among them [Acts 20.29],' and there is no one to drive them out. 'She that was great among the nations . . . sits solitary and a widow . . . , and hath none to comfort her [Lamentations 1.1, 2].' He who is all truth has said: 'The harvest truly is great, but the labourers are few; pray ye therefore the Lord of the harvest, that he would send forth labourers into his harvest [Luke 10.2].'

And I say to you my dear friend: the harvest truly is great among Christ's people, but in some places there are no reapers. You therefore pray the lord of the harvest, that is, my beloved David, that he would send forth reapers into his harvest, that when you have prayed him he may say to them, as his own protector and one supreme friend Christ Our God said to his disciples: 'Go your ways, behold I send you forth [Luke 10.3].' He is the lord of the vineyard: let him send labourers into his vineyard and say: 'Go ye also into my vineyard, and whatsoever is right I will give you for the work of my vineyard [Matthew 20.4].' His is the power and ordering of Christ's vineyard, that is, the churches of God. His is the praise and the glory and the everlasting reward, that they be well ordered and governed, that they have shepherds, as many as can be found that are worthy and pleasing to God. He it is in this kingdom who can preach to all men and to all the churches —— [some words are missing here]— to have rewards and blessings on earth and eternal bliss and blissful eternity with Christ and his saints.

35 Alcuin to Charles the Great, 796–7

Source: Duemmler, 121; *EHD* I, 201, p. 786.

Professor Whitelock points out that Alcuin borrows the language of the Song of Songs, 4.12 f.; 4.16; and 5.1 f. in the last paragraph of this extract.

I, your Flaccus [*i.e.* Alcuin himself], according to your exhortation and encouragement, am occupied in supplying to some under the roof of St Martin the honey of the sacred scriptures; am eager to inebriate others with the old wine of ancient learning; begin to nourish others on the fruits of grammatical subtlety; long to illumine some with the order of the stars, like the painted ceiling of a great man's house; becoming many things to many men [*cf.* I Corinthians 9.22], that I may instruct many to the profit of the Holy Church of God and to the adornment of your imperial kingdom, that the grace of the

Almighty be not void in me [*cf.* I Corinthians 15.10], nor the bestowal of your bounty in vain.

But I, your servant, miss to some extent the rarer books of scholastic learning which I had in my own country through the excellent and devoted zeal of my master [i.e. Ethelbert, afterwards archbishop of York] and also through some toil of my own. I tell these things to your excellency, in case it may perchance be agreeable to your counsel, which is most eager for the whole of knowledge, that I send some of our pupils to choose there what we need, and to bring into France the flowers of Britain; that not in York only there may be a 'garden enclosed', but in Tours the 'plants of Paradise with the fruit of the orchard', that the south wind may come and blow through the gardens by the River Loire, and the aromatical spices thereof may flow; and finally, that there may come to pass what follows in the Canticle from which I have taken this metaphor: 'Let my beloved come into his garden and eat the fruit of his apple-trees'; and he may say to his young men: '"Eat, friends, and drink and be inebriated, my dearly beloved." I sleep, and my heart watcheth'; or that admonitory utterance of the prophet Isaiah on the teaching of wisdom: 'All you that thirst, come to the waters. And you that have no money, make haste, buy and eat. Come ye: buy wine and milk without money and without any price [Isaiah 55.1].'

36 Alcuin to Charles the Great, *c.* 801

Source: Duemmler, 238.

To the most pious lord king, David, Albinus of everlasting bliss sends greeting.

May God in highest Trinity reward your goodness with everlasting bliss, O best beloved David, for all the devotion and kindness you have shown to me your servant. All that in your mercy you promised at the first news of my arrival you have faithfully fulfilled; and to the store of fullest truth which rests always in the treasure house of your heart you have added a hundred fold, so that it shines clearer than light for all to see and through distant lands resounds in the ears of many. What more could be done for the happiness of my sojourn? What better token of your goodness towards me, than all these generous gifts? What thanks can I offer worthy of your kindness, other than with constant and assiduous prayer to call upon Almighty God in his great compassion and goodness, that with the eternal reward of heavenly bliss he may repay you many times over for all the benefits which you have in your bounty lavished upon my humble self?

That I may be allowed to spend my days at St Martin's I beseech you in all submissiveness, in all humility, in all devotion. So weak and infirm am I that I can undertake no more travel and no more work. To speak the truth, all the worth, all the strength has left my body, and daily retreats from me further: I fear it will not return in this life.

I had hoped and prayed that when my days were spent I could look for one last time upon your blessed face. But as my poor weak body declines I know for certain that it cannot be.

And so I call upon your mercy and unfailing goodness, that your pious heart and kindly will may not be angry at my infirmity, but may in holy compassion allow me to rest in my weariness, to devote myself to prayers on your behalf, and to come before the face of the eternal judge with penitential tears; so it may be that in the mercy of the Lord Jesus I may escape the fearsome accusations of the old enemy, and merit the aid of one of the saints to stand with me and intercede for my frailty, lest I be given into the hands of my enemies.

O, how must every man fear that day, and how necessary it is for each of us to prepare to meet his God, encouraged by that light which lighteth every man and cries to us: 'Walk while ye have the light, lest darkness come upon you [John 12.35].' How we should walk in the light he tells us in another place, when he says: 'Let your light so shine before men, that they may see your good works, and glorify your Father which is in heaven [Matthew 5.16].'

> May the grace of Christ be with you for ever, O David,
> That you may flourish and be strong, a powerful conqueror
>   in the world,
> And that after this you may in bliss attain the celestial
>   kingdom,
> And dwell forever with the saints on the heavenly hill.
> May Christ in his gentleness give you manifold reward
> For all the gifts your goodness has bestowed on me.
> As many as the grass blades in the earth, and the sands on
>   the sea shore,
> So many be your blessings, David, from a merciful God.
> May David through the everlasting years live always
> By holy merit glorious and happy in Christ.

Letters from the *Codex Carolinus*

We have selected the following three papal letters in an attempt to illustrate the tone of Hadrian I's approach to Charles the Great, and the wide range of matters brought to the Frankish king's attention. The last letter has a special interest for English readers.

37 Pope Hadrian I to Charles the Great, 776

Source: Codex Carolinus 59.

Hadrian, pope, to our lord and most excellent son Charles, king of the Franks and Lombards and patrician of the Romans.

We have received the words of the distinguished utterance of your divinely founded royal power, and have given thanks to Almighty God for assuring us of the well-being of your divinely protected kingdom, together with that of our spiritual daughter the queen, your most gentle wife, of your children also, and of all the bishops and clergy, the senate and all the divinely protected people of the Franks; for God, who 'trieth our heart and reins [Psalm 7.9]', will bear witness how, though wholly undeservedly, we yet remain in the honey-sweet affection of your royal power. And together with our bishops and priests, our clergy and senate and all our people, we pray Almighty God in his mercy unceasingly to give you victory and extend your kingdom, to the exaltation of your spiritual mother, God's Holy Church of Rome, and to the salvation of the people entrusted to us by God: for in your exaltation is our joy. And it is our constant wish and desire that our news of your divinely protected kingdom be good and favourable and of benefits received by all the Frankish people, for after God there is nothing but your mighty arm in which we put our trust. Just as our predecessor, the lord pope, Stephen, put a sure trust in your father, the lord king Pippin of pious memory, so all the more do we put our trust in your most mighty kingdom, and rest assured therein.

We find in your sweet letter a mention of the sale of slaves, to the effect that they were sold by our Roman people to the unspeakable race of Saracens. We have never sunk to such a disgraceful act, and God forbid that we should; nor was it done with our approval. The unspeakable Greeks have always sailed along the coasts of Lombardy, and they it was who bought some families from the region and struck up friendships with the Lombards themselves and through their agency received the slaves in question. When this happened we sent straightway to Duke Allo, instructing him to prepare a large fleet, arrest these Greeks and destroy their ships by fire; but he would not obey our command, because we have neither the ships nor the sailors able to make the arrest. Nevertheless, we did our utmost, and call God to witness that we strove mightily in our desire to prevent this scandal; the ships belonging to the Greeks we had burned in the harbour of our city of Civitavecchia, and we kept the Greeks themselves in prison for some considerable time. But, as we have said, many families were sold by the Lombards at a time when famine was pressing them hard; indeed, some of the Lombards went on board the Greek ships of their own accord, having no other hope of staying alive.

As to our priests: those men who have dared falsely and against God and their own hearts to accuse them, 'their iniquity lieth unto itself [Psalm 27.12]'. There is, the Lord be thanked, no corruption among our priests, nor should your loftiness believe such things, seeing that with the Lord's help and through the intercession of the holy and for ever virgin Mary Our Lady and of St Peter the chief of the apostles you have seen fit to join us in a bond of love and affection. Our enemies, who have always sown tares, are now seeking, since God is against them, to sow some mischief between our two sides; yet, with the Lord's help and through the intercessions of St Peter the apostle, they will in no wise prevail, such is the confidence which we have in the Lord's goodness and in your royal eminence. For, as the psalmist says, 'The Lord shall destroy all deceitful lips, and the tongue that speaketh evil [Psalm 12.3]'; so will it be with those who bring such unheard of charges before you and lay accusations against our priests.

May our God see fit to preserve you by the right hand of his protection, to the exaltation of God's Holy Church of Rome.

May the Divine Grace preserve your excellence in safety.

38 Pope Hadrian I to Charles the Great, 788

Source: Codex Carolinus 83.

Hadrian, pope, to our lord and most excellent son and co-father in God, Charles, king of the Franks and Lombards and patrician of the Romans.

It was with a heart full of love that we received your sweet, most agreeable and exalted royal letter. And when we opened it and learned of your royal good health and that of our spiritual daughter, the lady queen, and of the well-being and prosperity of your most noble children, we gave great thanks to Almighty God, who, through the intercessions of St Peter the apostle your patron and the continual prayers of our own unworthy self on your behalf, assigns to you everywhere victories unceasing and makes all around you flourish, your territories and borders alike.

Even more did we rejoice at the subjection of the Bavarians, as we foretold and hoped that we would; so also it was with expectation that we heard of your outstanding royal victory and triumph.

You will recall, we believe, the apostolic letter which we sent to you earlier concerning the men of Capua who came to us through your royal assistance. Some days after we had sent that letter to you, we made these men of Capua swear, at the tomb of your protector St Peter, the chief of the apostles, an oath of loyalty to that same apostle of God and to the authority of us and your royal self. And when the oath had been administered, one of the Capuans, the priest Gregory, requested to speak with us privately, declaring: 'Now I can in no way hide anything, since such is the oath you put me to.' And when we had questioned him more precisely he told us his story:

When the lord and mighty king Charles had returned last year from the city of Capua, his duke Arichis, God being against him, sent messengers to the emperor,[2] seeking his help and asking for the honour of the patriciate together with the duchy of Naples in full tenure, and requesting also that his kinsman

---

[2] *i.e.* the emperor at Constantinople.

Athalgisus be sent to assist him with a strong force of men; and he promised that both in his tonsure and in his mode of dress he would follow the usage of the Greeks at the emperor's bidding. On hearing this the emperor sent to him two envoys, that is to say two *spatharii*,[3] together with the governor of Sicily, bearing with them vestments worked in gold and also the sword, comb and scissors for making him patrician in accordance with the promise that Arichis had made in the matter of dress and tonsure, and requesting Romuald the son of Arichis as a hostage. As to Athalgisus his kinsman, he sent him a message saying: 'We have not sent him to you, but have dispatched him with the army to Treviso and Ravenna.' When these men arrived they discovered that through God's ordinance and the intercessions of the apostles the counsels of the wicked had been brought to nought: for they found that Duke Arichis and his son Romuald were dead.

Now while your most faithful envoy Atto had been at Salerno the men of Benevento were not willing to receive the Greeks, but after the return of the said deacon they brought them from Greece by the land route and received them into Salerno. They remained there for three days, taking counsel with Athalberga the widow of Arichis and with the chief men of Benevento; and the Beneventans advised the Greek envoys as follows: 'We have sent our envoys to King Charles, requesting Grimoald as our duke, and we have in addition sent a request through Atto the deacon, who himself gave us an assurance that we would indeed have him as duke in due course. It is best therefore that you should remain at Naples until we can receive Grimoald as duke; then Grimoald, when he has attained the office which his father Arichis held, will do what his father was unable to do, and with him to help us carry out our promises we will meet the emperor's wishes in each and every respect, as was agreed with his father.' So they escorted them with great pomp to Naples by the land route, and the people of Naples received the Greeks with banners and standards; and while they stayed there awaiting the outcome they did not cease to devise mischief, along with Stephen the bishop and those of the Neapolitans who supported him. The Greeks themselves sent messengers to the emperor telling him of the deaths of Arichis and his son, and awaited his instructions as to what they should do.

But in all these things, O sweetest of sons, may your most excellent, divinely protected and most enlightened royal power shine forth in its actions, not only for the exaltation of your spiritual mother the Holy Church of Rome and for our salvation, but also, with God as your protector and with St Peter the bearer of the keys of the kingdom of heaven as your leader, for the security and triumph of your own invincible kingdom.

But to return to your most faithful envoys, namely the devout abbot, Magenarius, Joseph, Count Liudericus and Gotteramnus the *ostiarius*;[4] as it was

---

[3] High officials of the Byzantine court: literally 'sword-bearers'.

[4] A high court official: literally, 'door-keeper'.

told to us by Gregory the priest of Capua, after returning from Benevento to Spoleto they fled from there also, because the Beneventans had laid plans against them together with the Neapolitans and the Sorrentines and the people of Amalfi. The plans were to have your envoys stopped on the sea coast outside the city of Salerno, and for the Beneventans and the Neapolitans to make a sudden attack on them by night and kill them; later it was to be announced that the Neapolitans had come upon them and had killed them secretly, thinking them to be Beneventans. Your envoys got to know of this and therefore assembled together and fled, wishing to avoid your royal scorn; for, if they had gone to Salerno the Neapolitans and the men of Amalfi and Sorrento were hidden there under arms, ready to rush out on them along with the Beneventans and kill them. This is what we have been told: and all their evil counsels have been brought to nought, such is the most full confidence and deep-seated love and affection that we know is felt by your royal power towards us and towards St Peter, the chief of the apostles. And so all things are subject to you, as we pray to the same apostle of God day and night that they should be, and are put in submission under your shining royal feet.

As to our health, about which you inquired, it is (with the Lord's help) as good as your own, and we do not cease to offer prayers on your behalf, that both in this world you will enjoy many more years of governing your kingdom, and in the heights above, together with our lady the queen and your most noble children, you may win a reign without end.

May the Divine Grace keep your excellence in safety.

39 Pope Hadrian I to Charles the Great, 784–91

Source: Codex Carolinus 92.

Hadrian, pope, to our lord and most excellent son and co-father in God, Charles, king of the Franks and Lombards and patrician of the Romans.

Most wise and most sweet was the letter sent to us by your all-surpassing and triumphant royal power, and we have received its gentle message. On opening it with even more than our usual love our first concern was to have confirmation of what we had continually hoped for, that is to say the excellent health and prosperity of yourself and our spiritual daughter the lady queen, together with that of your distinguished royal children and of all their loyal household. For just as you in your royal mercy have expressed your great desire that we should by our apostolic letters or by envoys inform you frequently of our condition, so we also are constantly longing and eager to hear, whether through your royal letters or through your excellent envoys, of your triumphant victories and prosperity and of the good health and safety of our lady the queen, your noble children and all your faithful subjects. Indeed, you may rest assured that by our apostolic intercessions at the tomb of St Peter the bearer of the keys of the kingdom of heaven we never cease to implore the Divine Mercy on your behalf; for we too are assured that your unwavering royal benevolence does not cease either to strive for the exaltation of your mother the Holy Church of Rome, which is the head of all churches, and for the prosperity of your apostolic father. Such is the rule that your father adopted, the lord Pippin, gentle king of pious memory, and as he began so he continued unchanging until his end; and by following his example your royal power has grown more lofty in all respects, through the mediation of the apostles and our own continual intercessions.

Now it was recounted in your royal letter that Offa, king of the English, had sent to your royal excellence certain information, namely, that some enemies of himself and yourself had brought to our apostolic notice that the same king Offa was suggesting to you that with his advice and encouragement you should (which God forbid) remove us from the holy seat of our office and place another upon it from among your own people. This information was to your mind most wicked and hurtful, and was judged by your excellence to be most certainly false, since neither would Offa ever encourage you to such a thing nor would any other thought enter his mind than that we in our fatherhood should be able in his day by God's mercy to rule and govern the Holy Church of God for the benefit of all Christian people.

We also, relying on your royal power, are utterly assured that its benevolent and unassailable and orthodox loyalty towards our apostolic fatherhood will remain preeminent, fervent in the Holy Spirit as a burning fire, and that the guile of the old enemy will never prevail with any heresy to shake its adherence to the Catholic, apostolic and orthodox faith, but rather that like 'the unspotted mirror' [Wisdom 7.26] it will remain forever a true and brightly shining defender of that same orthodox faith and of our own high office.

Of these foul assertions recounted by Offa, which it is a sin to acknowledge or mention, we have until now heard nothing, and now that we hear them we do not believe them: for who would think of committing such acts, even if (which God forbid) he were a pagan? So much the more, seeing that his royal ancestors have always been submissive in obedience and loyal affection to the holy pontiffs our predecessors, should this unheard-of treachery be thought incredible in our sight.

Yet, 'If God be for us, who can be against us? [Romans 8.31].' 'The Lord is on my side; I will not fear: what can man do unto me? [Psalm 118.6].' And again, 'The Lord is my light and my salvation; whom shall I fear? The Lord is the strength of my life; of whom shall I be afraid? [Psalm 27.1].' For every plant which our heavenly Father hath planted, no man shall prevail to root it up, seeing that 'all things were made by him, and without him was not anything made that was made [Matthew 15.13; John 1.3].' We for our part, who have, though unworthy, attained the apostolic see, and who in succession to St Peter

133

the chief of the apostles have received and hold it and rule over the whole Christian people entrusted to us by God, were not chosen by men or through any man, but were called through Jesus Christ Our Lord. We have been predestined in his gospel, as St Paul the apostle, the instrument of our choosing, has taught us: 'Whom he did foreknow, he also did predestinate. Moreover, whom he did predestinate, them he also called: and whom he called, them he also justified; and whom he justified, them he also glorified [Romans 8.29–30].' And again, St James the apostle instructs and teaches us: 'Every good gift and every perfect gift is from above, and cometh down from the Father of lights, with whom is no variableness neither shadow of turning. Of his own will begat he us with the word of truth [James 1.17–18].' And so like an adamant and a flint we fulfil the word of the prophet, and fearing nothing we cease not to preach the word of God to the nations, as it is written: 'I have made thee a watchman unto the house of Israel: therefore hear the word at my mouth, and give them warning from me [Ezekiel 3.17].' For in accordance with the precepts of St Peter the bearer of the keys of the kingdom of heaven we cease not to preach to kings and peoples the word of truth and life.

For love of which, together with the most loyal envoys whom you sent to us, we received the envoys of King Offa with willing heart, and looked upon them with a joyful countenance out of respect for your own distinguished excellence, fulfilling their requests, so that they might be able to bring back to your triumphant and divinely fostered royal power the welcome news that we are accustomed to take as much trouble in carrying out your wishes as you in ours. And so you observe such habits to the end, may the Divine Majesty grant you, together with our lady the queen and your most noble sons, in this world to enjoy long years of rule over your kingdom and thereafter for ever to rejoice in triumph with all the saints.

May the Divine Grace preserve your excellence in safety.

40 Charles the Great to Queen Fastrada, 791

This letter is included for its intrinsic interest and also as a representative of a miscellaneous group of correspondence published in *MGH, Epp.* IV, ed. E. Duemmler (mentioned above).

Source: MGH, Epp. IV, *Epistolae Variorum*, 20.

Charles, by the grace of God king ot tne Franks and Lombards and patrician of the Romans, to our dear and well beloved wife, Queen [Fastrada]:[5]

We wish by this letter to send you affectionate greeting in the Lord, and through you to our sweet daughters and to those other faithful subjects of ours who are

---

[5] Here, as elsewhere in the letter, the name is omitted in the MS.

with you. We would have you know that (God be thanked) we are safe and sound.

A messenger from our beloved son [Pippin], by name ——, has brought us news that he is well, and also the apostolic father and all our kinsmen who live in those parts. At this we were greatly pleased.

In addition he informed us that our forces, which we earlier instructed to go from Italy into Avar territory and to encamp in the region of ——, arrived there on 23 August and joined battle with the enemy. Almighty God in his mercy gave them victory and they killed a great multitude of the Avar force—so great, they say, that no greater slaughter has been inflicted upon the Avars for many a year. They ravaged the defences themselves, and encamped there all night until the third hour of the following day. Then they took up their spoils and withdrew in peace, taking with them one hundred and fifty Avar captives which they were keeping to await our instructions. The loyal subjects of God and ourselves who achieved this success were Bishop ——, Duke ——, and Counts ——. The duke of Istria, we are informed, also did good service there with his men. The names of our vassals were ——.

We for our part with the Lord's help performed litanies for three days, that is from 5 to 7 September, being Monday, Tuesday and Wednesday, beseeching God in his mercy to grant us peace, health and victory and a successful journey, and in his mercy and goodness to be our helper and counsellor and defender in all our difficulties. Our clergy gave instructions that all who, having regard to their health or age or youth, could abstain from meat and wine should do so; of those who wished to be excused and to have permission to drink wine during those three days the more wealthy should pay a shilling for each day on which they did so, and the less wealthy according to their means; and if a man wished to drink wine and could give nothing more, he should at least give a penny. Each man also was to give alms in accordance with his own good will and with his means. Every priest was to offer a special mass, except where infirmity prevented it; and those clerks who knew the psalms were each to sing fifty, and during the time that the litanies were being performed they were to go unshod. This our clergy thought proper, and we for our part applied ourselves and with the Lord's help carried it out.

We would ask you therefore to consider, along with —— and —— and our other loyal subjects, how these same litanies may be performed there also. As for yourself, we leave it for you to decide how much your health will permit.

It was a surprise to us that no messenger or letter of yours reached us after [we had left?] Regensburg; we would ask you therefore to inform us more frequently of your health and of anything else that you please. And again we send you our greeting in the Lord.

IV Charters and Allied Material

A surprising amount of charter and allied diplomatic material has survived from the Carolingian period though it is not easy to separate the authentic from the later forgery, nor—a more difficult task again—the authentic from the later partial forgery. Charles the Great was the most popular of names for later forgers to use when they drew up documents purporting to grant property or privileges to great churches or abbeys. Some originals, however, still exist, such as the St Denis immunity (48) in two copies, and the gift of Luzarches and Messy to the same abbey (46). Most grants naturally are preserved in later cartularies (41, 42, 47, 51, 52) or other codices (44, 45, 49, 50). Document 43 exists in a seventeenth-century transcript, and 53 gives a good example of an authentic charter which has received an 'emendation' from a later scribe.

It is difficult to evaluate the importance of the secretariat in the reign of Charles the Great. Few scholars now would refer to it as a chancery in the full sense of the term. Clerks drawn from the royal chapel were the active agents, and came to constitute a regular group of *notarii* or *cancellarii*, essentially ministerial in function. Their task was the relatively humble one of drawing up the royal diplomas, though from their number a single officer emerged to be known clearly by the end of the reign as the chancellor. The most prominent among them took on the special responsibility of recognition in relation to the charters, that is to say of bearing witness to the authenticity and validity of the document. Hitherius (42, 44, 46–8) fulfilled this function in the early years of the reign to January 777, with Wigbald on occasion acting as deputy. Hitherius, who had been an active servant of Pippin as early as 760, became abbot of Tours in 775, and was employed on Italian embassies in 770 and again in 781. Others to occupy the role were Rado from 777–99 (49 and 51) with Giltbert (wrongly spelled in both documents) as a deputy; Ercambald from 799–812, known as *notarius et cancellarius* (52 and 53) with Genesius and Blado as deputies; and in the last year of the reign Hieremias, who became archbishop of Sens.

We have chosen documents to illustrate the range covered in these diplomas, most of which resulted from suits or petitions, often, to judge from internal evidence, from petitions to restore ancient rights and liberties. Grants of immunities to great religious houses are illustrated in the charters to Corbie (42), Lorsch (44), and St Denis (48). More routine grants are to be found in 41, 45, 46, 47, 49, and 52. Matters of political interest are touched on in 43 (protection of

Scottish monks) and **51** (a reward for campaigning against the Saracens of Spain). Document **50** emphasizes the difficulties attending the Bavarian situation after the fall of Tassilo, and **53** gives splendid insight into the means by which the Frankish king successfully asserted his authority over the Lombard people.

We have added to this section three documents which are not strictly diplomas but notices (*notitiae*) or records of suits heard to decide questions of ownership and rights over property. Professor Bullough in *The Age of Charlemagne*, pp. 17–18, has drawn attention to this type of document, still perhaps inadequately taken into account in general interpretations of the reign.

Dr Percival has translated the charters from MGH *Die Urkunden der Karolinger*, ed. Engelbert Muehlbacher (2nd edn., Berlin 1956), which is referred to as Muehlbacher below, and the *notitiae* from *I Placiti del 'Regnum Italiae'*, ed. Cesare Manaresi, Fonti per la Storia d'Italia (Rome 1955), which is referred to as Manaresi below.

41 The tithes of the church of Utrecht are confirmed, 1 March 769

Source: Muehlbacher, 56.

Charles, by the grace of God king of the Franks, illustrious. It is our belief that if in all matters we grant the petitions of the clergy the Lord will reward us for it. Wherefore the venerable bishop Gregory brought for our perusal a confirmation of our lord and father of glorious memory, the former king Pippin, concerning the property of his church of St Martin which is built in the town of Utrecht on the River Rhine, and relating to those properties which our ancestors the earlier Pippin, Charles, Carloman and the same our father aforementioned granted to the said church of God and to the said bishopric, assigning and confirming to the said God's church of St Martin all the tithes, that is to say from lands or slaves or tolls or marketing or from any other source from which revenue might be expected for the fisc, for the provision and sustenance of the monks and clergy who there convert the gentiles to Christianity and in the mercy of Our Lord give teaching to those they have converted, to the end that other Christians may carry on the Christianity that is theirs. So the said Gregory did petition us that we should renew the confirmation, and this with willing heart we have duly done. Wherefore by this our ordinance we decree and command that whatever our aforesaid ancestors did by their instruments lawfully and properly grant to the said church of God, these the said pontiff, Gregory, shall by our new confirmation, without contradiction from any person, have granted and conceded to that same church. And that this authorization of our confirmation may be more strictly observed and better maintained through the years we have instructed that it be endorsed hereunder with the mark of our hand.

Mark of the most glorious king Charles.

Issued the first day of March, in the first year of our reign; enacted in the royal palace at Aix.

42 The immunity of the monastery of Corbie is confirmed, 16 March 769

Source: Muehlbacher, 57.

Charles, king of the Franks, illustrious. If by our utterances we reaffirm those things which were conceded and granted in former times by our royal predecessors to the places of religion for the benefit of God's servants, by this we exercise the royal custom and are confident that such actions redound to our favour and to the stability of our kingdom. Wherefore the venerable Hado—abbot of the monastery of Corbie, which is situated in the district of Amiens and which our ancestors, the former king Chlothar and Baltechildis his wife had built from its very foundations—has brought it to the attention of our royal mercy that the aforementioned prince and his queen granted to the said monastery by their order this concession, that all those properties which they themselves had confirmed to it for their own salvation, as well as those which might be added or made over to it by succeeding kings or by any other god-fearing men and those which by whatever means had been acquired for it by the abbots of the said monastery themselves, in whatever districts or territories, all these the monastery for its part should possess for all time in undisputed right, with full immunity and without giving access to justices or the claims of the public fisc. So all the instructions and confirmations of our predecessors—of the kings Childeric, Theoderic, Clovis, Childebert, Dagobert and our father also, up until the present time—the said abbot brought to us for our perusal, and asserted that this privilege had been maintained from that time to this. But in a desire for firm assurance he besought our highness that by our authority it should be more fully confirmed to him and to the aforementioned monastery. Know then that we have with willing heart confirmed and granted this petition of his in all respects. Wherefore by this present order we ordain and decree that whatever was granted or conceded to the aforementioned monastery by our predecessors, in whatever places or territories it was, and whatever was added or conveyed to it by god-fearing men, or was acquired for it, by whatever means, by the abbots themselves who there give service to God, or will in the future with God's aid be given or bestowed by any man whatsoever, all these properties, both those which the monastery for its part is now known to possess and own and those which in the future with God's aid may be bestowed upon it or assigned to it by whatever legal instrument, they shall, after inspection of the instructions of the princes aforementioned, have authority to possess and own in undisputed right in full immunity and without access to justices, in such a way that no public justice shall under any circumstances presume to enter the estates of that monastery or to approach its men who are known to live on its lands, whether it be to hear cases or to demand payment for the infringement of the peace [*fredus*] or to arrange provisioning or billetings or to require or receive any payments on the part of our fisc; rather, as we have said, they should enjoy full possession and ownership in undisputed right and in full immunity, with all payments for the infringement of the peace [*fredus*] conceded to them both now and for the future, to the end that these servants of God may better take delight in imploring the mercy of God for the stability of our kingdom. And that this order may be more strictly observed and in all respects maintained through the years we have ordained that it be confirmed hereunder with the signature of our hand.

Hiterius witnessed and signed.

Issued the sixteenth day of March, in the first year in which I began to reign; enacted at Orville; in the name of the Lord.

43 The property of the Scottish monastery on the island of Honau is restored, 772–4

Source: Muehlbacher, 77.

Charles, by the grace of God king of the Franks, illustrious, enjoins upon all who have received anything from the church of the Scots which is situated on the island of Honau to give back everything that they have received or taken by force without permission of the abbot Beatus. And if anyone wilfully withholds such property the king ordains that all the justices of that land should duly seek out all the property of the church in accordance with the law of the Franks, since the property of monks is the proper concern of the king. Wherefore let all these aforesaid things be restored to the church of the Scots, without any hindrance, whether they be lands or vineyards, cattle or men, silver or gold. And if anyone does not do this, let him recognize that it is the king's orders which he disobeys, since the kings of the Franks have given freedom to all the Scottish monks, that no one should seize anything of their property, nor should any people other than they have possession of their churches. So do in these matters as you wish to keep our favour.

44 A gift to the monastery of Lorsch, 2 September 774

Source: Muehlbacher, 82.

Charles, by the grace of God king of the Franks and Lombards, illustrious. Whatever, in keeping with the love of God, we grant or confirm to the resting places of the venerable saints, this we believe without doubt redounds to our eternal bliss through the protection of Our Lord. Wherefore be it known to the multitude of all our faithful subjects that in the name of the Lord and for the redemption of our soul we give to our monastery called Lorsch, where the body of the most holy martyr Nazarius is buried and where Gundelandus holds office as abbot, and wish to be given to that place in perpetuity, an estate called Oppenheim, situated in the district of Worms on the River Rhine, in its entirety, with all its benefit and with whatever is known lawfully to belong and pertain to it, that is to say, with its lands, houses and buildings, its tenants, serfs, vineyards, woods, fields, meadows, pastures, islands, waters and watercourses, its movable and immovable belongings and all its appurtenances and appendages, and with all its bounds and marches; whatever lawfully pertains to the estate above mentioned we, for our part, grant and confirm in all respects from this day forth wholly and in full, for the love of God and in reverence for the exalted martyr Nazarius, on the day of dedication of his holy church and of the translation of his body; likewise the land lying in the area belonging to Dexheim, as it has done from ancient times to the present day, is to belong to the church which is built at Oppenheim. So we have ordered this our confirmation to be written on the matter, that the aforementioned abbot who is now in office there, and also his successors and those having charge of the said church, shall from this day have, hold and possess the said estate of Oppenheim wholly with all its appurtenances and appendages in a condition of immunity, and whatever they may choose to do with it for the benefit of the church or for the sustenance of the monks they are to enjoy freedom of decision in our mercy and that of our wife and children, that it may with the Lord's help redound to their increase both now and in future times. This order, that it may be more firm, we have endorsed hereunder with our own hand and have ordered to be sealed with our ring.

Mark of the most glorious king Charles.

I, Rado, was witness on behalf of Hitherius.

Issued the second day of September in the sixth year of our reign; enacted in the royal city of Worms; so be it.

45 The right of the monastery of Fulda to choose its own abbot, 24 September 774

Source: Muehlbacher, 86.

Charles, by the grace of God king of the Franks and Lombards, illustrious, to all our faithful subjects both present and future. It behoves our royal mercy that amid the petitions of others we should lend a kindly ear to the clergy, and that such things as are asked in the fear of God's holy name should be put beyond doubt and brought to effect, so that when some proper request for the relief of God's servants is granted it may redound to our credit, seeing that perfect faith fails not to obtain the favour of the Most High, which according to Our Lord's own teaching is given especially to ordinary men whose minds are devoted to the faith. As it is written, 'Blessed are the poor in spirit; for theirs is the kingdom of heaven [Matthew 5.3].' Be it known to you therefore, in your gentleness and eager concern, that the venerable Sturmio, abbot of the monastery of Fulda, which is built in honour of St Boniface the martyr in the district of Grabfeld in the wastes of *Boconia*, where rest the bodily remains of that most precious lord and saint, has besought our royal mercy that, for the increase of our merit, the watchful protection of God and the divine mercy of the Most High, we should grant an indulgence and concession to the said monastery, to the effect that, as the same abbot Sturmio now lives with a great crowd of monks in that monastery in accordance with a holy rule, so from henceforward, both now and in the future, the same holy community of St Boniface should live and work for ever in accordance with their order and holy rule, lest it should happen (which God forbid) that the religious devotion which has been acquired and strengthened through the good examples of the holy fathers should become lax and fall away to nothing. This we should strive to prevent, and therefore he besought us that out of love for the reverend martyr we should make this concession, namely, that whenever the abbot of the said monastery leaves this mortal life the holy community should itself choose a shepherd or abbot from its number subject to the approval of God, who will know how to lead this his flock into the way of truth, that in unity and concord they may attain pardon and eternal life. Wherefore we, for the increase of our merit and for the stability of our kingdom and our nobility, have without hesitation duly granted the petition of the clergy and of Abbot Sturmio and of the community of monks of the most holy martyr Boniface. This request we have, for the protection of God and the Divine Mercy, both granted and in all respects confirmed, to the effect that, so long as the community is known to be living and working in accordance with the holy rule, and so long as they mutually preserve and maintain their sacred order and show themselves loyal to us, whenever the abbot of the monastery leaves this mortal life the brothers shall have permission to choose from their number a shepherd or abbot with God's favour and with our consent, who can rule and govern the monks in accordance with their holy rule. So may it please the said monks continually to invoke the boundless goodness of God, for the eternal safety and felicity of our country and for the well-being of ourselves, our wife and our children. This our instruction and decree, in order that with Christ being in all things our helper it may be more firmly observed, and with Our Lord's aid be better maintained both now and in the future, should, we have directed, be endorsed hereunder with the mark of our hand.

Mark of the most glorious king Charles.

Issued to Abbot Sturmio, the twenty-fourth day of September, in the sixth year of our reign; enacted in the royal palace at Düren; so be it. Amen.

46 A gift to the monastery of St Denis, 25 February 775

Source: Muehlbacher, 92.

Charles, by the grace of God king of the Franks and Lombards, to all our faithful subjects both present and future. Seeing that the scriptures admonish us that each man ought steadfastly so to prepare himself that when he comes into the sight of the Judge on high he may deserve to hear of his Lord those words of kindness in which all just men through their good acts will rejoice, for this reason we have made, we believe, a salutary decision, that from those earthly possessions with which the Divine Grace has seen fit abundantly to endow us in this life we should make donations, however small they may be, to the end that we may so obtain mercy of the Most High. Wherefore, to the church of St Denis, where that precious master rests in bodily remains along with his fellows, and where the venerable Fulrad is abbot, and which we ourselves with Christ's favour have built anew and have ordered lately to be dedicated with great honour, we give, and wish to be given in perpetuity for the salvation of our soul, our two villas, the one in the place called Luzarches, which is situated in the district of Paris on the river called *Folunca*, together with the church in honour of St Cosmas and St Damian, and the other in the place called Messy, which is situated in the district of Meaux, both these villas with all their bounds and appurtenances, that they may be used for the increase of the said monastery and the monks that serve there, for the furnishing of the church itself and for the maintenance of the poor. These we give in their entirety, that is to say, with their lands, houses and other buildings, their tenants, slaves, vineyards, woods, meadows, pastures, waters and water courses, flour mills and all movable and immovable belongings: all this, as we have said, the monastery and those in charge of it are for their part to have, hold and possess, and shall have licence to do with as they wish both now and for the future, so long as it shall please these servants of God earnestly to pray both day and night for the Lord's mercy upon us and our descendants. And that this our authority may be more strictly observed and better maintained throughout the years, we have directed that it be confirmed hereunder in our own hand and sealed with our ring.

Mark of the most glorious king Charles.

I, Wigbald, witnessed and signed on behalf of Hitherius.

Issued the twenty-fifth day of February in the seventh and first years of our reign; enacted in the monastery of St Denis; in the name of God, so be it.

47 Freedom from tolls for the monastery of St Denis, 14 March 775

Source: Muehlbacher, 93.

Charles, by the grace of God king of the Franks and Lombards, to all our faithful subjects both present and future. Be it known to all of you, loyal in your devotion, that the venerable abbot Fulrad of the monastery of St Denis the martyr, where rest the bodily remains of the saint himself, has brought before us the grants and confirmations of earlier kings, and of our lord and father King Pippin, by which they conceded to the said church of God from of old all tolls, whether concerning the estates of the said church, or its men who live on its lands, or those who are known to be engaged on its business. And we, after reading in the confirmations and instructions of the earlier kings what grants were made from of old, have by this our present authority confirmed them anew, to the effect that throughout the realms of Frankia and Italy which are ours by God's favour, with regard to ships sailing upstream and downstream along the rivers, or carts and their loads, or the monastery's men or those known to be engaged on the business of the said church of God, wherever and to whatever region they may travel, in cities, castles, villages, harbours, public bridges and other places of business, or its men who live on its lands, or its estates and lands themselves, or the men who travel outside its estates on business or to purchase wine, no toll nor weir-passage nor tithe nor ship-money nor wheel-money nor bridge-toll nor damage nor gratuity nor trading-tax nor post-money shall be exacted; from ships or carts and their loads, or from what men carry on their back, or from those known to be engaged on the business of the said church of God, or from its estates or fields, or from the men who travel outside its estates on business or for the purchase of wine, no toll or passage-money whatever within our kingdoms of Frankia and Italy nor any tithe should you exact or demand, be it for our profit or for yours or for that of your subordinates or successors, but, as we have said and as is ordained in their charters, they are to have this grant and concession within the two kingdoms which are ours by God's favour. And that this our order may be more strictly observed we have directed that it be endorsed hereunder and sealed with our ring.

Mark of the most glorious king Charles.

Wigbald witnessed on behalf of Hitherius.

Issued the fourteenth day of March, in the seventh and first years of our reign; enacted at the royal palace of Quierzy; in the name of God, so be it. Amen.

48 A grant of immunity to the monastery of St Denis, 14 March 775

Source: Muehlbacher, 94

Charles, by the grace of God king of the Franks and Lombards. From the beginning of our reign and with effect from the time of our elevation, we were with the Lord's full help watchful, and with a view to good works took counsel with our pontiffs and elders and nobles whether, to confirm our kingdom and to attain the reward of eternal life, we should renew the immunities; and this we have done.[1] For it behoves our royal mercy before all other petitions to grant a willing ear and to put beyond doubt and bring to good effect such things as are prescribed for our salvation and asked in God's name, to the end that through the transitory things of this life we may attain eternal reward, according to Our Lord's instruction, saying: 'Make to yourselves friends of the mammon of unrighteousness [Luke 16.9].' So in accordance with his word we must through the mammon of unrighteousness obtain an eternal place in heaven, and by granting suitable benefits to the clergy become worthy in return of Our Lord's reward in the everlasting tabernacles. Wherefore the venerable Fulrad, abbot of the church of our special patron, the lord and martyr St Denis, where rest the bodily remains of that precious master, has sought our royal benevolence concerning the immunity granted from of old by preceding kings to all the estates of the aforesaid holy church; he declares that he has in his hands the orders themselves and affirms that they have until now been scrupulously observed. He therefore asks that we should by our authority grant and confirm anew to the said church those things which were granted and confirmed by their several authorities by earlier kings, concerning the said abbot, the holy place itself, and such men as deliver and assign themselves and their substance to the said church. Be it therefore known to all of you in your most valued good judgement that from respect for the holy place itself and for the freedom of those who there serve God we have most willingly granted his request and have confirmed it in all respects. Wherefore by this our instruction, which we declare to be of special force and wish to remain so for ever, we direct that neither you yourselves, nor your subordinates or successors, nor anyone invested with powers of justice, in the estates of the aforesaid church of St Denis, wherever and in whatever district they may be in the kingdoms acquired by us through the favour of God, namely the part of Italy called Lombardy and the Valtelline, whether those estates have been assigned by us to that house of God in recent times and are known to be in the possession and ownership of the monastery, or have been granted to it by God-fearing men by lawful instruments, or shall be so granted or assigned to it in

---

[1] The syntax of this sentence is far from clear.

the future, shall under any circumstances presume to make entry or demand payment at any time, be it to hear cases or to raise sureties or to exact the payment for the infringement of the peace [*fredus*] or to arrange billeting or provisions or to seek any payment whatsoever or anything which our fisc would normally expect to receive therefrom; all these things from all sources, together with the peace-payment which (as we have said) is wholly conceded to them, and whatever that holy place has been known to possess until now and whatever in the future may be added or assigned to it by God-fearing men or by ourselves, together with all such as may lawfully and properly commit themselves with all their substance to the monastery and bequeath and confirm their property to it by lawful deed—all these things are, for the increase of our merit, after the inspection of the charters themselves of earlier kings and in accordance with what this our present authorization contains, to remain with them in full immunity from this day forth without any claim being made upon them. And, as we have said, whatever our fisc might perhaps expect to receive from it, whether in candle-dues or in provisions or from the alms of the poor of the monastery, is by this our charter to be conceded and granted to it in full and in all respects and from all sources, that it may please them to pray the more earnestly to Our Lord in his mercy for the stability of our kingdom and for the peace of all our people. And that this our authority concerning this holy place may both now and in the future remain for ever firm and inviolate and be observed and maintained unimpaired through the years and be better believed in by all the justices, we have ensured that it be confirmed by the mark of our own hand.

Mark of the most glorious king Charles.

I, Wigbald, witnessed on behalf of Hitherius.

Issued the fourteenth day of March in the seventh and first years of our reign; enacted at the royal palace of Quierzy. In the Lord's name, so be it.

49 The properties of the church of Salzburg are confirmed, December 790

Source: Muehlbacher, 168.

Charles, by the grace of God king of the Franks and Lombards and patrician of the Romans, to all our faithful subjects both present and future. If we confirm by our authority those things which rightly belong to the places of religion we are exercising royal custom, and this we believe to redound to the increase of our merit and to the stability of our kingdom in God's name. Wherefore, be it known to your good understanding that the venerable Arno, bishop of the city of the Pinzgau which is now called Salzburg, has petitioned our royal highness that we should by our authority confirm all the property of his episcopal church, which is built in honour of St Peter, both that which has been given and bequeathed in lawful and proper manner over a long period of time by kings, queens, dukes and other God-fearing persons, and that also which the Divine Goodness may add to it in the future through the generosity of goodly people. This petition of his we have so confirmed, for the increase of our merit. Wherefore we order and instruct that whatever lawfully and properly belongs to the said bishopric, and whatever the said Bishop Arno may possess at the present time, together with all that may be given or bequeathed to them in the proper manner in the future, all this the said Bishop Arno and his successors are henceforth to have, hold and possess in full by our order, and it shall be for the increase of the said church for so long as it may please them continually to pray for the Lord's mercy upon us and our wife and children. And that this our authority may be more strictly observed we have decreed that it be confirmed hereunder by our own hand and sealed hereunder with our ring.

Mark of the most glorious king Charles.

I, Gildulfus, have witnessed on behalf of Rado.

Issued in the month of December in the twenty-sixth [XXVI for XXIII?] and eighteenth [XVIII for XVI?] years of our reign; enacted at ———; in the Lord's name, so be it. Amen.

50 The properties granted by Tassilo to the monastery of Kremsmünster are confirmed, 3 January 791

Source: Muehlbacher, 169.

Charles, by the grace of God king of the Franks and Lombards and patrician of the Romans. If we give willing ear to the petitions of priests and other servants of God concerning those matters which are brought to our hearing, and bring them to good effect in God's name, we are exercising royal custom, and this we believe to redound to our merit and to the stability of our kingdom. Be it therefore known to all our faithful subjects both present and future that the venerable abbot Fater has appealed to our royal mercy, in that Tassilo, formerly duke of Bavaria, had caused a monastery to be newly built in honour of St Salvator within our forest at the place called Kremsmünster in the district of Traungau, and had by deed of gift granted to that holy place certain properties in the said district and within the said forest, namely Sulzbach, Sippbach, Leombach, and all that lies between the two rivers called Ipfbach, together with one canton of those Slavs of whom Taliup and Sparuna were the administrators, and along-side the river called Dietach 30 Slavs and a stretch of territory which belongs to the said canton, which was sworn to by Phisso and has been formally inspected by Bishop Arno and Abbot Fater, together with Count Hleodrus and Chunibert the justice. Also, the land at Dietach and Sierning which those Slavs have cleared without the permission of Tassilo. Likewise in another place called Eberstallzell some land which was similarly cleared without the permission of Tassilo, and which was formally inspected by his envoys, Saluhho, Wanilo and Gaerbert. However, the men who live on this land at Eberstallzell should, if they wish to hold the said land, do service for it to the monastery, and if they do not wish to do so they are free to go. He also gave land at Pettenbach, from the spring as far as the river called Almfluss, that is (as Tassilo assigned it), up to the mountain slopes where he had granted them the pasture. Also, a villa called Alkoven, wholly with all its appendages and appurtenances, and at Alburg the chapel built in honour of St Martin with all the things pertaining to it, and at Sulzbach another church with all its appurtenances, and north of Vils a third church with the things pertaining to it at Donaugau. Also, in the abovementioned district of Traungau, in the place called Aschach, two vineyards with two vine-dressers, and in another place called Rodelbach three vineyards with three vine-dressers and two fishermen and also two other men who look after the bees and six smiths. All these things above mentioned the said abbot Fater declares that he is holding and possessing in free tenure on behalf of the said monastery. But because this could scarcely remain firm and stable by the grant of the said Tassilo alone he has petitioned our highness that in our mercy and by our authority we should grant and confirm it anew and more fully to the holy place; and this we have done. Wherefore we order and instruct, after inspecting the donation of Tassilo, that the said abbot Fater and his successors as abbots of the said monastery of St Salvator shall by this order and confirmatory grant of our highness be authorized to hold and possess it in the terms set out in the donation, wholly and freely without any impediment, so that now and for ever in the future it may redound to the increase of our merit and to the increase of that house of God. And that this our authority may be more strictly observed and the better maintained through the years by the favour of Christ, we have confirmed it hereunder with our own hand and have ordered it to be sealed with our ring.

Mark of the most glorious king Charles.

Issued the third day of January, in the twenty-third year of the reign of our lord and most serene king Charles; enacted at Worms; in the name of God, so be it. Amen.

51 A victory is rewarded, March 795 (?)

Source: Muehlbacher, 179.

In the name of the Father and of the Son and of the Holy Ghost. Charles, by the grace of God most serene king of the Franks and Lombards and patrician of the

Romans. Be it known to all our bishops, abbots, dukes, counts and all our faithful subjects both present and future. It is right that our royal power should provide assistance for those whose need is attested. Be it therefore known to you all in your proficiency that John came to us and showed us a letter which our beloved son Louis had written for him and sent by him to us. And we found recounted in this letter how he had fought a great battle against our heretics or Saracen infidels in the district of Barcelona, and defeated them in the place called *Ad Ponte* and killed certain of the said infidels and took spoils from them, some of which he brought to our beloved son, namely a fine horse, a fine coat of mail, and an Indian sword, together with a casket made of silver, and asked of him a deserted property known as *Fontes* in the district of Narbonne to cultivate; and he gave him the property and sent him to us. And when he had come to us with the letter which our son had written for him, the said John our faithful subject commended himself to us, and besought us to make him a formal grant of the property which our son had given him. We therefore granted the property to him in full with all its bounds and appurtenances, and with it all the land in the villa of Fontjoncouse that he and his men have or shall occupy or reclaim from the waste, and also such land, whether within its territory or in other villas and properties, as he and his men may occupy or take possession of. All this we grant to him as our gift, to the effect that he and his heirs shall hold it without dues or charges for as long as they remain loyal to us and to our sons. And that this our authority may be more strictly observed we have sealed it hereunder with our ring.

Gilabert witnessed and signed on behalf of Rado.

Issued in the month of March in the twenty-fifth [XXV for XXVII?] and eighteenth [XVIII for XXI?] years of our reign; enacted in our palace at Aix; in the name of God, so be it. Amen.

52 Freedom from tolls for two ships of the monastery of Cormery, 2 June 800

Source: Muehlbacher, 192.

Charles, by the grace of God king of the Franks and Lombards and patrician of the Romans. To all our bishops, abbots, counts, agents, *vicarii, centenarii* and all other our faithful subjects both present and future, be it known that we have granted the request of our most beloved and faithful subject Albinus, abbot of the venerable monastery of St Martin, where rest the bodily remains of the saint himself, to the effect that the monks who live according to the rule of St Benedict in the monastery built in honour of St Paul the apostle in the place called Cormery shall be permitted to sail two ships on necessary business to and fro along the Rivers Loire, Mayenne, Sarthe, Loir and Vienne, and shall not themselves or their men be made to pay or give any toll in any place whatsoever, be it of salt or of anything at all. Wherefore we have ordered this present authority to be drawn up, whereby we order for all time that neither you yourselves nor your subordinates nor your successors should presume to make any charge for these ships upon the said venerable abbot Albinus or his successors or the monks or their men from the aforementioned monastery of St Paul, nor make any claim upon them, nor require nor exact any toll nor mooring- nor harbour-dues nor levy nor any other payment, but rather that through our beneficence this privilege should both now and in all future times be used for the betterment of that holy place of Cormery and of the brothers themselves. And that this our authority may be held in greater respect and be better observed throughout the years, we have ordered it to be sealed hereunder with our ring.

Witnessed by Genasius on behalf of Ercambald.

Issued the second day of June, in the thirty-second and twenty-seventh years of our reign; enacted in the monastery of St Martin at Tours.

53 The property of Manfred of Reggio is restored, 17 July 808

The name 'Manfred' is added over an erasure by a later scribe.

Source: Muehlbacher, 208.

In the name of the Father and of the Son and of the Holy Ghost. Charles, most serene Augustus crowned by God, mighty and peaceable emperor, ruler of the Roman empire and through the mercy of God king of the Franks and Lombards. Be it known to the multitude of all our faithful subjects both present and future, that through the favour of God and the interceding merit of the apostles, the chiefs of the saints, we acquired the kingdom of the Lombards, and brought certain Lombard men out of their country into Frankia as a surety, and afterwards, through the intercession of our son, the glorious king Pippin, sent them back to their country and gave orders that to some of them their lawful inheritance, which we had called in to our fisc, should be returned. One of whom, [Manfred] by name, of the city of Reggio, has approached our clemency and made request of our serenity that by our instruction and authority we should concede and confirm afresh by full and formal grant all those things which, at the time when he was brought to Frankia, he justly and reasonably and in lawful inheritance possessed, and which we directed should afterwards be returned to him. This request we have been unwilling to deny, but know rather that for the increase of our merit and through the beneficence of our aforesaid son we have so granted and confirmed it in all respects. Wherefore we give these orders and instructions, which we desire to hold good for all time in his case, that so long as he gives faithful service to us and to our beloved son he shall, by this our authority, both hold and possess in fullest right all his property, that is, as we have said, whatever he in lawful manner possessed at the time when he was brought into Frankia on our orders, which we directed should afterwards be returned to him, and shall do with it as he wishes and shall have full and free enjoyment of it in all respects. And that this our instruction and confirmation may remain inviolate both now and for the future we have directed that it be endorsed hereunder by our own hand and have ordered it to be sealed with our ring.

Mark of the lord Charles, most pious and serene emperor.

I, Blado, signed on behalf of Ercambald.

Issued the seventeenth day of July, in the eighth year by Christ's mercy of our emperorship, and the fortieth year of our reign in Frankia, and our thirty-eighth in Italy, of the first indiction; enacted in our palace at Aix; in the name of God, so be it. Amen.

Notices of Judgements

The following three documents, *notitiae* or notices of judgements, indicate how Charles used his preeminence in law, both as king and later as emperor, to settle disputes in his territories. In the first instance he delegates judicial authority to the duke of Spoleto, in the second he acts directly himself, and in the third his *missi* perform the judicial function for him. The first account gives a particularly revealing insight into the judicial processes of the day.

54 Hildebrand, duke of Spoleto, decides a case of disputed property, Spoleto, July 781

Source: Manaresi, 5.

In the name of Almighty God. At the time when our lord Charles, most excellent king of the Franks and Lombards, was returning from Rome and from the churches of the blessed apostles St Peter and St Paul, and had come to *Vadum Medianum* in the territory of Florence, and when the lord and most glorious duke Hildebrand was present there with him to do him service, Paul, the son of Pando of Rieti, made a complaint to the lord king concerning the monastery of San Angelo which is situated near the town of Rieti, saying that it had belonged to his parents. And he showed a royal order issued by the lord king Liutprand, which made confirmation concerning the property of a certain Gutta, their aunt: 'And yet', he said, 'our duke has unlawfully taken the monastery from us and has given it to bishop Guigpertus.' Straightway the duke was questioned about these things by the exalted lord king, how the case had arisen, and he replied: 'This monastery of which you speak I found to be in the possession of the palace, and I gave it to bishop Guigpertus; moreover, I confirmed it in the monastery of the Holy Mother of God at *Acutianum*, and it is there confirmed by the order of your exalted authority.' The lord king therefore instructed him that when he returned to Spoleto he should with his justices inquire carefully into the case and settle it. And when he had returned there he called together his bishops and justices—the venerable bishop Arnefridus, the two Adeodati, Peter, Iustolfus and Sinualdus, and among the justices the *gastaldii* and Counts Sintarus, Maiorianus, Gumpertus, Hilpidius, Halo, Lupo, Herfemarus, Barusus and Vuifrid, with many others also attending—and when Pando had come into our presence with his sons and their associates he showed us the royal order which, when it was read out, contained the confirmation to them of the property of a certain Gutta, but no mention of the monastery of San Angelo. Then the aforementioned duke, with the bishops and justices named above, made inquiry of him saying: 'How is it that you did not show that order when bishop Teuto your brother was disputing with you concerning the monastery, at the time when he was claiming it on behalf of the palace and won the judgement against you concerning it in the presence of Duke Teudicius?' The reply of Pando and his sons and their associates was: 'At that time we did not have the order, but found it later.' To this the monastery, that is Abbot Ragambaldus and his monks, replied: 'The monastery in dispute, namely the monastery of San Angelo, was as you say confirmed on oath to the palace in the time of Duke Teudicius by Probatus your brother and Martinianus the *sculdhais* and Goderis of *Sub Muro*, and judgement was given concerning it by the hand of Dagarinus the *gastaldius* and referendary on the order of Duke Teudicius.' And when we asked Pando and his sons and their associates, namely Agio the priest and Ursus, to show us the judgement they replied: 'Bishop Teuto, when he came to the day of his death, called us to him and gave us the judgement, and we straightway burned it in the fire.' They were therefore asked by us and by the aforementioned justices and bishops what was contained in the judgement. Pando replied: 'If it had not been against us we would certainly not have burned it.' Agio the priest said: 'I read it, but I cannot remember whether the judgement was given in favour of the palace or of the church.' Ursus said: 'The judgement was burned in the fire in my presence; in whose favour it was given I do not know.' After this the aforementioned duke inquired of Dagarinus the *gastaldius* whether he had written out the judgement and which party had won the case. And he told us: 'I was present at the hearing when Duke Teudicius heard the case, and the victory went to the palace; oaths were entered into concerning it, and I wrote out the judgement with my own hand.' We, the aforementioned justices, asked Pando if this was true, and Pando agreed that it was, and said: 'All those things are true, as

Dagarinus the *gastaldius* has said; oaths were entered into concerning it, and we burned the judgement. You must now judge as you see fit, since from now on I speak the truth, namely that the judgement contained a statement that the case was won on oath by the palace, and that it was for this reason that we burned it in the fire.' They were further asked by us if they had any other documents concerning the matter to show them; and they denied it in our presence, saying: 'We have no other documents concerning it.' When all this has been done in our presence in the manner described we decreed what seemed to us and to our bishops and justices to be most proper: that Pando and his associates should give a surety to Dagarinus the *gastaldius* to make a settlement to our palace, in accordance with the decree contained in the page of the judgement which had been burned and lost, and Hilderic the *sculdhais* stood as surety; that the aforesaid abbot for his part should have and possess in its entirety the aforementioned church of San Angelo in the terms in which it had been granted to him by the palace; and that Pando and his associates for their part should be content with this settlement of the case. And so it was decided. Wherefore, to put an end to the dispute, this brief notice of the judgement, on the order of the above-mentioned authority and at the dictation of Dagarinus the *gastaldius*, was written by me Totemannus the notary, in the month of July of the fourth indiction.

I, Hildebrand, most glorious duke, have signed this judgement with my own hand.

I, Adeodatus, unworthy bishop, have signed with my own hand.
I, Senuald, bishop, have signed with my own hand.
I, Adeodatus, bishop, have signed with my own hand.
I, Iustolphus, bishop, have signed with my own hand.
I, Sintarus, *gastaldius*, have signed with my own hand.
I, Halo, magnificent count, have signed with my own hand.
I, Herfemarus, *gastaldius*, have signed with my own hand.

55 Charles, as emperor, decides a case of disputed authority over a church, 29 May 801

Source: Manaresi, 21.

In the name of the Father and of the Son and of the Holy Ghost. Charles, most serene Augustus crowned by God, mighty and peaceable emperor and ruler of the Roman empire and by the mercy of God king of the Franks and Lombards. When in God's name we came to the territory of Bologna on our return from Rome, and there on the River Reno met in session with our bishops, abbots, dukes, counts and other notables and the rest of our faithful subjects to hear the suits of all men and administer right justice, then did Vitalis, bishop of the holy church of the city of Bologna, bring charges against the venerable Anselm, abbot of the monastery which is built in the place called Nonantola in honour of Our Lord and Saviour Jesus Christ and the holy apostles and St Silvester the pope, saying that he had unlawfully driven his priest, Urso by name, out of a baptismal church built in honour of St Mamma in the village called Lizzano and pertaining to his bishopric, and moreover that the abbot himself and his monks had unjustly removed from it all the belongings which the priest had at the church, and had allowed neither the bishop himself nor his priest to have any authority over the said church. But the aforesaid venerable Anselm appeared in person and gave the following reply, saying that Aistulf, the former king of the Lombards, had by his order assigned the aforesaid village of Lizzano to him in its entirety on behalf of the aforesaid monastery, together with the men belonging to it, free men as free and slaves as slaves, and that afterwards he and the inhabitants of the place had built the church with the consent of Romanus, bishop of the aforementioned city of Bologna, and that the said Romanus had consecrated it at his request. And when there arose between them no small dispute the aforesaid Anselm brought before us the order of the aforementioned king Aistulf, in which was contained the statement that he had assigned and confirmed the aforementioned village, together with other property belonging to him, to the aforesaid monastery. To this bishop Vitalis and his clergy replied that the church had been consecrated by his predecessor and should therefore belong by law to his diocese. But in reply to this Abbot Anselm said: 'We do not deny, nor do we wish to deny, the consecration and confirmation and preaching which were carried out by his predecessor in that holy church of God in accordance with canonical authority; nor did we drive the aforementioned priest Urso out of the church, but rather he turned to flight and left the church of his own accord; and if the priest can carry out his ministry in accordance with the canons we shall willingly allow him to hold the church in which he was ordained.' Therefore it seemed good to us and to our faithful subjects, and we deemed it just, that the aforementioned Vitalis, venerable bishop of the holy church of the city of Bologna, should without anyone's unlawful hindrance and in accordance with canonical authority perform consecration and preaching in the church, and should make inquiry of his priest in the matter of his ministry in accordance with the canons and correct him, and that the aforementioned priest Urso should be given back his church and its belongings; but that the aforesaid venerable abbot Anselm and his successors should hold and possess in full the gift which the former king Aistulf had as a grant of his largesse assigned and confirmed to his monastery, together with all the buildings and everything lawfully and properly belonging to it; and that for the future this dispute between them should be put at rest and settled. And so that this order and decision may be more strictly adhered to and better observed through the years we have instructed that it be sealed hereunder with our ring.

I, Genesius, signed on behalf of Ercambald.

Issued 29 May, in the first year in Christ's mercy of our emperorship, and the thirty-third year of our reign in Frankia and the twenty-eighth in Italy; enacted in the aforementioned territory of Bologna, on the River Reno. In the name of God, so be it. Amen.

56 A case of disputed property is decided by the royal *missi* Ardemannus and Gaidualdus, Rieti, 22 February 807

Source: Manaresi, 21.

In God's name. Notice of a judgement given when we, Ardemannus and Gaidualdus, royal *missi* on orders from our lord the emperor Charles and King Pippin, had come to this city of Rieti, and when there sat in judgement with us in the house of Leo the *sculdhais*, to consider and decide the suits of individual people, Hisimundus, bishop of the holy church of Rieti, and Liuto the *gastaldius*, Leo and Teudipertus the *sculdhais*, Scaptolfus and Spento, the brothers Statius and Toto, Leutherius and Audolfus, Mango of Valva and many other justices. There came into our presence Guelantus, monk of the monastery of Mary, Holy Mother of God, in the Sabine territory, and with him Scaptolfus, advocate of the same monastery, who had a dispute with Gaido the priest and Opteramus the notary and Hildericus, the son of a certain Magnolfus, concerning the property of one Palumbus, their uncle. And the aforementioned Scaptolfus the advocate said: 'Palumbus your uncle entrusted all his property to the monastery of St Mary, and to the monks Guelantus and Fratellus, for the salvation of his soul, and you have unlawfully entered upon that property and have dispossessed us of it.' To this Gaido the priest and Opteramus and Hildericus replied: 'We wish to dispute that Palumbus gave or entrusted his property to you.' Scaptolfus the advocate replied: 'It is so; we can prove that this same Palumbus your uncle put all his property and belongings into the hands of the monks Guelantus and Fratellus in the aforesaid monastery of St Mary for the good of his soul, and we have witnesses here before you, namely Constantinus and Probatus and Gudipertus.' These men were asked by the justices what they knew of the matter, and with one voice all gave the same testimony: 'We were there and saw the said Palumbus put his house in the city with all his belongings and property into the hands of the monks Guelantus and Fratellus and of the monastery of St Mary in the Sabine territory for the good of his soul.' The justices made Constantinus and Gudipertus and Probatus swear to this effect in their presence, and they declared: 'As we have given testimony so is the truth.' And the aforementioned brothers gave their oath to Scaptolfus the advocate, and for their oath received from him in formal exchange a pair of gauntlets. And so we, the aforementioned justices and hearers, did have Scaptolfus the advocate and the monk Guelantus reinvested that same hour with the said property and belongings, and may this decision remain good both now and for ever hereafter, and let Gaido the priest and Opteramus and Hildericus pursue this case no further. It has been settled between them. This notice of judgement was written at the dictation of the aforementioned Ardemannus and Gaidualdus, *missi* of our lord the king, by me, Hisimundus, notary, on the twenty-second day of February of the fifteenth indiction.

✠ Mark of the hand of Ardemannus, *missus* of our lord the king, who made this sign of the holy cross.

✠ I, Gaidualdus, was present at this enactment.

✠ I, Teudipertus, *sculdhais*, was present at this enactment.

✠ I, Spento, was present at this enactment.

✠ I, Statius, was present at this enactment.

Introductory Reading

Among many modern general works on the Carolingian period the following books and articles appear especially important for English-speaking readers:

BOUSSARD, J.   *The Civilization of Charlemagne*, London 1968.

BULLOUGH, D.   *The Age of Charlemagne*, London 1965.

'*Europae Pater:* Charlemagne and his achievements in the light of recent scholarship', *EHR* 1970.

FICHTENAU, H.   *The Carolingian Empire*, Oxford 1957.

GANSHOF, F. L.   *Frankish Institutions under Charlemagne* (trs. Bryce and Mary Lyon) Providence, Rhode Island 1968.

The Carolingians and the Frankish Monarchy; Studies in Carolingian History (including a list of Professor Ganshof's own extensive and penetrating contributions to Carolingian studies) London 1971.

GRIERSON, P.   'Money and Coinage under Charlemagne', *Karl der Grosse*, Band 1, 3 vols., Dusseldorf 1965.

LATOUCHE, R.   *The Birth of Western Economy*, London 1961.

SULLIVAN, R. E. *The Coronation of Charlemagne* (Problems in European Civilization Series), Boston 1959.

ULLMANN, WALTER   *The Carolingian Renaissance and the Idea of Kingship*, London 1969.

WALLACE-HADRILL, J. M.   *The Long-Haired Kings*, London 1962.

'The *Via Regia* of the Carolingian Age', in B. Smalley, editor, *Trends in Medieval Political Thought*, Oxford 1965.

Early Germanic Kingship in England and on the Continent, Oxford 1971.

Index